# Peer work in Australia

## A new future for mental health

**Edited by**

Janet Meagher AM

Anthony Stratford

Fay Jackson

Erandathie Jayakody

Tim Fong

© RichmondPRA Ltd ACN 001 280 628 trading as Flourish Australia Services (Flourish Australia) and Mind Australia Ltd ACN 005 063 589 (Mind Australia).

The views expressed in this publication have been formed from the experience and research of the contributors and authors. Not all views in this book necessarily reflect the views of Flourish Australia, Mind Australia or the publisher. While the authors have taken care to thoroughly research all aspects of the content in this book to ensure the conclusions and views formed are evidence and experience based, no warranty is given as to the correctness of the information contained in this book, or of its suitability for use by you.

This book is copyright and all rights are reserved. Apart from any use as permitted under the Copyright Act 1968, no part may be reproduced or communicated to the public by any process without prior written permission.

For all requests and enquiries concerning reproduction and rights please contact the chief information officer at communications@mindaustralia.org.au or info@flourishaustralia.org.au or by mail to:

| Flourish Australia | or | Mind Australia |
| --- | --- | --- |
| 5 Figtree Drive | | PO Box 592 |
| Sydney Olympic Park NSW 2127 | | Heidelberg VIC 3084 |
| Australia | | Australia |

First published 2018

Suggested citation
Meagher, J., Stratford, A., Jackson, F., Jayakody, E., & Fong, T. (Eds.). (2018). *Peer work in Australia: A new future for mental health*. Sydney: RichmondPRA and Mind Australia.

ISBN: 978-0648441700

Cover design: Bench Creative
Copy editing: Juliet Richters

Printed in Australia

# Dedication

Peer work in mental health is certainly not a new concept, as it can be traced back to the days of revolutionary France. In 1793, Philippe Pinel, later to be known as the father of psychiatry, reported in his diary that the governor of the Bicêtre Asylum, Jean-Baptiste Pussin, was hiring past patients to work in the asylum. Pinel wrote at the time, 'As much as possible, all servants are chosen from the category of mental patients. They are at any rate better suited to this demanding work because they are usually more gentle, honest, and humane'.

We were to wait until the mid-1960s for the belief that recovery from serious mental health challenges was indeed possible and real. This promoted the unique and powerful contribution of the lived experience of mental distress and recovery. From this foundation the modern peer workforce was born.

There have been many peers who have contributed to the professionalism and pioneered the growth of this workforce. We also need to thank those champions who are not peers but have supported the growth of the lived experience workforce.

We dedicate this book to those peers who have gone before us and on whose shoulders we now stand.

# Foreword

I wish you a warm welcome to an ever-expanding community of like-minded people who understand and wish to build on the value of lived experiences of recovery. This book fills an important gap in the literature on peer work. Australia has been a leader in peer work since its inception twenty years ago, and you have learned valuable lessons here that can benefit your fellow lived experience leaders across the globe, because peer work has become a truly global phenomenon. It is cropping up and spreading in every part of the world, and expanding more rapidly than anyone could have predicted. That is why I am writing to you from the opposite end of the planet.

It is within this context that I hope you appreciate the value of what has been produced, because others will be following this lead. There has been a considerable amount of academic research conducted on peer work to date, showing that peers can engage persons who have been difficult to reach and who have not benefited from traditional services, that peer workers can decrease the use of costly acute services like emergency room visits and hospitalisations, while increasing the use of outpatient care, and that peer work can reduce demoralisation and the use of alcohol, while increasing hope, empowerment and self-care. This evidence has been important in establishing the credibility and effectiveness of peer work, but it does not tell people how to do it, how it works, or what it looks like in practice. This book will begin to fill that important gap in the literature, enabling others to transform their own pain and suffering into a constructive tool to alleviate the pain and suffering of others, as you have yourselves been able to do. You have been afforded, and taken advantage of, that valuable opportunity. This book will extend that opportunity to others around the world. You can take pride in using your own lived experience in this generous and instructive way, inspiring others to do the same in their own local communities. For doing so transforms both individual lives and systems of care, as recovery becomes a reality for everyone.

*Professor Larry Davidson*
Director, Yale Program for Recovery and Community Health, Yale University, School of Medicine, New Haven, CT, USA

# Contents

Dedication — iii
Foreword — v
Abbreviations — viii
Acknowledgements — ix
Introduction — x

**Section 1: Peer work in mental health in Australia: its scope, role and contribution** — 1
Scope, role and contribution of peer work: derived, synthesised and analysed from selected peer work literature — 3
*Janet Meagher and Gerry Naughtin*

**Section 2: Changing culture and growing peer work** — 41
Flourish Australia — 43
*Fay Jackson and Tim Fong*

**Section 3: The long walk** — 69
Peer work in Mind Australia — 71
*Erandathie Jayakody and Anthony Stratford*

**Section 4: Examples of involvement in peer work by states and territories** — 109
Research promoting and supporting the peer workforce: how to use it, how to create it — 111
*Louise Byrne*

The lived experience workforce in Central Adelaide Local Health Network: A South Australian experience of developing a peer workforce in clinical mental health services — 127
*Matthew Halpin*

Western Australia's peer workforce: principles, practice and opportunities — 141
*Rhianwen Beresford and Vivien Kemp*

Honouring, developing and growing Victoria's lived experience workforce — 155
*Vrinda Edan and Emma Cadogan*

**Section 5: Values and experiences in implementing peer work** — **173**

Why peer workers do their work — 175
*Darren Jiggins*

Peer work and climate change — 187
*Tim Heffernan*

The world according to me: a Western Australian peer work journey, some history, reflections and thoughts — 202
*Lyn Mahboub*

**Section 6: Specialised developments in peer work** — **217**

How a collective consumer and carer voice shaped a national qualification for mental health peer work — 219
*Michael Burge*

Brook RED — 237
*Eschleigh Balzamo*

Youth peer work: building a strong and supported youth peer workforce — 250
*Nicholas Fava, Bridget O'Bree, Rose Randall, Hamilton Kennedy, Jesse Olsen, Emily Matenson, Sarah Fitzpatrick and Magenta Simmons*

Intentional Peer Support: some notes from a roller-coaster ride in Victoria — 266
*Flick Grey*

Peer supervision: stumbling blocks and ways forward — 280
*Aimee Sinclair*

**Section 7: A force for change** — **295**

Collated from the proceedings of a workshop held in April 2018 — 297
*Leanne Craze and David Plant*

The hearts and minds of the peer workforce — 328
*Leanne Craze and David Plant*

**Appendix** — **333**
Authors and contributing authors — 333
Workshop contributors — 334

# Abbreviations

| | |
|---|---|
| AHS | Area Health Service |
| AOD | alcohol and other drugs |
| HVN | Hearing Voices Network |
| LGBTI | lesbian, gay, bisexual, transgender and intersex |
| LHD | Local Health District |
| LHN | Local Health Network |
| MHJHADS | Mental Health, Justice Health and Alcohol and Drug Services |
| MIEACT | Mental Illness Education Australia Capital Territory |
| NDIA | National Disability Insurance Agency |
| NDIS | National Disability Insurance Scheme |
| NGO | non-government organisation |
| NSW | New South Wales |
| OECD | Organisation for Economic Co-operation and Development |
| PHaMs | Personal Helpers and Mentors |
| SA | South Australia |
| SROI | social return on investment |
| UK | United Kingdom |
| UN | United Nations |
| US/USA | United States |
| VMIAC | Victorian Mental Illness Awareness Council |

# Acknowledgements

Flourish Australia and Mind Australia believe in the power of peer work.

As two leading community mental health organisations, we were delighted to collaborate in a project that has gathered the evidence that supports the practice of peer work in Australia into one publication. This book highlights the breadth and diversity of the peer work profession and, most importantly, the contribution of peer work to a person's recovery journey.

Our collaboration has been a clear demonstration of a very simple, yet powerful message, that the supports we provide are led by people with lived experience.

It gives us great pleasure to acknowledge and thank the editorial working group who have provided leadership and guidance for this project. The outstanding result is a world first publication of a book solely dedicated to the practice of peer work in Australia.

We hope you are as inspired as we are.

Robyn Hunter
**CEO, Mind Australia Limited**

Mark Orr
**CEO, Flourish Australia**

# Introduction

This book is a landmark on the journey of peer work in the mental health sector in Australia. It is the first of its kind in Australia: a co-produced book on peer work. It is arguably the first of its kind in the world.

This book fulfils the need for a deeper understanding of peer work. The growth of the peer workforce, along with the development of new areas of engagement such as the National Disability Insurance Scheme and expansion of the evidence base supporting peer work, highlighted the need for documenting the progress, achievements and future outlook of peer work in the mental health sector in Australia.

The publication of this book is both timely and courageous. Timely, because the mental health sector in Australia is currently engaged in the activities and stresses of mental healthcare reform. The growth and maturity of peer work is at a point where its further development and policy structures are intersecting with broader disability sector reforms, leading to new understandings and acknowledgement of the value of quality peer worker. Courageous, because it sets out to produce a quality and substantial book on peer work in Australia, without anything other than enthusiasm and commitment to fulfil a desperate need for such a resource. Also courageous is the reiteration of the fact that there is now good evidence that peer work is an effective and high-quality intervention, and that mental health services require new approaches, such as peer work, in order to deliver effective services.

The book is the brainchild of Janet Meagher AM and Dr Gerry Naughtin. They authored a discussion paper on peer work to educate the National Disability Insurance Agency on the value of peer work and its possible relevance to services and supports in a future disability peer work scenario. They did this in their capacity as members of the Independent Advisory Council for the National Disability Insurance Agency. This substantive paper drew heavily from the peer work literature and became a synthesis of what the literature was saying and what the evidence was. That original paper went through several iterations and eventually a much simpler version was decided upon as the one to focus the deliberations of the Agency's board. During the substantive efforts to produce this discussion paper it became apparent that there is a need for a more comprehensive publication on Australia's peer work. The discussion paper in its original form is included in this book and the book is built on that.

A coalition was formed between Janet Meagher, Mind Australia and Flourish Australia. (Mind Australia and Flourish Australia are leading specialist mental health service providers in Australia.) Both organisations were deeply committed to the production and bore production costs equally. The publication did not receive any external funding.

The editorial working group included of representatives from both organisations. It consisted of: Janet Meagher, Tim Fong (Flourish Australia), Fay Jackson (Flourish Australia), Erandathie Jayakody (Mind Australia) and Anthony Stratford (Mind Australia), and was supported by Kim Jones with administrative assistance.

A commitment to co-production of the book was established from the outset. This is reflected in the membership of the editorial working group and the contributing authors. (Three of the editorial working group members are peer workers, as are twenty-seven of the authors.)

Key individuals and organisations were invited to write an original paper for the book. Authors are predominantly experts by experience. They have lived through and thrived (not just survived) in the experience of recovery from mental health challenges; they are recognised for using the insights and expertise from their personal expertise to inform their work and are known for doing so in paid professional roles. They have documented their work and experience in the paid lived experience workforce and research with eloquence, courage and professionalism.

The few contributors who brought clinical or management expertise were invited because they have been allies who have opened doors to enable the lived experience and peer workforce to take its rightful, respected place in mental health services. They have supported lived experience advocates to bridge the gaps between advocacy for peer work and the healing it can bring, and employment into these much-needed positions.

In addition to the contributing authors, approximately forty-five peers across Australia contributed to the book by participating in a workshop to discuss key issues and future directions on peer work. Their contribution is documented in the chapter 'A force for change', written by Leanne Craze and David Plant.

On the whole, the production of this book is a massive voluntary task on the part of the editorial working group members, contributing authors and workshop participants across Australia. All gave most generously of their time and expertise. All have stretched their capability and time to give of their best to enable this to come about. The book taps into the vast wellspring of expertise, knowledge and practice in the lived experience workforce. It is inspiring to see that many authors who contributed articles for the book had never written for publication previously.

Readers of this book will realise the powerful and deeply meaningful work that peer workers achieve. They will see the humble, empathic way in which peer workers walk alongside people who have experienced similar distress and support them without trying to 'fix' their situation; rather they help people believe in themselves, so that they discover their own solutions, self-agency, self-advocacy, strengths, capabilities and possibilities.

Readers will also come to an understanding that the peer workforce is an ever-increasing and vital component of multifaceted teams across all levels of the mental health sector, from service delivery to policy making to funding of services. They will gain understanding of how lived experience and peer work staff bring about much-needed cultural change in services and workplaces.

We hope the book will ignite a much stronger dialogue about the value of peer work that will enable the further development, growth and promotion of peer work in Australia not only in the mental health sector but also in new development areas such as the National Disability Insurance Scheme. We hope the book will be an inspiration for the emerging and future peer workers as they take on the mantle of the future of the peer workforce.

We commend this book to policy makers, funders, academics, clinicians, workforce leaders, peer workers and all with an interest who are committed to delivering recovery-focused mental health services.

# Section 1

**Peer work in mental health in Australia: its scope, role and contribution**

# Scope, role and contribution of peer work: derived, synthesised and analysed from selected peer work literature

*Janet Meagher and Gerry Naughtin*

*Janet Meagher AM has a long association with the mental health and disability sectors. She was a National Mental Health Commissioner, board member, lived experience adviser, author, mentor, trainer for many across the disability, mental health and consumer communities. Her history of institutionalisation led her to become an activist and advocate working for rights, equity, participation and respect for people living with mental health issues.*

*Dr Gerry Naughtin has many years of involvement in community mental health services. He is currently the strategic adviser to the National Disability Insurance Agency and is the former chief executive of Mind Australia. Gerry has contributed to the development of peer workers through his role at Mind and involvement with Janet Meagher in the preparation of reports for the Independent Advisory Council for the NDIA.*

In the contemporary Australian context, we need to conceptualise elements of peer work activity and broaden current interpretations of it, not merely as a valued mental health support activity but as a developing service modality across a variety of human service jurisdictions as a new and effective professional role in multiple sectors. People who have lived through particular life situations and have learned much through that process are a rich resource—a resource that is as yet underutilised and untapped. A broader understanding of the principles of peer work may well open up this lived experience cohort as a potential new support workforce across many sectors.

Beyond this point in time, peer work will have proven its worth and will be looking at its place in the much wider service and support context. Going forward, it will not be an 'either/or', it will be an essential element within the suite of service offerings across the entire human service arena. Whether in disability, addictions, justice, parenting, education, health or mental health, it will be a stream of work that will be a critically important component of one-

## 1: Peer work in mental health in Australia: its scope, role and contribution

on-one service delivery. It will be supporting people to rebuild their lives, develop a personal sense of control, master their emotional strengths and work as models, guides and companions on people's journeys towards a contributing life.

This chapter pulls together ideas, concepts and findings derived and synthesised from a broad range of literature related to the topic of peer work. In the interest of retaining context and flow we have merged the writings into a conceptual framework that hopefully makes the richness of the literature available to a wider readership. We do not claim ownership or authorship of the concepts herein, merely owning the task of drawing them together for your convenience.

### Introduction

Mental health practice in Australia has not given enough attention to the experience and management of the challenges of mental ill-health from the perspective of the person with mental health issues. Often, people have been taught that others are the experts in their mental health, that professionals have 'the answer' and know what is best and that there are only limited, rigid versions of a way forward. In fact, people with mental health issues are and can be supported to become the experts in coping with, surviving and even thriving in their lives despite their challenges. Professional peer work is a philosophy and also a service model and employment practice that focuses on the person accessing the service and supports them in their management of their mental health challenges. It impacts on their sense of control over their life opportunities. Peer work is an approach to engaging people with mental health issues as the central actors in the management of their mental wellbeing and in building meaningful and purposeful lives.

In spite of over thirty years of active discussion of the importance of lived experience in mental health practice, those living with mental health issues continue to report that many service providers do not recognise the personal impacts of their mental health issues or give enough weight to their coping and managing strategies. Few have been asked to discuss what their experiences have taught them. Few have found service providers to be interested in the personal talents or gifts they have developed, nor have they been helped to process ways of finding meaning in their life experiences. The problems encountered along people's life paths have typically been regarded as the result of their faulty bodies, malfunctioning brains or social histories. Insufficient focus is given to the ways people have been affected by a variety of negative and positive bureaucratic, professional, community and environmental factors, not the least of which would be breaches of their human rights. Service providers have frequently operated from a sense of responsibility, lacking confidence in people and harbouring fears related to their own personal safety and professional liability that have driven decisions and limited tolerance of a person's agency and risk taking. Negative perceptions of the person's capacity to manage and concerns about harm to self and others have often restricted or entirely eliminated the person's choices. All too often, people have been taught to have low expectations and focus on maintenance of the status quo rather than the prospect of recovery or a full life.

The development of peer work in Australia has a thirty-year history. Peer work in mental health in Australia has evolved from being a disruptive consumer-led practice to being accepted as an important part of good recovery, clinical and psychosocial disability support practice by consumers, families and carers, governments and professional associations. People with mental health issues and service providers now expect peer work to be a part of the mix of support offerings that are available. Peer work has evolved significantly over the past decade and there have been many views about what peer work is and what it can achieve. There is an emerging consensus about what Australian peer work is, and this chapter seeks to articulate the need for further development some of the elements of contemporary peer work practice.

In Australia, there has been phenomenal growth in the mental health peer workforce in the past five years. In the community sector, for instance, there is evidence of growth of numbers of peer employees from single digits to triple digits in the space of three years. However, peer work is still a comparatively under-utilised approach to service delivery, and evaluation has lagged behind implementation of peer workforce roles. Given this, it is important to consider and use the available evidence regarding the utility and value of a peer workforce. This can assist agencies and organisations to apply best practice models and contribute to the further development and diversification of the workforce.

## 1: Peer work in mental health in Australia: its scope, role and contribution

This chapter explores the concept of the peer worker role and outlines the values, ethics and contribution of peer work. It summarises the wealth, the richness and the diversity of peer work literature. It offers strategies and suggestions of how to build lived experience and peer work into a range of disability organisations, based on an ethical value base and accepted principles.

A focused approach to the employment of people living with mental health issues (provided they are appropriately skilled and actively engaged in their personal recovery) offers effective strategies to assist people to live contributing lives and reduce their reliance on formal services. People with lived experience of mental health issues can play effective roles as support coordinators or facilitators, support providers and mentors. They can, by their professionalism, intent and status as lived-experience experts, model aspects of how to challenge oneself, offer encouragement and raise people's awareness of their personal potential. The expertise that such people offer is vital and under-recognised (Galbally, 2011). We argue that policy and practice in disability, mental health and other human service streams needs to integrate peer work practice and build on the experience of peer work over the past decade to develop service responses that will deliver better mental health and practical outcomes for service users.

**Peer work**

*What is peer work?*

Each of us in our life situation has many peer groups, based on age, work, hobbies and other facets of our identity, for example, our Facebook 'friends', our work colleagues, our social circles. In mental health systems, peer work is offered by an individual who identifies as a peer through having personal lived experience of trauma, mental health issues, psychiatric diagnosis and/or severe and long-lasting emotional distress. According to the *Macquarie dictionary*, one sense of the word 'peer' is 'an equal in any respect'.

In the context of peer work, the use of the term 'peer' indicates that the role requires the appointment of a person who meets an essential job criterion of having personal 'lived experience'. In such positions, the peer is regarded as bringing a particular and valued expertise to the role through their personal experience of dealing with and managing emotional distress, enabling them to become a specialist support provider with unique dimensions of that experience and of recovery to bring to the required tasks.

The validity of peer work has been established by the United Nations Convention on the rights of persons with disabilities (2006), which states

> Article 26.1: Parties shall take effective and appropriate measures, including through *peer support*, to enable persons with disabilities to attain and maintain maximum independence, full physical, mental, social and vocational ability, and full inclusion and participation [emphasis added].
>
> Article 27.1e, 1h: Promote employment opportunities and career advancement for persons with disabilities ... Promote the employment of persons with disabilities ... through appropriate policies and measures, which may include affirmative action programmes, incentives and other measures.

The Australian Government has been a strong supporter of peer work for over a decade and was a major contributor in the development of peer work through its Personal Helpers and Mentors Program. They have more recently defined the role as 'a professional role that is distinguished from other forms of peer support by the intentionality, skills, knowledge and experience that peer workers bring to their role. They are employed as professional subject matter experts who can be a key conduit between a consumer, their other support people, and the services they use.' (Australian Government Department of Health, 2016).

Peer work is 'providing support, encouragement and hope to another'. It aims to promote hope and to focus on strengths and supports rather than illness or disability. It is different from other types of support work in that the source of support is a person who identifies as having lived through similar related and relevant experiences to those of the consumers. An example of peer support is people with specific health conditions meeting others who have been through treatment for a similar condition and who can share experiences and talk about what works for them.

The empathy and experience that the peer brings to the group is a key element in helping people to build their own emotional resilience, to understand the ways in which others have dealt with the health condition and to frame and sustain their response to the health condition. It is an element of practice that

## 1: Peer work in mental health in Australia: its scope, role and contribution

helps people to build their own sense of control and choice over their life situations. Peer workers may play a particular role as part of a support or treatment team. Lived experience has long been a part of support groups such as breast cancer support groups and 12-step programs for addictions. Peer work provides a professional role for such lived and shared experiences.

Over an extended period of time, the literature and experienced peer workers indicate that the following six qualities are required in an **effective peer worker**:

1. integration of their experiences of mental distress into their lives so they see value in them and do not feel ashamed or disempowered
2. ability to think critically and reflect on what they do and why they do it, and be capable of making judgements based on reasonable possibilities
3. having values consistent with the peer values of the service for which they work
4. having a good understanding of marginalisation issues, exclusion and discrimination
5. being empathetic, emotionally mature and objective
6. being skilled at utilising personal lived experience purposefully to support people in recovery and to develop more empathetic service practices.

Formalised peer work is support provided by **paid** peer support workers who are people with personal experience of living with a disabling, traumatic, health or living situation. Through their processing of and learning from this personal experience, they may be able to offer empathetic support, empowerment and validation to other people with comparable experiences. In addition, it is common for people with similar lived experiences to offer each other practical advice, emotional support and suggestions for strategies that professionals may not consider, offer or have time to share.

In the literature and in practice, to this point, it can be seen that a peer worker or peer support position uses the term 'peer' to indicate that it is one that requires the person appointed to the job to be one who meets an 'essential job criterion' of having **personal** lived experience. In these positions, the person is regarded as bringing a particular and valued expertise to their role through their **personal experience** of a mental health issue, enabling them to become a specialist support provider with unique experiences to bring to the job.

It needs to be said, however, that in carer or family member peer support there is a differential. That difference is, importantly, that in a specified 'carer' position, the requirement is that the 'carer peer worker' must bring lived experience as having been a primary carer for a person with enduring mental health issues. These two roles are quite specialised and intrinsically different. They must not be confused.

In the future, we will take this aspect as a 'given' and our reflections on peer work will move us to more esoteric places where we will further develop the focus, the scope and expectations of peer work.

Beyond this point in time, peer work will have proven its worth and will be looking at its place in the much wider service and support context. Going forward, it will not be an 'either/or', it will be an essential element within the suite of service offerings across the entire human service arena. Whether it be in disability, addictions, justice, parenting, education, health or mental health, it will be a stream of work that will be a critically important component of one-on-one service delivery. It will be supporting people to rebuild their lives, develop a personal sense of control, master their emotional strengths and work as models, guides and companions on people's journeys towards a contributing life.

Peer work is *not* voluntary work. It is professional work for which specific salaries, training, development and peer supervision are desirable. In peer work roles there are expectations of productivity, accountability and performance similar to those of other professional staff. It is regarded as essential that those with peer work responsibilities must be paid for their expertise and have and maintain ethical and performance standards commensurate with sector expectations.

In understanding what peer work is, it is important to understand how it differs from other roles.

A peer worker is not you, as an employer, 'being kind' to an individual by giving an unemployable or disadvantaged individual a 'sort of a job', to make them feel better. It certainly is not a 'cheaper' way of staffing or the gesture of employing someone with less experience to save 'professional' staff from doing menial tasks. And, most significantly, it is *not* unpaid or voluntary work.

A peer worker understands the parameters of their role. In it, they know they are not:

- a counsellor. Peer workers may use some counselling skills, but it is important that they know that they are not counsellors.
- an adviser. Peer workers may be called upon to give advice, but it is important to remember that they are not advisers. The focus should be sharing, encouragement and experience rather than giving advice.
- an advocate. By definition, an advocate is someone who pleads or speaks for another, which is not part of a peer worker's role.
- a friend. Although some aspects of friendship may enter into the peer relationship, there are clear differences between friendship and peer work boundaries. For example, a friend can be contacted at home and at any reasonable time, whereas a peer worker would be available during agreed hours and would not be contactable in their private 'home time'.
- a 'friendly ear'. Although providing participants with non-judgemental listening is part of the peer worker role, the ability to empathise while remaining emotionally focused on the reason for their being present is a very important part of being a peer worker.
- a sympathetic listener. Peer workers express *empathy* with participants, not sympathy.
- a 'role model'. Peer workers may be seen as 'inclusion guides' by offering their life experiences and activities as exemplars, but will also point participants to a range of community identities for broader modelling.

**Lived experience and peer work**

In a presentation on peer work and its value given to the Queensland Consumer Advisory Group in Brisbane in 2001, Michael Burge described lived experience as 'the expertise that comes from firsthand experiences … that experience places the peer in the best position to provide hope and support and encourages [others] to participate and to voice their needs and concerns based on their individual … journey'. Lived experience of mental ill-health is an asset: 'A peer worker is an occupational title for a person [who has lived with a] problem, who is working to assist other people with a [similar issue]. Because of their life experience, such persons have expertise that professional training cannot replicate; they are important sources of information, a potential source of motivation, and may serve as mentors to others' (Dodie Bennett and Janet Meagher at a leadership retreat in 2010).

However, it is important to recognise that having 'lived experience' alone is not the only competency required of a peer worker. As well as lived experience, a person's overall life experience, employment and education history, emotional maturity and ability to engage and communicate are all important elements of the competencies peer workers need to bring to their roles.

Our experience highlights what a complex and demanding job peer work is. Enabling positive growth in people who are experiencing a significant mental health condition is a complex and difficult task. It is by its nature relationship-based and rarely works if it is undertaken in a formulaic way. There is much art and a lot of science in effective peer work. But what is known from thirty years of peer work experience in Australia is that peer work is a distinctive contribution and important element of good mental health outcomes in a range of medical, therapeutic, rehabilitation and recovery-oriented interventions and supports for people with chronic health conditions.

Peer-to-peer work is primarily about how people connect to and interact with one another in a mutual relationship. These roles are different from traditional roles that happen to be filled by someone with a similar lived experience. A person working in a traditional role, such as a clinician, manager or support worker, may have had similar experiences to those who are using their services (for example, a clinician, manager or support worker may also be a cancer survivor or have had a mental health issue). This does *not* make that person a 'peer' in the sense that we are discussing here. They may share their personal experience, but they are still operating within their primary role as a manager, clinician or support worker. In their primary role their obligations are to fulfil stated professional responsibilities. There remains a substantive difference between peer and non-peer roles, and although each is important both have to be carefully managed on the front line for their respective significant contributions to be most effectively made.

## 1: Peer work in mental health in Australia: its scope, role and contribution

Mead and MacNeil elegantly describe the difference between lived experience and peer work:

> peer support has been defined by the fact that people who have like experiences can better relate and can consequently offer more authentic empathy and validation. It is also not uncommon for people with similar lived experiences to offer each other practical advice and suggestions for strategies that professionals may not offer or even know about. Maintaining its non-professional vantage point is crucial in helping people rebuild their sense of community when they've had a disconnecting kind of experience (2006, p. 29).

### Scope of peer work

Peer workers undertake a variety of functions in diverse settings that include:
- vocational support
- personal support, social integration
- preparing, implementing or coordinating recovery or support plans
- educative programs or classes
- rehabilitation, habilitation and recovery facilitation
- community integration activity
- accommodation support
- transitional support from hospital or other care to reintegration into the community
- assisting people to access and manage their participation in the National Disability Insurance Scheme (NDIS).

### Goals of peer work

The supporting peer work literature outlines a number of specific goals for peer work. For example:

1. Helping people rediscover and activate their own personal, innate resources, enabling them to:
   - share their life challenges with those who understand
   - grow in confidence and be encouraged to share and explore their issues in increasing breadth and depth
   - believe that they can have control over their own life, inclusion and happiness

- take on responsibility for their own journey towards participation and integration
- gain and share knowledge of skills, activity pathways and tools that may be useful
- be strengthened, and take that strength into their lives.

2. Experiencing benefits from collective wisdom, providing people with:
   - access to accumulated knowledge from multiple perspectives
   - new insights, widening the basis of understanding their particular issues and helping people to build purpose and meaning in their lives
   - a source of support, inspiration and empowerment, reducing perceived limitations and helping to build self-confidence and control
   - self-respect, knowing that they are valued
   - opportunities to understand themselves and their issues, enabling them to have the freedom to be themselves without fear of rejection, failure or humiliation and to gain knowledge of their rights and an understanding that their lived experience is accepted and valued.

3. Receiving and giving hope, inspiration and empowerment for inclusion by providing:
   - proof that inclusion and recovery are possible, gained from observation and learning from the stories of others
   - encouragement from others
   - an understanding that inclusion, observation, understanding, recovery and health are all part of a life-long journey.

4. Helping people develop a renewed sense of self-respect, understanding and belonging through being part of a caring community, so that they gain:
   - knowledge that they are not isolated and are not the first to be in their position
   - strength from the realisation that they are an important part of the community
   - opportunities to make authentic connections that increase wellbeing socially, mentally, physically and spiritually
   - opportunities to give help to others, as equal to equal, through:
     - sharing what they have learnt
     - encouraging listening as well as being listened to

1: Peer work in mental health in Australia: its scope, role and contribution

- potentially offering support to others from their lived experience
- experiencing the personal strength and healing that come from helping others and contributing to the greater good of their community
- self-respect and having knowledge of (and valuing) collective wisdom.

5. Accessing a pathway to growth that is:
- non-threatening
- affordable
- complementary to existing provider goals
- either complementary to existing services or stand-alone
- open to freedom of participation.

6. Reducing people's social isolation and improving their economic and social participation.

These goals are addressed through practice guidance that preferably has the following elements:
- actively advocating and supporting people to find and use their own voice
- sharing experiences, strengths and wisdom without giving unsolicited advice
- acknowledging those being supported as their primary responsibility
- avoiding discussion of diagnoses or the use of pathologising language by not referring to people using words like 'client', 'consumer' or other consumer-systematised terms
- respecting the power of simply 'being with' people in their efforts
- supporting others in peer roles and those working in isolated environments
- staying connected to others and their work by participating in peer worker meetings, events and gatherings and acquiring knowledge and new ideas (This an essential responsibility.)
- treating each other with compassion through a commitment to honesty, transparency and a willingness to work through issues or conflict
- acting as change agents, sharing new ideas and challenging existing ideas as required
- supporting a culture of questioning to understand and be well-informed about how practices and beliefs are shaped

- being committed to being aware of, and transparent about, their own power and privilege in these roles
- understanding the obligations of 'working with'—not 'working for'—a peer.

## Peer support

Peer support is one element of peer work. It is an important element and is about *how* people connect to, and interact with, one another. It involves people drawing on shared personal experiences to provide knowledge, social interaction, emotional assistance and personal or practical help to each other in a way that is often mutually beneficial.

Peer support is based on the belief that people who have faced, endured and overcome adversity can offer useful support, encouragement, hope and, perhaps, mentorship to others facing similar situations (Davidson et al., 2006). It has been defined as: 'Any organised support provided by and for people with similar conditions, problems or experiences' (O'Hagan, 2011), and Orwin (2008) states 'it should be noted that peer support … is about understanding another's situation empathically through the shared experience of [disability, trauma or] emotional and psychological pain'.

Shery Mead, in her comprehensive definition of peer work from 2003, defines peer support as:

> a system of giving and receiving help founded on key principles of respect, shared responsibility, and mutual agreement of what is helpful. Peer support is not based on … models and diagnostic criteria. It is about understanding another's situation empathically through the shared experience of emotional and psychological pain. When people find affiliation with others whom they feel are 'like' them, they feel a connection. This connection, or affiliation, is a deep, holistic understanding based on mutual experience where people are able to 'be' with each other without the constraints of traditional (expert/patient) relationships. Further, as trust in the relationship builds, both people are able to respectfully challenge each other when they find themselves re-enacting old roles.

The peer support approach done well promotes a coping, inclusion and wellness mindset. Fostering responsibility and critical self-awareness, it assists a person to find and develop their own personal interior resources, enabling them to be empowered with the knowledge and belief that they can and do have control over their life. For some people, being ready and willing to take responsibility for their own journey towards recovery, participation, inclusion, wellbeing and growth means having access to peer support as a fundamental element of their recovery.

It has been proposed that the following three areas of focus are essential for effective peer support work:

1. mutuality. Here, 'mutuality' refers to operating from an equal a playing field, where connection is the focal point and neither person is the 'fixer'.
2. being a change agent. Based on wisdom gained from personal experience, people in peer roles advocate for growth and facilitate learning within the individual served, the service system and beyond.
3. remaining 'in' but not 'of' the system. This refers to working in the service system while holding values that are specific to the peer role and not taking on responsibilities that dilute those values or widen their purpose (Mead, 2003).

**Values and philosophical base of peer work**

There is a strong ethics, values and philosophical base to peer work practice. While there are a number of statements of these values, we summarise the essential elements in the following manner.

- Human potential and vision: We believe in the probability that all of us can and will be able to have a contributing and fulfilling life. Our focus is on the vision of a full and meaningful life for all, not just day-to-day functioning and survival.
- Self-determination and choice: We put a high value on the healing power of simply having choices and refuse any participation in force or coercion.
- Dignity of being a whole person: We, the people who have personal lived experience, are the experts on our own experience. We regard each person as whole, with many strengths and contributions to make.
- Easy-to-understand language: We value clear, human, non-clinical language that creates space for each person to explore and find their own meaning in life and their experiences.
- Mutuality: We are committed to reciprocity and being honest and real in our connections. We recognise the fluidity of human experience and our

various roles, and the ability of each of us to learn from one another.
- Approach each other with genuine curiosity: We seek to understand each participant's worldview. We are dedicated to learning about people from themselves, and not from files or meetings where they are not present.
- Honesty, truth and transparency: We believe in people's fundamental resiliency and are up-front with them about limitations, concerns and conflicts. We are never complicit in decisions about people, in decisions being made about people, without their knowledge and input.
- Seeing challenges as growth and learning opportunities, not as crises: We choose to regard our times of greatest frustration or distress as a potential sign of change to come and as an opportunity for growth. This is not intended to deny the deep pain that people may experience, but rather to value and have faith in what can emerge from that experience.
- Transformation: We recognise the need for transformation in support systems and the community. We believe that, for change to be sustainable and real, it must happen within our communities and systems. It is not solely the responsibility of each participant.
- Focus on moving forward: We seek the development of something better and healthier than the power structures and approaches that have harmed and limited many of us in the past. We will consciously avoid compromising our values or replicating past wrongs.
- Connectedness: We recognise our connectedness. Our work is a part of a human rights movement. We strive to have our fundamental connectedness to a history of disempowerment and oppression and fight for inclusion and for disability rights to be recognised, implemented and understood.
- Importance of community involvement: We believe in the importance of human connection in healing and inclusion. A person in a peer role can support someone to find resources within and from the community to meet this need and make sustained change.

These values translate into the following practice guidelines:
- enabling empowerment for service users
- never being judgemental of people's choices
- having peer worker reporting and support expectations
- not imposing personal limits on others

- encouraging freedom of choice
- acknowledging that a peer worker is not 'all things to all people'—peer workers must know their personal and professional limitations and be honest about them
- exhibiting high standards of personal conduct with regard to:
  - ensuring their own safety and wellbeing
  - maintaining emotional and personal control
  - maintaining integrity in 'professional' relationships
  - exhibiting respect
  - respecting and protecting participants' dignity and avoiding substance misuse
- protecting participants' privacy and confidentiality
- exhibiting personal integrity and honesty
- enhancing their own knowledge constantly.

Agreement on the philosophy, ethics and principles that underpin the employment of those with lived experience in the support workforce is pivotal as a starting point. To enable that, services and organisations will need to:

- enable key stakeholders to understand and appreciate the value and power of peer work as a cost-effective part of the support system and as a means of preventing the escalation of personal, support or inclusion issues and of promoting adjustment and inclusion by improvement in emotional, physical and spiritual wellbeing
- emphasise the value and power of lived experience, placing it in its proper context as a specialist knowledge base—an expertise. Having it valued and utilised alongside other types of expertise will enhance the provision of relevant supports to individuals, increasing their opportunities and participation goals
- highlight the validity and value of peer work as an integral and valued method of service delivery
- promote personal involvement, participation and empowerment.

Services and organisations moving in this direction need to champion the inclusion of those with lived experience by an overt and direct policy commitment to employing them. There are useful resources available for organisations working towards introducing a peer workforce at the 'Peer work hub' at www.peerworkhub.com.au.

## Contribution of peer work

The value of self-help support groups, social and friendship groups, telephone support trees and consumers connecting individually with each other on an informal basis, whether in the community, establishments or hospital, has been recognised across our sector for over sixty years. An extension of this more recently is that international research literature has provided the evidence base for professional peer work and peer support as being effective in upholding and enhancing the quality of participants' lifestyles and personal choices.

Across a range of human service sectors, it is acknowledged that good-quality peer work is a means of individualised interaction that is known to be successful in preventing the escalation of personal, support or inclusion issues, and in promoting recovery, adjustment and inclusion by enhancing the participant's emotional, physical and spiritual wellbeing.

Peer support in a broader context is known to be a particularly effective and positive intervention strategy for people who have lost children, people with alcohol and substance misuse problems, and people with cancer. It has proven to be a tremendously important mechanism towards helping many people move through difficult personal situations (Riessman, 1990; Roberts et al., 1999). In alcohol and other drug services and organisations it is offered as an intervention type that is seen as more practical and effective than generic, clinical or traditional methods of support.

In the contemporary Australian context, we need to conceptualise the elements of peer work activity and broaden current interpretations of it, not merely as a valued mental health support activity but as a developing service modality across a variety of human service jurisdictions as a new and effective professional role in multiple sectors. People who have lived through particular life situations and have learned much through that process are a rich resource—a resource which is as yet untapped and underutilised. A broader understanding of the principles of peer work may well open up this lived experience cohort as a potential new support workforce across many sectors.

## 1: Peer work in mental health in Australia: its scope, role and contribution

More immediately, there is an imperative that current and future National Disability Insurance Scheme participants are encouraged to include in their support plan support items that enable them to engage a peer worker to assist them in developing their plan and in implementing their support package. This is a particularly important issue for practice and funding of supports over the next five years.

Peer workers offer an approach that can be either complementary to clinical services or, in some situations, effective as a stand-alone intervention. It is acknowledged that to promote peer support work as a valued service type in its own right has validity because, as mentioned above, it is a proven means of preventing the escalation of isolation and emotional issues, and promotes help-seeking behaviours and improved wellbeing in the people it supports. Giving peer support, like receiving it, results both in increased self-esteem and increased levels of hope (Ratzlaff et al., 2006). Peer work has added value in that it can provide a meaningful career option for some people living with mental health issues or other difficulties. For many people, work provides structure and meaning, and Hutchison et al. (2006) suggest that, for peer workers, employment can provide an identity shift from patient, consumer or client to that of valued worker and contributing citizen. Moran et al. (2012) report that peer providers discovered personal strengths that they were not aware of previously, and that their sense of themselves as capable human beings was augmented through their work. As a London manager of peer workers commented, 'It's very powerful how it lifts people out of that sick role, to say, "let us give them a job, here's some responsibility, I believe in you, you can do this" ' (Gillard et al., 2013).

Peer work has also been shown to assist organisations in the development and maintenance of a sensitive support service culture. Organisations emphasise that, through their peer workforce, they acknowledge the value and power of lived experience. They see this lived experience in the context of a specialist knowledge base, an expertise. Having that expertise valued and utilised alongside other types of expertise is an effective way to bring relevant supports to a range of participants, enhancing their opportunities and participation goals.

## Evidence base for peer work

A substantial body of research on peer work has been undertaken over the past twenty years. Research has focused more on some areas of peer work and service delivery than others. More studies have been undertaken on consumer peer workers than on carer peer workers, and research has often focused on peer support as a specific element of lived experience peer work. Where research specifically concerns peer support, efforts have been made in literature reviews to ensure that this is clear. However, there are significant differences in the definitions of peer work used in research. Research has also concentrated on peer work in the context of adult services; there are fewer studies on which to draw with regard to children, young people and older people. For particular age groups, the definition of 'peer' may also involve a person of a similar age or developmental stage, as well as personal disability or lived experience of mental ill health (Daley et al., 2013). As the research base grows, knowledge of the utility of peer work for people across the lifespan, as well as for their families and carers, will be enhanced.

In the United Kingdom, the review *Peer Support: what it is and what it does* was undertaken by an independent organisation, the Evidence Centre (National Voices, 2015). The review process followed best practice for identifying and summarising trends in research. Two reviewers searched ten bibliographic databases independently to identify studies published between January 2000 and January 2015. Research of any type was eligible, as long as it was published in English and focused on peer support in Organisation for Economic Cooperation and Development (OECD) countries (to allow some comparability with the UK). Research with people with long-term physical or mental health conditions or their family carers was prioritised, but other studies were included to illustrate how widely peer support has been used.

More than 20,000 studies were screened, of which 1023 were identified for inclusion; 524 of these studies examined the outcomes of peer work and the others described processes. They came from the UK (23%), Europe (27%), North America (41%) and many other parts of the world (9%). There were 27 reviews compiling findings from multiple studies and 147 randomised trials (which are thought to provide high-quality evidence). The rest were lower-quality, non-experimental studies. All 1023 studies were used to develop a simple 'typology' showing the variety of initiatives that are labelled 'peer support'. The researchers then looked at the results of the 524 outcome studies to identify which types of peer support or peer work were associated with improvements in people's experience (including knowledge and satisfaction), health behaviour and outcomes and service use and costs.

Systematic processes were used to identify and analyse the material, but the review was not exhaustive. It showed trends in the research evidence and sparked discussion rather than providing definitive answers about the most effective peer support or peer work model or the findings of every study.

Using the 1023 studies to classify the types of peer support or work available, the reviewers found that it varied in terms of who was involved (target group, who set up the support, who provided support, training and payment of facilitators), what type of support was provided (support activities, support type), why support was provided (rationale), how support was provided (mode of delivery, number of people involved), where support was provided (location) and when support was provided (duration, frequency).

Widespread acknowledgement of the usefulness of lived experience roles exists throughout the literature, with better outcomes, increased quality of life for consumers and reduction of service costs frequently cited (Anderson et al., 2009; Commonwealth of Australia, 2009; Happell & Roper, 2007; Mental Health Commission of New Zealand, 2005; National Mental Health Consumer and Carer Forum, 2010; WHO, 2010). However, major barriers to the development of the lived-experience workforce were also identified (Anderson et al., 2009; Craze Lateral Solutions, 2010).

On the subject of barriers, Goldman and Lefley (1996) found that the attitudes of mental health professionals towards mutual support services prevented their clients from accessing peer support services. Many were reluctant to refer people and even perceived such services as being potentially detrimental to their overall functioning. Davidson et al. (1999) stated that partnerships struck between professional and peer support services are necessary for the peer work role to have a substantial effect on the majority of mental health consumers. Another significant barrier is funding. Despite the strong evidence base and potential gains of peer work, only a minority of consumers with severe mental health issues, that is, up to a third of individuals, participate in activities offering mutual support. A significant contributor to this phenomenon includes a lack of funding for peer services and the challenges this presents.

Several studies of peer work report raised empowerment scores by consumers (Repper & Carter, 2011). One study found that both providers and recipients of peer support reported an increased sense of independence and empowerment, which may have related to increased stability in work, education and training (Janzen et al., 2006). Personal empowerment can be regarded as a positive process parallel to the negative processes associated with self-stigma. Repper et al. (2013) note that peer workers embody the possibility of acceptance and success, so they can challenge the barriers created by self-stigmatisation. Engaging in peer work can alter attitudes to mental health issues and break down stigma, as well as fostering hope (Mowbray, Moxley & Collins, 1998).

Studies have found that consumers involved in peer support initiatives have higher levels of community integration (Repper & Carter, 2011). Forchuk et al. (2005) found that people who received peer support demonstrated improved social support, enhanced social skills and improved social functioning. As a person involved in a peer support program run by the Mental Illness Fellowship Victoria put it: 'I've done a complete turnaround in my life. Even just going to a restaurant or a shopping centre, I don't feel that anxiety and stress any more. Yeah, I'm a citizen, whereas before, I didn't feel as if I was' (Health Workforce Australia, 2014, p. 9).

Importantly, for the peer workers themselves there is evidence that peer work assists with 'increased confidence, self-esteem, increased knowledge … increased levels of employment leading to better financial situations, increased volunteering, social support and networking and increased aspirations for life' (Peters, 2010). This aligns well with a community provider's mission to support people who are affected by mental health issues and who have complex needs, and to resource their journey towards living a fulfilling life in the community. It illustrates a clear business case for embracing a peer work workforce strategy.

Studies report that peers can be very effective at establishing connections with those people who are 'hard to reach'. Sells et al. (2006) reported that peer workers were highly skilled and effective at engaging and communicating acceptance. They were able to increase treatment participation among the more disengaged in case management for consumers with co-morbid mental health and alcohol and other drug issues. Davidson et al. (2012) note that peer staff can be especially effective in engaging people into care and acting as a bridge between those people and other staff. In this and other ways, peer work can be an important and useful complement to existing mental health services.

In terms of specific groups, in the mental health context, researchers have reported that Māori, Pacific and Chinese participants say that peer support translates well across cultures but requires adaptation to the cultural needs or expectations of each group. Peer support for specific groups or populations should have sufficient operational independence to ensure that the unique and cultural aspects of the service are respected and preserved.

Overall, the evidence with regard to cost-effectiveness and peer work is limited, largely due to the fact that not enough rigorous studies have been undertaken. A report by the Centre for Mental Health in the UK (Trachtenberg et al., 2013) specifically examined whether peer workers could reduce psychiatric inpatient bed use and thus prove cost-effective. The study found that peer support workers brought about significant reductions in bed use among the patients they supported, leading to financial savings that were well in excess of what it cost to employ the peer workers. The study concluded that the use of peer workers is justified on value-for-money grounds.

Additionally, a cost-benefit analysis has shown that 'peer support workers cost less than clinicians—suggesting they are cost effective' (Peters, 2010). Generating cost-effectiveness while utilising an expert resource that is central to achieving a provider's mission makes sound business sense. Peer workers may be cost-effective in a range of ways. They may complement the non-peer workforce, allowing both peers and non-peers to focus on using their respective expertise. Supporting health practitioners to use their full scope of practice can improve satisfaction, retention and productivity (Rogers, Kash-MacDonald, & Brucker, 2009). In terms of risk management, some studies have shown that peer work has no effect; however, there are no studies to date to show that it has any *adverse* effects (O'Hagan, 2011).

A literature review undertaken by Canadian researchers (Leung & DeSousa, 2002), revealed that, although past research findings are limited due to the

lack of rigour in their methodologies, participants of groups offering peer support have described the following significant gains:
- self-esteem
- better decision-making skills
- improved social functioning
- decreased psychiatric symptoms (resulting in decreased rates or lengths of hospitalisation)
- lower rates of isolation
- larger social networks
- increased support seeking
- greater pursuit of educational goals and employment (Davidson et al., 1999; Humphreys & Rappaport, 1994; Froland et al., 2000).

Research undertaken by Health Workforce Australia (2013) on behalf of the National Mental Health Commission (in an unpublished report on the Mental Health Peer Workforce Project) included a small-scale survey of 305 people who identified as peer workers. Of this sample, 18% worked casually, 29% full-time and 53% part-time. About half of the sample worked for non-government organisations, while 17% worked in public hospitals, 11% in a Commonwealth-funded mental health service or program and 10% in a state- or territory-funded public mental health service or program.

Although, as has been stated, many studies are qualitative, some randomised control trial findings are available. The quantitative and qualitative evidence suggests that the peer workforce can be as effective as the professional mental health workforce in some roles, and may offer particular benefits to consumers, peer workers, families, carers and service providers. There is newer and growing evidence base that is articulating strong indicators of greater efficiencies and solid recovery outcomes when peer workers are in the staffing mix.

## History of peer work

Peer work has its origin in self-help and mutual support movements that were volunteer in nature (Davidson et al., 2006). People came together to help one another or to advocate for better services. In recent times peer work has evolved into more formalised approaches, and people are employed as peer workers in varying roles. Today, referring to 'peer work' is different from the 'self-help' activities that were the embryonic beginnings of that mutual support which we now recognise as 'professional' lived-experience peer work, a paid employment role.

## Australian efforts towards peer work

**1980s**: A push to incorporate peers into organisations and to participate in policy formulation and service evaluation was not welcomed. People with lived experience were tolerated as volunteers and needed to show their worth to the groups they were involved in. Over time, most community organisations began to include lived-experience and carer volunteers in such positions as board member, but there were no formal involvement opportunities and no funded roles in staff, policy or support areas.

**1990s**: In late 1992 a small committee of people who had personal lived experience of mental health issues met with Jan Whalan, manager of the large Sydney Rozelle Psychiatric Hospital, to discuss the development and creation of positions in the hospital that would utilise and value those with personal lived experience. This meeting was followed by the historic employment of consumer peer advocates at the hospital, with appropriate employment conditions and salary rates. These peer worker roles are acknowledged as the earliest nominated roles for people with lived experience of mental health issues, and the people who performed them are recognised as the first paid peer workers in Australia. They were a cohort of part-time and casual consumer advocates (peer workers) under the leadership of the valiant late Helen Blum. Historically, this innovation coincided with the landmark publication of the *Report of the National Inquiry into Human Rights of People with Mental Illness* (National Inquiry, 1993) from which followed the development of the first National Mental Health Strategy and related reform activities and policies. The most relevant development relates to the requirement for government and agencies to consult with the community, in particular consumers and carers. They set up formal consultative and advisory structures across Australia. Every state and territory formed community advisory groups and each of them was represented in a National Community Advisory Group. These led to organised groups for consumers and carers proliferating across the country. This period also saw an increase in the variety of consumer and peer engagements and opportunities. Victoria and a few other states followed, with various forms of paid roles for lived-experience consumers being created in organisations and in services.

**2000s**: By 2008 it was clear that the diversity of roles (and, in some places, the distortion, dilution and corruption of the integrity of such roles) had the potential to undermine the higher values that they represented. A peak lived-experience organisation, the Australian Mental Health Consumer Network, created a working group to set out standards and ethics to underpin peer work in Australia. However, they were unable to complete that work. It remains incomplete.

The founder of the United States' Georgia Peer Support Network, Larry Fricks, visited Australia in 2008 and again in 2011 to discuss peer work and establishing enhanced peer workforce training and employment opportunities, as there had been a push to see such things become established here. He spoke about 'certified' peer specialist training and the variety of peer roles, and said that following US federal legislation in 2007 such certified peer workers were able to bill Medicaid for specific services. The Georgia Peer Support Network's certified peer worker training course was the core training requirement for peer workers in twenty-three states at that time. The takeaway message from Fricks to us in Australia was: 'I am an expert in lived experience; I am the evidence of recovery'.

**2010s**: Professor Larry Davidson (of Yale University, USA) visited Australia several times, promoting peer work and the academic case for integrating it into service provision. He outlined both the academic research and the evidence base that backs up such concepts as the value of lived experience and, particularly, the efficacy of peer worker roles. His work reminds us that integrity and truthfulness, aligned to the core values of peer work, need to underpin everything we do.

In this current decade, mental health commissions (national and state) have shone a new spotlight onto the peer workforce and its potential, particularly its part in improving the 'contributing lives' of those who can benefit from peer work activity. The mental health commissions reinforce that what is needed now is a greater commitment on the part of providers to expand on their peer workforce and establish career structures to enable those staff in specialist peer roles to continually improve and look to future career developments. The peer workforce is now the most rapidly growing workforce in the mental health sector in Australia, with many working in the non-government sector.

**Training and professional supervision for peer work**

Many mental health peer work courses and curricula can be found in the US, Canada, New Zealand and parts of Europe. Several of these are accredited to certain agencies, but there is wide variation in their expectations, consistency and levels of competencies. That is why peers in Australia emphatically wanted to develop a single qualification; they wanted consistency of expectation, agreed value sets, agreed standards of practice and a quality set of standardised core information units for those in the peer workforce.

Development of the nationally accredited Certificate IV in Mental Health Peer Work was completed in 2012 through the Community Services and Health Industry Skills Council, and the course was approved by Australia's National Register of Vocational Education and Training. In 2014 and 2015, registered training organisations and technical and further education colleges began to offer this qualification. Graduates gave enthusiastic feedback about how challenging and effective the training and assessment process was. Also, and more importantly, they said how much it enhanced their work and supported their awareness of maintaining integrity in their practice of peer work.

Separate units of training are available for personal lived experience peer workers and for carer peer workers. A suite of peer-developed open-access training resources supports delivery of the course, thereby maintaining its quality and integrity. The certificate course has an approved curriculum, developed with strong stakeholder leadership and involvement in its content.

In the general sense, training, development and professional supervision opportunities for peer workers are essential. In mental health, there are multiple opportunities for peer-led or peer-organised training opportunities, through recovery colleges in multiple states and through larger community organisations, some registered training organisations or specialist peer-focused training consultancies and conferences.

One of the key insights from Health Workforce Australia's review of the mental health peer workforce (National Mental Health Commission, 2013) is that training on its own is insufficient. The review found that training and development must be accompanied by continuous appropriate support and peer supervision:

> Peer support encompasses a range of potential relationships ... There is equal potential in each type of relationship for Peer Workers to be exposed to suicidal intent or experiences that are distressing or traumatising. 'You can't just have a bit', a provider argued, 'just training is not enough. There must be continuous support. Depth of training is probably less important than having a safe structure to work within. That means supervision'.

The same review emphasised that several participants argued

> strongly that the non-professional [that is, non-health, non-clinical] character of peer support—such as mutuality and equality in relationship—should not be lost with the emergence of a trained and paid peer support workforce. Peer support by definition is non-professional support. One provider, for example, adopts a motto 'experts at not being experts' to describe the role. Few in the sector would want peer support taught within tertiary institutions by tutors who may have little or no practical experience in providing peer support.

Effective supervision helps maintain integrity for the peer worker. A skilled supervisor, knowledgeable about the peer role, can help the peer worker to 'stay peer'. External supervision especially can assist the peer worker to step out of their role to understand and reflect both on what they do and on the personal reactions and motivations that may be influencing their work effectiveness. Effective supervision is crucial.

Supervision for a peer worker should take the form of:
- monthly one-to-one formal line management supervision with the team leader
- monthly one-to-one supervision with an external supervisor
- fortnightly structured group supervision
- fortnightly less structured group supervision.

Supervision is critical to the success of peer work and yet is the process that is most likely to be neglected or cancelled due to time constraints. Supervision is a specialised, professional process that needs to be conducted with skill and understanding. Although supervision in peer work is no different in process

## 1: Peer work in mental health in Australia: its scope, role and contribution

from clinical supervision, its content is different. This is not just because peers already carry vulnerability from their lived experiences, but also because the peer work role is so different from traditional support or rehabilitation roles.

Peer workers' supervisors need:
- an understanding of, and belief in, the peer work role and the service model and philosophy
- to be, ideally, people with similar lived experiences, to have worked as a peer worker, and to have undertaken the same peer training as those they supervise
- training and experience in supervision
- to be external to the peer workers' team and, ideally, be external to the organisation.

These opportunities have not always existed. They arose in response to the growth in the numbers of peer workers and the demand for appropriate training, development and professional supervision options.

To this end, in 2017 a number of Australian peer work leaders agreed to work together to establish a national professional association for mental health peer workers, and other initiatives are sure to follow as this element of the workforce develops and grows.

## Conclusion

There is strong support for peer work in clinical mental health services, community-based and specialist organisations as well as in the opening up of new opportunities, such as initiating new peer-operated service models and integrating peer work supports into the National Disability Insurance Scheme. Client choice in the Scheme does open up many more potential opportunities for peer work. There is an imperative that current and future NDIS participants are encouraged to include support items in their support plan that enable them to engage a peer support worker to assist them in developing their plan and in implementing their support package. This is a particularly important issue for practice and funding of supports over the next five years.

It is important that the advocates of these concepts of peer work and peer support are successful in promoting peer work across a range of human service areas and that the work is shown to provide optimum outcomes for people. Beyond this point in time, peer work will have proven its worth and will be looking at its place in the much wider service and support context. Going forward, it will not be an 'either/or', it will be an essential element within the suite of service offerings across the entire human service arena. Whether it be in disability, addictions, justice, parenting, education, health or mental health, it will be a stream of work that is a critically important component of one-on-one service delivery. It will be a catalyst to enable people to rebuild their lives, develop a personal sense of control, master their emotional strengths and work as models, guides and companions on people's journeys towards a contributing life, thereby strengthening our communities.

It is our contention that a cutting-edge support service would be one that utilises such a 'disruptive technology' as peer work in order to maintain quality leadership and supports across a suite of services.

After all, what we believe in and promote is the motto 'Nothing about us without us'.

## References and further reading

Anderson, J., Collins, I., Edan, V., Fossey, E., Green, J., Grigg, M., … Roper, C. (2009). Real lives, real jobs: Developing good practice guidelines for a sustainable consumer workforce in the mental health sector, through participatory research (Final report). Retrieved from http://www.ourconsumerplace.com.au/files/real_lives_real_jobs.pdf

Anderson, T., Ogles, B., Patterson C., Lambert, M., & Vermeersch, D. (2009). Therapist effects: Facilitative interpersonal skills as a predictor of therapist success. *Journal of Clinical Psychology, 65*(7), 755–768.

Ashcraft, L., & Anthony, W. (2007). The value of peer employees. New York: Behavioral Healthcare Executive. Retrieved from http://www.behavioral.net/article/value-peer-employees

Association of Participating Service Users. (n.d.). The peer model manual: Consumer participation in action. Association of Participating Service Users. Retrieved from http://sharc.org.au/wp-content/uploads/2013/11/FINAL-PEER-MODEL-MANUAL.pdf

Australian Government Department of Health. (2009). *Fourth national mental health plan: An agenda for collaborative government action in mental health 2009–2014*. Canberra: DoH. http://www.health.gov.au/internet/main/publishing.nsf/Content/mental-pubs-f-plan09

Australian Government Department of Health. (2016). *PHN primary mental health care flexible funding pool implementation guidance: Primary mental health care services for people with severe mental illness, and Regional approach to suicide prevention*. Canberra: Department of Health. Retrieved from http://www.health.gov.au/internet/main/publishing.nsf/content/phn-mental_tools

## 1: Peer work in mental health in Australia: its scope, role and contribution

Balzamo, E., Roberts, J., Green, S., Heffernan, T., Tucker, S., & Parker, G. (2017). Peer work leadership statement of intent: A national professional association for mental health peer workers. Retrieved from http://www.iimhl.com/files/docs/IIMHL-Updates/20170618.pdf

Baptist Care (SA), & Mental Illness Fellowship South Australia. (2009). Employer tool-kit: Employing peer workers in your organisation. MIFSA. Retrieved from http://sharc.org.au/wp-content/uploads/2016/11/12-MIFSA_PWP_toolkit_for_employers.pdf

Bassett, T., Faulkner, A., Repper, J., & Stamou, E. (2010). Lived experience leading the way: Peer support in mental health. London: Together. Retrieved from https://amhp.org.uk/app/uploads/2017/08/livedexperiencereport.pdf

Bergeson, S. (n.d.). Cost effectiveness of using peers as providers. Retrieved from http://www.fredla.org/wp-content/uploads/2016/01/Cost_Effectiveness_of_Using_Peers_as_Providers.pdf

Bologna, M. J., & Pulice, R. T. (2011). Evaluation of a peer-run hospital diversion program: A descriptive study. *American Journal of Psychiatric Rehabilitation, 14*(4), 272–286.

Bouchard, L., Montreuil, M., & Gros, C. (2011). Peer support among inpatients in an adult mental health setting. Issues in Mental Health Nursing, 31(9), 589–598.

Bradstreet, S. (2009). Harnessing the 'lived experience': Formalising peer support approaches to promote recovery. *Mental Health Review, 11*(2), 33–37.

Bradstreet, S., & Pratt, R. (2010). Developing peer support worker roles: Reflecting on experiences in Scotland. *Mental Health and Social Inclusion Journal, 14*(3), 36–41.

Burdekin Report *see* National Inquiry Concerning the Human Rights of People with Mental Illness (1993).

Burge, M. (October 2016). Valuing the lived experience. Presentation at Recovered Futures, 12th Biennial Asia Pacific International Mental Health Conference, Brisbane 2016. Abstract retrieved from http://aspacmentalhealth16.com.au/wp-content/uploads/2016/03/ASPAC-Conference-Abstracts-A4-FINAL.pdf

Byrne, L. (2013). Grounded theory study of lived experience mental health practitioners within the wider workforce (PhD thesis). Central Queensland University. Retrieved from https://www.researchgate.net/publication/277803269_A_grounded_theory_study_of_lived_experience_mental_health_practitioners_within_the_wider_workforce

Campbell, J. (2005). The historical and philosophical development of peer-run programs. In: S. Clay, B. Schell, P. W., Corrigan, & R. O. Ralph (Eds.), *On our own, together: Peer programs for people with mental illness*. Nashville, TN: Vanderbilt University Press.

Campbell, J., Lichtenstein, C., Teague, G., Banks, S., Sonnefeld, J., Johnsen, M., ... COSP Steering Committee. (2004). Consumer-operated services program (COSP) multi-site research initiative: Overview and preliminary findings. Missouri Institute of Mental Health at the University of Missouri School of Medicine. Retrieved from https://www.mentalhealthamerica.net/sites/default/files/COSPVAREPORT.pdf

Centre of Excellence in Peer Support. (2013). Considerations when operating a peer support service. ARAFEMI. Retrieved from http://www.peersupportvic.org/index.php/2014-12-15-22-42-49/2014-12-16-02-22-27/func-startdown/173/

Chinman, M., George, P., Dougherty, R. H., Daniels, A. S., Shoma Ghose, S., Swift, A., ... Delphin-Rittmon, M. E. (2014). Peer support services for individuals with serious mental illness: Assessing the evidence. *Psychiatric Services, 65*(4), 429–441.

Chinman, M., Rosenheck, R., Lam, J., & Davidson, L. (2001). Comparing consumer and non-consumer provided case management services for homeless persons with serious mental illness. *Journal of Nervous and Mental Disease, 188*(7), 446–453.

Chinman, M., Weingarten, R., Stayner, D., & Davidson, L. (2001). Chronicity reconsidered: Improving person–environment fit through a consumer-run service. *Community Mental Health Journal, 37*(3), 215–229.

Chinman, M., Young, A. S., Hassell, J., & Davidson, L. (2006). Toward the implementation of mental health consumer provider services. *Journal of Behavioral Health Services & Research, 33*(2), 176–195.

Chisholm, D., & Evans, D. B. (2010). Improving health system efficiency as a means of moving towards universal coverage. Geneva: World Health Organization. Retrieved from http://www.who.int/healthsystems/topics/financing/healthreport/28UCefficiency.pdf

Clay, S., Schell, B., Corrigan, P., & Ralph, R. (2005). *On our own, together: Peer programs for people with mental illness*. Nashville, TN: Vanderbilt University Press.

Cook, J. A. (2011). Peer-delivered wellness recovery services: From evidence to widespread implementation. *Psychiatric Rehabilitation Journal, 35*(2), 87–89.

Cook, J. A., Copeland, M. E., Corey, L., Buffington, E., Jonikas, J., Curtis, L., ... Nichols, W. H. (2010). Developing the evidence base for peer-led services: Changes among participants following WRAP education in two state run initiatives. *Psychiatric Rehabilitation Journal, 34*(2), 113–120.

Corrigan, P. (2006). Impact of consumer operated services on empowerment and recovery of people with psychiatric disabilities. *Psychiatric Services, 57*(10), 1493–1496.

Craze Lateral Solutions. (2010). Scoping study to inform establishment of a new peak national mental health consumer organisation. Retrieved from http://consumersaustralia.org/wp-content/uploads/2015/10/nmhcorep_scoping-study_2010.pdf

Cyr, C., Heather, M., O'Hagan, M., & Priest, R. (2010). Making the case for peer support: Report to the peer support project committee of the Mental Health Commission of Canada. Mental Health Commission of Canada. Retrieved from https://www.mentalhealthcommission.ca/sites/default/files/2016-07/MHCC_Making_the_Case_for_Peer_Support_2016_Eng.pdf

Daley, S., Newton, D., Slade, M., Murray, J., & Banerjee, S. (2013). Development of a framework for recovery in older people with mental disorder. *International Journal of Geriatric Psychiatry, 28*(5), 522–529.

Daniels, A., Grant, E., Filson, B., Powell, I., Fricks, L., & Goodale, L. (Eds.). (2010). Pillars of peer support: Transforming mental health systems of care through peer support services. Retrieved from http://www.pillarsofpeersupport.org/final%20%20PillarsofPeerSupportService%20Report.pdf

Davidow, S. (2011). A handbook for individuals working in peer roles. Substance Abuse and Mental Health Services Administrations & Western Massachusetts Recovery Learning Community, USA. Retrieved from http://www.psresources.info/images/stories/A_Handbook_for_Individuals_Working_in_Peer_Roles.pdf

Davidson, L., Belamy, C., Guy, K., & Miller, R. (2012). Peer support among persons with severe mental illnesses: A review of evidence and experience. *World Psychiatry, 11*(2), 123–128.

## 1: Peer work in mental health in Australia: its scope, role and contribution

Davidson, L., Chinman, M., Kloos, B., Weingarten, R., Stayner, D., & Kraemer, T. J. (1999). Peer support among individuals with severe mental illness: A review of the evidence. *Clinical Psychology: Science and Practice, 6*(2), 165–187.

Davidson, L., Chinman, M., Sells, D., & Rowe, M. (2006). Peer support among adults with serious mental illness: A report from the field. *Schizophrenia Bulletin, 32*(3), 443–450.

Dixon, L., Krauss, N., & Lehman, A. (1994). Consumers as service providers: The promise and challenge. *Community Mental Health Journal, 30*(6), 615–634.

Eiken, S., Campbell, J., & Campbell, J. (2008). Medicaid coverage of peer support for people with mental illness: Available research and state examples. Thomson Reuters Healthcare. Retrieved from http://www.wicps.org/uploads/1/8/1/4/1814011/peersupport_reuters.pdf

Faulkner, A., & Basset, T. (2010). *A helping hand: Consultations with service users about peer support.* London: Together. Retrieved from http://www.together-uk.org/wp-content/uploads/downloads/2011/11/helpinghand.pdf

Felton, C. J., Stastny, P., Shern, D., Blanch, A., Dohahue, S. A., Knight, E., … Brown, C. (1995). Consumers as peer specialists on intensive case management teams: Impact on client outcomes. *Psychiatric Services, 46*, 1037–1044.

Forchuk, C., Martin, M. L., Chan, Y. L., & Jensen, E. J. (2005). Therapeutic relationships: From psychiatric hospital to community. *Psychiatric Mental Health Nurse, 12*(5), 556–564.

Froland, C., Brodsky, G., Olson, M., & Stewart, L. (2000). Social support and social adjustment: Implications for mental health professionals. *Community Mental Health Journal, 36*(1), 61–75.

Galbally, R. (2011). Foreword. In *Charter of peer support*. Retrieved from http://www.peersupportvic.org/index.php/2014-12-15-22-41-32/2014-12-15-22-46-46

Gates, L. B., & Akabas, S. H. (2007). Developing strategies to integrate peer providers into the staff of mental health agencies. *Administration and Policy in Mental Health and Mental Health Services Research, 34*(3), 293–306.

Gillard, S. G., Edwards, C., Gibson, S. L., Owen, K., & Wright, C. (2013). Introducing peer worker roles into UK mental health service teams: A qualitative analysis of the organisational benefits and challenges. *BMC Health Services Research, 13*(1), 188.

Goldman, C. & Lefley, H. (1996). Working with advocacy, support, and self-help groups. In J. V. Vaccaro and G. H. Clark (Eds.), *Practicing psychiatry in the community: A manual* (pp. 361–386). Washington, DC: American Psychiatric Press.

Grant, P. M., Huh, G. A., Perivoliotis, D., Stolar, N. M., & Beck, A. T. (2012). Randomized trial to evaluate the efficacy of cognitive therapy for low-functioning patients with schizophrenia. *Archives of General Psychiatry, 69*(2), 121–127.

Happell, B., & Roper, C. (2007). Consumer participation in mental health research: Articulating a model to guide practice. *Australasian Psychiatry, 15*(3), 237–241.

Hardiman, E. R., Theriot, M. T., & Hodges, J. Q. (2005). Evidence-based practice in mental health. *Best Practices in Mental Health, 1*(1), 105–122.

Health Workforce Australia (2014). Mental health peer workforce literature scan. HWA. Retrieved from http://www.peersupportvic.org/index.php/2014-12-15-22-42-49/2014-12-16-02-22-27/Research/Mental-Health-Peer-Workforce-Literature-Scan/

Hinton, T. (2009). Experts by experience: Strengthening the mental health consumer voice in Tasmania. Hobart: Anglicare Tasmania in association with the Tasmanian Mental Health Consumer Network. Retrieved from https://www.anglicare-as.org.au/sites/default/

files/Experts_by_experience_-strengthening_the_mental_health_consumer_voice_in_Tasmania.pdf

Holter, M. C., Mowbray, C. T., Bellamy, C. D., MacFarlane, P., & Dukarski, J. (2004). Critical ingredients of consumer run services: Results of a national survey. *Community Mental Health Journal, 40*(1), 47–63.

Humphreys, K., & Rappaport, J. (1994). Researching self-help/mutual aid groups and organizations: Many roads, one journey. *Applied & Preventative Psychology, 3*, 217–231.

Hutchinson, D. S., Anthony, W. A., Ashcraft, L., Johnson, E., Dunn, E. C., Lyass, A., ... Rogers, E. S. (2006). The personal and vocational impact of training and employing people with psychiatric disabilities as providers. *Psychiatric Rehabilitation Journal, 29*(3), 205.

Jackson, F., & Fong, T. (2017). Why not a peer worker? *Mental Health and Social Inclusion, 21*(3), 176–183.

Janzen, R., Nelson, G., Trainor, J., & Ochocka, J. (2006). A longitudinal study of mental health consumer/survivor initiatives: Part 4—Benefits beyond the self? A quantitative and qualitative study of system-level activities and impacts. *Journal of Community Psychology, 34*(3), 285–303.

Kyrouz, E. M., Humphreys, K., & Loomis, C. (2002). A review of research on the effectiveness of self-help mutual aid groups. In B. J. White & E. J. Madera (Eds.), *American self-help clearinghouse self-help sourcebook* (7th ed., pp. 71–85). Cedar Knolls, NJ: American Self-Help Group Clearing House. Retrieved from http://nipspeersupport.org/?page_id=588

Landers, G. M., & Zhou, M. (2011). An analysis of relationships among peer support, psychiatric hospitalization, and crisis stabilization. *Community Mental Health Journal, 47*(1), 106–112.

Lawn, S., Smith, A., & Hunter, K. (2008). Mental health peer support for hospital avoidance and early discharge: An Australian example of a consumer driven and operated service. *Journal of Mental Health, 17*(5), 498–508.

Legere, L. (2014). *The provider's handbook on developing and implementing peer roles*. Substance Abuse and Mental Health Services Administrations & Western Massachusetts Recovery Learning Community, USA. Retrieved from http://www.psresources.info/images/stories/A_Providers_Handbook_on_Developing__Implementing_Peer_Roles.pdf

Leung, D., & DeSousa, L. (2002). A vision and mission for peer support: Stakeholder perspectives. *International Journal of Psychosocial Rehabilitation, 7*, 5–14.

Lyass, A., & Chen, R. (2007). Effects of participation in consumer-operated service programs on both personal and organizationally mediated empowerment: Results of multisite study. *Journal of Rehabilitation Research and Development, 44*(6), 785–800.

McDiarmid, D., Rapp, C., & Ratzlaff, S. (2005). Design and initial results from a supported education initiative: The Kansas consumer as provider program. *Psychiatric Rehabilitation Journal, 29*(1), 3–9.

McLean, J., Biggs, H., Whitehead, I., Pratt, R., & Maxwell, M. (2009). *Evaluation of the delivering for mental health peer support worker pilot scheme*. Edinburgh: Scottish Government Social Research. Retrieved from http://www.gov.scot/resource/doc/291864/0089933.pdf

Mead, S. (2003). Defining peer support. West Chesterfield, NH: Intentional Peer Support. Retrieved from https://docs.google.com/document/d/1WG3ulnF6vthAwFZpJxE9rkx6lJzYSX7VX4HprV5EkfY/edit

## 1: Peer work in mental health in Australia: its scope, role and contribution

Mead, S., & MacNeil, C. (2006). Peer support: What makes it unique? *International Journal of Psychosocial Rehabilitation, 10*(2), 29–37.

Mead, S., Hilton, D., & Curtis, L. (2001). Peer support: A theoretical perspective. *Psychiatric Rehabilitation Journal, 25*(2), 134–141.

Meagher, J., Beattie, V., & Farrugia, P. (2013). Embracing inclusion—employment of people with lived experience (policy paper). Sydney: RichmondPRA. Retrieved from www.flourishaustralia.org.au/embracing-inclusion-lived-experience

Mental Health Commission. (2005). *Service user workforce development strategy for the mental health sector, 2005–2010*. Wellington, New Zealand: MHC.

Mental Health Coordinating Council (2015). Peer work qualification project. Resources for Certificate IV Mental Health Peer Work. Community Mental Health Australia. Retrieved from https://www.mentalhealthcommission.gov.au/our-work/mental-health-peer-work-development-and-promotion.aspx

Mental Health Coordinating Council (n.d.). Workforce development pathway 5—Consumer workers and care workers. Sydney: MHCC. Retrieved from http://www.mhcc.org.au/media/10529/wfdg-pathway-5-consumer-workers-carer-workers.pdf

Moran, G. S., Russinova, Z., Gidugu, V., Yim, J. Y., & Sprague, C. (2012). Benefits and mechanisms of recovery among peer providers with psychiatric illnesses. *Qualitative Health Research, 22*(3), 304–319.

Mowbray, C. T., Moxley, D. P., & Collins, M. E. (1998). Consumers as mental health providers: First-person accounts of benefits and limitations. *Journal of Behavioral Health Services & Research, 25*(4), 397–411.

Mowbray, C. T., & Tan, C. (1993). Consumer-operated drop-in centers: Evaluation of operations and impact. *Journal of Mental Health Administration, 20*(1), 8–19.

National Disability Insurance Agency. (2016). Rural and remote strategy 2016–2019. NDIA. Retrieved from https://www.ndis.gov.au/medias/documents/h2c/hb0/8800389824542/Rural-and-Remote-Strategy-991-KB-PDF-.pdf

National Empowerment Center and the Recovery Consortium (2006). *Voices of transformation: Developing recovery-based statewide consumer/survivor organizations.* Center for Mental Health Services (CMHS), Substance Abuse and Mental Health Services Administration (SAMHSA), US Department of Health and Human Services (DHHS). Retrieved from https://power2u.org/wp-content/uploads/2017/09/VoicesTransformationRS.pdf

National Inquiry Concerning the Human Rights of People with Mental Illness (1993). *Human rights and mental illness: Report of the national inquiry into the human rights of people with mental illness.* Brian Burdekin, David Hall, Margaret Guilfoyle, Human Rights and Equal Opportunity Commission. Canberra: Australian Government Publishing Service.

National Mental Health Commission (2013). *A contributing life: 2013 national report card.* NMHC. Retrieved from http://www.mentalhealthcommission.gov.au/media/94321/Report_Card_2013_full.pdf

National Mental Health Consumer & Carer Forum (2010). Supporting and developing the mental health consumer and carer identified workforce—A strategic approach to recovery. Canberra: NMHCCF. Retrieved from https://nmhccf.org.au/sites/default/files/docs/mhca_carewf_layout_16-9_0.pdf

National Mental Health Consumer & Carer Forum (2011). Advocacy brief: The peer workforce. Canberra: NMHCCF. Retrieved from https://nmhccf.org.au/sites/default/files/docs/final_peer_workforce.pdf

National Voices (2015). Peer support: what it is and does it work. National Voices and Nesta. Retrieved from https://www.nationalvoices.org.uk/publications/our-publications/peer-support

Nelson, G., Ochocka, J., Janzen, R., Trainor, J., Goering, P., & Lomotey, J. (2007). A longitudinal study of mental health consumer/survivor initiatives: Part V—Outcomes at 3-year follow-up. *Journal of Community Psychology, 35*(5), 655–665.

New Zealand Ministry of Health (2008). *Let's get real: Real skills for people working in mental health and addiction.* Wellington: New Zealand Ministry of Health. Retrieved from https://www.health.govt.nz/system/files/documents/publications/letsgetreal-sep08.pdf

Nicholas, A., & Reifels, L. (2014). Mental health and the NDIS: A literature review. Melbourne: MIND Australia. Retrieved from https://www.researchgate.net/publication/277016484_Mental_Health_and_the_NDIS_A_Literature_Review

Nicolellis, D. (2015). Vocational peer support: Bringing psych rehab, employment, and peer support together. *PsyR Connections, 1.* Retrieved from https://www.psychrehabassociation.org/newsletters/psyr/vocational-peer-support-bringing-psych-rehab-employment-and-peer-support-together

Norden-Powers, C. (1994). *Empowerment: How to succeed with vision, leadership and change.* Melbourne: Longman Professional.

NSW Mental Health Consumer Workers Committee & NSW Consumer Advisory Group—Mental Health Inc. (2013). Framework for the NSW public mental health consumer workforce. NSW Consumer Advisory Group. Retrieved from http://being.org.au/wp-content/uploads/2015/06/Framework-2013-sent-to-CAC-270913.pdf

O'Donnell, M., Parker, G., Proberts, M., Matthews, R., Fisher, D., Johnson, B., ... Hadzi-Pavlovic, D. (1999). A study of client-focused case management and consumer advocacy: The community and consumer service project. *Australian & New Zealand Journal of Psychiatry, 33*(5), 684–693.

O'Hagan, M. (2011). Peer support in mental health and addictions: A background paper. Retrieved from http://sharc.org.au/wp-content/uploads/2016/03/Peer-Support-Overview-OHagan.pdf

Orwin, D. (2008). Thematic review of peer supports: Literature review and leader interviews. Wellington, New Zealand: Mental Health Commission. Retrieved from http://d20wqiibvy9b23.cloudfront.net/resources/resources/000/000/600/original/Thematic_Review_of_Peer_Supports_Orwin.pdf?1468359846

Ostrow, L., & Leaf, P. J. (2014). Improving capacity to monitor and support sustainability of mental health peer-run organizations. *Psychiatric Services, 65*(2), 239–241.

Peters, J. (2010). *Walk the walk and talk the talk: A summary of peer support activities in some IIMHL countries.* Te Pou: National Centre of Mental Health Research, Information and Workforce Development. Retrieved from http://d20wqiibvy9b23.cloudfront.net/resources/resources/000/000/593/original/Peer_Support_in_English_Speaking_Countries_Peters.pdf?1468359841

Pickett, S. A., Diehl, S. M., Steigman, P. J., Prater, J. D., Fox, A., Shipley, P., ... Cook, J. A. (2012). Consumer empowerment and self-advocacy outcomes in a randomized study of peer-led education. *Community Mental Health Journal, 48*(4), 420–430.

Pitt, V., Lowe, D., Hill, S., Prictor, M., Hetrick, S. E., Ryan, R., & Berends, L. (2013). Consumer-providers of care for adult clients of statutory mental health services. *Cochrane Database of Systematic Reviews, 3*, CD004807.

RaffertyWeiss Media (n.d.). Leveraging the lived experience of peer support staff in behavioral health (Video file). Retrieved from https://resourcesforintegratedcare.com/Behavioral_Health/Peer_Supports/Video/Lived_Experience

Ratzlaff, S., McDiarmid, D., Marty, D., & Rapp, C. (2006). The Kansas consumer as provider program: Measuring the effects of a supported education initiative. *Psychiatric Rehabilitation Journal, 29*(3), 174–182.

Repper, J., & Carter, T. (2010). *Using personal experience to support others with similar difficulties: A review of the literature on mental health in peer support services*. Nottingham: University of Nottingham and Together, Nottingham. Retrieved from http://www.together-uk.org/wp-content/uploads/downloads/2011/11/usingpersexperience.pdf

Repper, J., & Carter, T. (2011). A review of the literature on peer support in mental health services. *Journal of Mental Health, 20*(4), 392–411.

Repper, J., Aldridge, B., Gilfoyle, S., Gillard, S., Perkins, R., & Rennison, J. (2013). *Peer support workers: Theory and practice*. London: Centre for Mental Health.

Resnick, S. G., & Rosenheck, R. A. (2008). Integrating peer-provided services: A quasi-experimental study of recovery orientation, confidence, and empowerment. *Psychiatric Services, 59*(11), 1307–1314.

Riessman, F. (1990). Restructuring help: A human services paradigm for the 1990s. *American Journal of Community Psychology, 18*(2), 221–230.

Roberts, L. J., Salem, D., Rappaport, J., Toro, P. A., Luke, D. A., & Seidman, E. (1999). Giving and receiving help: Interpersonal transactions in mutual-help meetings and psychosocial adjustment of members. *American Journal of Community Psychology, 27*(6), 841–868.

Rogers, E. S., Kash-MacDonald, M., & Brucker, D. (2009). *Systematic review of peer delivered services literature 1989–2009*. Boston, MA: Center for Psychiatric Rehabilitation, Boston University. Retrieved from http://www.bu.edu/drrk/research-syntheses/psychiatric-disabilities/peer-delivered-services/

Rokeach, M. (1973). *The nature of human values*. New York: Free Press.

Salzer, M. S., & Shear, S. L. (2002). Identifying consumer-provider benefits in evaluations of consumer-delivered services. *Psychiatric Rehabilitation Journal, 25*(3), 281.

Sells, D., Davidson, L., Jewell, C., Falzer, P., & Rowe, M. (2006). The treatment relationship in peer based and regular case management for clients with severe mental illness. *Psychiatric Services, 57*(8), 1179–1184.

Simpson, A. (2013). Collaborators, not competitors: Peer workers and professionals. *Journal of Psychosocial Nursing and Mental Health Services, 51*(10), 3–4.

Simpson, A., Flood, C., Rowe, J., Quigley, J., Henry, S., Hall, C., ... Bowers, L. (2014). Results of a pilot randomised controlled trial to measure the clinical and cost effectiveness of peer support in increasing hope and quality of life in mental health patients discharged from hospital in the UK. *BMC Psychiatry, 14*(1), 30.

Simpson, E. L., & House, A. O. (2002). Involving users in the delivery and evaluation of mental health services: Systematic review. *BMJ, 325*(7375), 1265.

Sledge, W. H., Lawless, M., Sells, D., Wieland, M., O'Connell, M. J., & Davidson, L. (2011). Effectiveness of peer support in reducing readmissions of persons with multiple psychiatric hospitalizations. *Psychiatric Services, 62*(5), 541–544.

Solomon, P. (2004). Peer support/peer provided services underlying processes, benefits, and critical ingredients. *Psychiatric Rehabilitation Journal, 27*(4), 392–401.

Story, K., Shute, T., & Thompson, A. (2008). Ethics in peer support work. *Journal of Ethics in Mental Health, 3*(1), 1–4.

Stratford, A. C., Halpin, M., Phillips, K., Skerritt, F., Beales, A., Cheng, V., ... & Kobe, B. (2017). The growth of peer support: An international charter. *Journal of Mental Health*. Online 6 July. doi: 10.1080/09638237.2017.1340593

Substance Abuse and Mental Health Services Administration (2007). Letter from Medicaid acknowledging that peer support is a 'best practice'. Center for Mental Health Services, US Department of Health and Human Services. Retrieved from http://cosb.countyofsb.org/uploadedFiles/admhs_new/resources/Systems_Change/Peer_Action_Team/CMS-8-15-07.pdf

Substance Abuse and Mental Health Services Administration (2011a). *Consumer-operated services: Evaluating your program*. HHS Pub. No. SMA-11-4633. Rockville, MD: Center for Mental Health Services, US Department of Health and Human Services. Retrieved from https://store.samhsa.gov/shin/content/SMA11-4633CD-DVD/EvaluatingYourProgram-COSP.pdf

Substance Abuse and Mental Health Services Administration (2011b). *Consumer-operated services: The evidence*. HHS Pub. No. SMA-11-4633. Rockville, MD: Center for Mental Health Services, US Department of Health and Human Services. Retrieved from https://store.samhsa.gov/shin/content/SMA11-4633CD-DVD/TheEvidence-COSP.pdf

Te Pou o te Whakaaro Nui (2017). Values informed practice. Te Pou o te Whakaaro Nui. Retrieved from https://www.tepou.co.nz/uploads/files/resource-assets/160126-values-informed-practice.pdf

Tondora, J., O'Connell, M., Miller, R., Dinzeo, T., Bellamy, C., Andres-Hyman, R., ... Davidson, L. (2010). A clinical trial of peer-based culturally responsive person-centered care for psychosis for African Americans and Latinos. *Clinical Trials, 7*(4), 368–379.

Trachtenberg, M., Parsonage, M., Shepherd, G., & Boardman, J. (2013). *Peer support in mental health care: Is it good value for money?* London: Centre for Mental Health. Retrieved from https://www.centreformentalhealth.org.uk/Blog/blog-peer-support-in-mental-health-care-is-it-good-value-for-money

UK Department of Health (2010). *Putting people first: Planning together—peer support and self-directed support*. London: DoH. Retrieved from http://www.helensandersonassociates.co.uk/media/43747/planning%20together%20-%20peer%20support%20and%20self%20directed%20support.pdf

United Nations (2006). *Convention on the rights of persons with disabilities*. Geneva: UN. Retrieved from www.un.org//disabilities/documents/convention/convoptprot-e.pdf

Van Tosh, L., Finkle, M., Hartman, B., Lewis, C., Plumlee, L. A., & Susko, M. A. (1993). *Working for a change: Employment of consumers/survivors in the design and provision of services for persons who are homeless and mentally disabled.* Rockville, MD: Center for Mental Health Services.

Van Tosh, L., Ralph, R. O., & Campbell, J. (2000). The rise of consumerism. *Psychiatric Rehabilitation Skills, 4*(3), 383–409.

Walker, G., & Bryant, W. (2013). Peer support in adult mental health services: A metasynthesis of qualitative findings. *Psychiatric Rehabilitation Journal, 36*(1), 28–34.

Whiteley, A. (1995). *Managing change—A core values approach.* Melbourne: Macmillan Education.

[WHO] World Health Organization. (2010). Mental health and development: Targeting people with mental health conditions as a vulnerable group. Geneva: WHO. Retrieved from http://www.who.int/mental_health/policy/mhtargeting/en/

# Section 2

# Changing culture and growing peer work

# Flourish Australia

*Fay Jackson and Tim Fong*

*Fay Jackson is general manager of Inclusion at Flourish Australia, deputy commissioner with the New South Wales Mental Health Commission and founder of Vision in Mind. Fay began her career in mental health as a volunteer advocate, then went on to be a peer worker, manager of peer work and director of Consumer, Carer and Community Affairs with the South East Sydney Illawarra Area Mental Health Service. Fay is a member of the National Consumer and Carer Reference Group and lived experience member of the NSW Health Agency of Clinical Innovation and Clinical Excellence Commission Council.*

*Tim Fong is general manager of human resources at Flourish Australia. He has extensive experience working in the not-for-profit sector, in project management and internationally in the corporate sector. He is a registered psychologist and has also worked in frontline mental health services as well as operational management, providing him with a unique blend of experience and training. He is passionate about building an inclusive workforce and recognises the valuable contribution people with a lived experience of a mental health issue can contribute to an organisation's mission.*

> All truth passes through three stages. In the first, it is ridiculed. Then it is opposed. And finally it is accepted as self-evident.
>
> *attributed to Arthur Schopenhauer (1788–1860)*

Flourish Australia are, arguably, one of the leaders in promoting and growing the peer workforce in Australia. They are well known for their longstanding commitment to growing the lived experience workforce, with over 50% of the workforce currently identifying as having a lived experience; of those, 179 are mental health peer workers. Achieving this is the result of many years of effort, encompassing cultural change, policy development, affirmative action and organisational leadership.

Flourish Australia believe that valuing lived experience across all levels of the organisation is key to developing an effective peer workforce that delivers positive outcomes for people accessing mental health supports. Every policy, program and significant decision made at Flourish Australia is made in

## 2: Changing culture and growing peer work

consultation with people with a personal lived experience of a mental health issue and recovery. Flourish Australia have a number of positions other than peer work that require a personal lived experience of a mental health issue across the organisation. These include positions on Flourish Australia's board of directors, executive and other senior management positions, frontline positions and advocacy roles.

Peer work offers people with a lived experience the opportunity to take trauma, abuse, emotional distress and hiatuses in life and to use these experiences in support of others, building relationships based in reciprocity and mutuality, being open, feeling safe and appreciated. It offers people the opportunity to do all this while continuing to grow their resiliency, bringing their whole selves to work.

**Some history**

In 2000, Psychiatric Rehabilitation Australia, one of Flourish Australia's founding organisations, commissioned a report on the organisation's approach to service delivery. It led to significant change, restructuring and reformation of policies and procedures. The resulting changes led to an unequivocal focus on people accessing services and changing the culture of the organisation.

A significant outcome of the review was a stronger focus on lived experience involvement across the organisation, including for the first time in staff training and development as well as in quality assurance activities. Of greatest importance was the dramatic increase in including direct lived experience expertise in all organisational activities. This eventually led, in 2002, to a number of positions being created that specified that applicants had to have personal lived experience of a mental health issue. These positions represented the first time such people were employed to work one-on-one as 'peers'. Their role was to support those utilising the organisation's employment programs.

Over the next several years we built on this initiative by making the employment of people with lived experience a success. Of course, there were challenges, but as a recovery-oriented organisation we were committed to the task of growing lived-experience involvement and, particularly at that time, the paid peer workforce.

## A brief comment on the evidence-base for peer work

Flourish Australia did not enter into peer work without recognising and acknowledging the growing evidence base for the efficacy of peer work. International research has drawn a strong conclusion that peer work is valuable in supporting people with mental health issues to recover. Researchers have concluded that peer support can bring about significant reductions in hospital bed use among patients they support, leading to financial savings well in excess of additional pay costs (Trachtenberg et al., 2013).

Chinman et al. (2014) found 'the effectiveness of peers added to traditional services and of peers delivering structured curricula was positive.' They found the following positive outcomes for people with a lived experience:

- reduced inpatient service use
- improved relationship with providers
- better engagement with care
- higher levels of empowerment
- higher levels of patient activation
- higher levels of hopefulness for recovery.

## Paid peer work

When Flourish Australia refer to a peer work position, they are referring to peer workers who are in paid positions, specifically designated as 'peer workers', and who have a personal lived experience of a mental health issue and recovery. This is an important distinction because not all organisations share this view of peer work.

Notably, while Flourish Australia believe that peer support provided by carers and family members to carers and family members is important, Flourish Australia's peer workforce does not include carers or family members who have had experience of caring for people with lived experience of mental health issues or unpaid volunteers. Nor does it include employees who hold a different position in the organisation who have a lived experience. An employee engaged as a 'peer worker' with Flourish Australia is paid at an award rate just like any other employee and fulfils an important role integrated into mental health service teams.

## 2: Changing culture and growing peer work

An important facilitator to growing the peer workforce was Flourish Australia's commitment to growing the lived experience workforce. Flourish Australia found that it was essential to first have designated lived experience roles embedded at all levels of the organisation. The presence of lived experience throughout the organisation supports the robust conversations that are sometimes needed to help people to open up to new possibilities. Having designated lived experience positions supports the transformation process needed to evoke organisational change. In turn that change facilitates the required reformation of traditional mental health supports, policies, procedures and work practices that must adapt if an organisation is to develop and grow a high-quality peer workforce.

The growth of the peer workforce is an important response to workforce issues in mental health services. The National Disability Insurance Scheme (NDIS) is Australia's solution to enhancing the decision-making authority of people living with disability in Australia. The NDIS can be characterised as a transition away from a grant or block funding model for Australian disability providers to an individualised funding model that puts the power of the dollars spent on disability supports and services directly into the control of the people living with significant disability. Eligible NDIS participants will now directly buy the services and supports they need to support them in their lives rather than what disability providers have to offer in their often limited or specialised suite of services.

The NDIS currently projects significant workforce shortages at its full rollout stage (Australian Government Productivity Commission, 2017). Peer workers and employees with a personal lived experience, in large enough numbers, with support and respect can address those challenges, and in turn, completely alter the culture of clinical and non-clinical services for the better. Arguably, the NDIS has provided one of greatest opportunities in recent time to support the growth of peer work in Australia and has the ability to change the way service providers deliver psychosocial supports. People with a lived experience of a mental health issues now have more freedom to select and purchase services and supports directly from providers who have a strong peer workforce ethos and culture.

## Language

The way an organisation communicates shapes the culture of the organisation and arguably the outcomes of people accessing mental health supports. Flourish Australia have long recognised the importance of organisational language in driving cultural change. As a result, they developed a *Strengths-based language guide* for use in all services (Flourish Australia, 2015). With a focus on what is possible, the *Guide* sets the foundation for how staff are expected to communicate with each other, with people accessing services and with external stakeholders. At Flourish Australia, terms such as 'consumer', 'user' or 'client' are replaced with 'people accessing our services' or just 'people'. Similarly, the use of slang, jargon or labels to describe behaviours or diagnosis (terms such as 'depressed' or 'manic') are actively avoided, and people are never referred to by diagnosis. Flourish Australia firmly believe that this type of communication alienates people and can result in unwanted or disruptive interactions when working with people. We say this because when people start to see themselves as a diagnosis or a behaviour trait, they start to lose their personal identity; this may be followed by a loss of dignity, rights and responsibilities. Flourish Australia call people 'people'. Simple, respectful and inclusive.

To support the application of the *Strengths-based language guide,* Flourish Australia have an organisation-wide agreement that provides permission for everyone to respectfully challenge each other if they inadvertently stray from using strengths-based language, offering an opportunity to reflect on more strengths-based words to use. Staff embraced this openness and encouraged each other. After the dominance and history of the medical model in psychiatry and mental health support services, the power of strengths-based language in the sector cannot be overstated.

## Planning

Changing culture and growing the peer workforce does not just happen. Flourish Australia identified that it was important to ensure that a detailed strategy was established, and that agreement was achieved across all levels of the organisation. Flourish Australia's peer workforce strategy is multifaceted. Considerable time and effort was invested in ensuring the strategy fitted with the organisation's strategic vision and was consistent with its mission, vision and values. Flourish Australia saw growing the peer workforce as part of its strategic direction to deliver effective, evidence-based and high-quality services to people who access its services, as the reason the organisation exists and explains how any return on investment will be measured in the future.

Given organisational culture is set and driven from the top, a commitment from the board and senior leadership team was fundamental. Having lived experience embedded through all levels of the organisation supported this endeavour and secured the commitment required. A series of conversations with managers and throughout the organisation paved the way for imagining the positive contribution peer workers could make to the organisation.

## Policy

Growth of the peer workforce was not only achieved through good planning and organisational commitment, but supported by a clear policy direction. Through the organisational conversations that occurred, a pioneering strategy called 'Why not a peer worker?' was developed. Jackson and Fong (2017) outlined Flourish Australia's journey and how the 'Why not a peer worker?' strategy was instrumental in promoting their peer workforce. There we described some of the challenges and learnings along the way and outlined practical ideas that have been successfully implemented by Flourish Australia.

Prior to this policy, two key governance directions were introduced that supported the development and growth of peer work. The first, *Embracing inclusion: Employment of people with lived experience* (Beattie, Meagher, & Farrugia, 2014), outlined the organisation's commitment to employing people with lived experience of a mental health issue. Fundamentally, the conclusion reached was that something active and positive needed to occur to pursue the growth required. The organisation's affirmative action policy received its mandate from this policy direction paper.

*Embracing inclusion* discussed the role of peer work in the organisation and a set of five principles for the implementation of peer work strategy were defined. These principles were:

1. Self-determination: the right to make free choices about life without external coercion (Scott, 2011, in O'Hagan, 2011)
2. Participation and equality: self-determination within a peer support initiative is often expressed through participation and equal relationships. There is direct participation of the members in the organisation's decision-making process (Segal et al., 2002, in O'Hagan, 2011) that is characterised by a lack of hierarchy (White, 2009, in O'Hagan, 2011).
3. Reciprocity: this describes the honest and genuine two-way helping relationships that occur in peer-run initiatives (Campbell et al., 2006, in O'Hagan, 2011) through the kinship of common experience (White, 2009, in O'Hagan, 2011). This is sometimes referred to as the peer principle whereby relationships are based on shared experiences and values that are characterised by reciprocity and mutuality (Clay, 2005, in O'Hagan, 2011)
4. Experiential knowledge: there is high value placed on experiential knowledge which is subjective as well as concrete, specific and commonsensical (White, 2009, in O'Hagan, 2011) as opposed to theoretical and scientific knowledge. High respect for experiential knowledge means that peers can share their problems and solutions with each other in a non-judgemental way. With this, knowledge is not controlled, but shared.
5. Recovery and hope: recovery in this context emphasises not recovery from symptoms but the recovery or discovery of a life worth living of one's own choosing.

The second key governance direction was the *Recovery action framework* (RichmondPRA, 2014). The framework was co-developed with people with lived experience and staff, and focused on answering two vital questions:

1. How do we inform attitudes and behaviours of staff, partners and the people who access our services to make them more supportive of recovery?
2. What do we need to do to achieve continuous improvement across the organisation to fully implement recovery-oriented practices?

These questions highlighted that an organisation not only needs to develop policies and practices to support the implementation and future growth of their recovery focus and subsequently of their peer work, it also needs to review and update existing policies and practices. Affirmative action was one of the important new policies.

## Affirmative action

An affirmative action policy was developed to ensure suitably qualified and experienced people with a personal lived experience of a mental health issue and recovery were considered during recruitment and employed. In summary, the policy states,

> Flourish Australia supports Affirmative Action. If two candidates present with suitability to a role, and one of those people has a lived experience, the person with the lived experience will be the preferred candidate.

## Position descriptions

Appointing people to any position without clearly defined position descriptions will inevitably lead to problems. Jackson and Fong (2017) and Davidson et al. (2012) outlined the importance of peer worker roles having specific position descriptions and described how these are central to establishing industrial protections for a strong peer workforce.

When Flourish Australia commenced the peer work growth strategy, mental health worker positions made up the majority of their frontline workforce. The workforce operated effectively, and core tasks and responsibilities of the frontline positions were well defined. In fact, the intention was to build upon the strong foundation of responsibilities that existed by complementing the balance of our workforce with the expertise that only peer work can add. A conversation with managers was had.

For each task and responsibility that was at the time performed by Flourish Australia's frontline mental health workers, a simple question was applied: 'Why can't a peer worker do that?'. Discussions with managers about each task and responsibility eventually led to a consensus that confirmed there was nothing a peer worker could not deliver that our existing frontline workers were currently delivering. In fact, peer work added an extra benefit of being required to purposely use a lived experience of a mental health issue and recovery in their work.

The discussion then centred on the question: 'If a peer worker can accomplish the same duties as the existing frontline workforce, there is no reason not to employ peer workers. But what is the reason to employ peer workers?' This led to discussions about the fidelity of peer work and the nature of the relationships and discussions between peer workers and people accessing services.

Peer workers talk about personal lived experience in purposeful ways to build a reciprocity in their working relationships, to carefully share experiences, give examples of recovery, and to mentor people and raise hope in their lives. Peer workers are a living example that people can and do recover. They show that people with lived experience can and do live contributing, meaningful, connected, valuable lives and they gently encourage the people they support to take the steps and the risks they need to take to achieve their optimal potential. Peer workers support people taking dignified risks to grow and to flourish.

When a peer worker uses their personal lived experience as an example of what a person can do, the barriers people may have established around their possible recovery can be brought down in conversations built on reciprocity, mutual experiences, shared understanding and hope. People who hear the experiences of a peer worker can be encouraged and hopeful about their own lives. They recognise that this person, this peer worker, must have had experiences similar to theirs and yet they are living a life of their choosing with roles and responsibilities that make them proud of who they are, including being aware of their lived experience.

Some of the duties of peer workers and mental health workers are practical, such as cooking and cleaning. Peer workers supporting people in these duties model the capabilities of people with a mental health issue to undertake and complete these tasks. The mutual discussions about past experiences that take place while sharing in these 'task building' relationships, camaraderie, pride and capabilities, further build respect and reciprocity. In addition, many people are more comfortable discussing their past, issues and hopes for the future while sharing in tasks.

Engagement with managers, having them reflect on role requirements and discussing with them what peer workers could do, was a game changer.

Subsequently the decision was made that Flourish Australia should actively employ more peer workers. These discussions formed the basis of the 'Why not a peer worker?' strategy that has underpinned Flourish Australia's recent work (see Jackson and Fong, 2017).

**Qualifications**

Implementing a peer workforce, like any other profession, requires suitably qualified people being appointed to peer work positions. The qualifications require a person to be able to appropriately apply lived experience and knowledge. If a peer worker enters the workforce without formal training and appropriate qualifications, initial and further training about the ethics and practice expectations of peer work needs to take place, even for those with other formal qualifications. For example, people who hold degrees in social work or nursing or psychology need to have training to know how to be a peer worker rather than a social worker, nurse or psychologist.

Training and professional qualifications is an area for which peer work is often criticised. The majority of the people attracted to working at Flourish Australia in peer work either have their Certificate IV in Mental Health Peer Work (National Mental Heath Commission, 2015) or are in the process of gaining it. 'Intentional Peer Support' training (see www.intentionalpeersupport.org) is also offered.

Although some people with lived experience have not had the opportunity for post-secondary education, a growing number of people in peer work have formal qualifications in various professional areas. However, they are required to do the Certificate IV in Mental Health Peer Work, because what distinguishes the Certificate from other qualifications is that it provides specific training in ethics, values and skills that are fundamental to the effective delivery of peer work that are not covered by other qualifications. In the Certificate curriculum peer workers learn how to use their lived experience purposely and appropriately, to manage boundaries that can be more complicated because of the nature of sharing personal experiences and other elements fundamental to the ethos and practice of peer work.

## Supervision and peer mentoring

Given that in Flourish Australia peer worker positions are fully integrated into mental health support teams, usual supervision by line managers is an important requirement. Just as an employer requires social workers to demonstrate that they can effectively apply theoretical knowledge pertaining to their positions in the workplace, this should also be an expectation of peer workers.

Professionalising peer work provides another layer of support and supervision for the peer workforce. It ensures that the peer work being delivered maintains a professional standing within the organisation and mental health services as a whole.

In addition, specific peer work mentoring and professional supervision are required for peer workers. There should never be an assumption that a peer worker knows how to apply their lived experience or share their recovery story purposefully, effectively and in a timely manner in the workplace. Professional supervision and mentorship is not intended to usurp day-to-day operational management. Instead, professional supervision and mentoring is seen as an added value not dissimilar to any other profession undergoing professional clinical supervision, such as psychologists and other allied health professionals.

Peer work supervisors are lived-experience professionals who have extensive experience and expertise in peer work. They have held peer work positions and have usually had management experience. They have exceptional interpersonal skills, are strategic in thinking, encouraging and calming in their manner, and determined to build up peer work expertise. They are 'bridge builders' between peer work and other professions such as mental health workers, psychologists, social workers, nurses and psychiatrists. They are linked with all sectors of support and have good networks with peer work both within and outside the organisation.

Peer supervisors stay abreast of all changes and issues happening within peer work both within and external to Flourish Australia that might pertain to peer work.

Topics that are discussed during professional peer work supervision include reflecting on work practices and situations, supporting peer workers to find solutions to problems, ensuring peer workers are working in the peer ethos not only with people we support but with all staff, and supporting peer workers to advocate systemically both within Flourish Australia and externally with partner services, collaborators, families, other stakeholders and the community.

Additional supports are also provided. Flourish Australia have established a community of practice for peer work. This community is open to all staff who want to learn more about peer work and acts as a discussion forum about peer work across the organisation.

Flourish Australia also operate an internal peer work online forum. This is a moderated forum where staff interested in peer work can ask questions and provide answers give advice, discuss ethics, and ways of purposefully utilising lived experience, and engaging in reflective practice. The forum is invaluable because the contributions are there for the entire staff to see and reflect upon.

**Integration in teams**

For the growth strategy to succeed, the organisational commitment to growing the peer workforce must be maintained at all levels of the organisation. Everyone needs to understand and value the contribution peer work brings to the organisation's services and, importantly, the specialist contribution peer work adds to a multidisciplinary team. It is the diversity and range of a skills that a multidisciplinary team provides that is the driver of successful outcome for people accessing mental health supports. Peer work is part of its diversity and strength.

An important skill that peer workers bring to a multidisciplinary team is their ability to talk with team members and people accessing services about their personal lived experience in purposeful ways in order to build a reciprocity in the relationships, to carefully share personal experiences and examples of recovery, to mentor and raise hope in people's lives. No other profession can provide this experience or these skills. Peer workers are a living example that people can and do recover. They show that people with lived experience can and do live contributing, meaningful, connected, valuable lives and they gently encourage the people they support to take the steps and the risks they need to take to achieve their optimal potential.

The impact of these conversations can be profound. When a person says 'I can't recover; I am a paranoid schizophrenic' (or any other diagnosis they have been labelled with) we understand that this may have thwarted their belief in themselves and in what they can achieve. In response a peer worker can say 'I have experienced a similar diagnosis, but I am working and striving to meet my optimal potential. I can work on my recovery and lead a good life and you can too'. When a peer worker says this, the barriers people may have established around their potential for recovery can be brought down in one beautiful sentence. People hearing this can feel encouraged and hopeful about their own lives. They understand that this person, this peer worker, must have had experiences similar to theirs and yet this person is living a life with roles and responsibilities that make them proud of who they are, including being proud of their lived experience.

Peer work encompasses experiences of trauma, mental health issues and treatment as a valuable part of a person's life and journey that enables them to serve others. Far from being ashamed of their journey, people use it to connect, support, and to bring hope to others. When people share their vulnerability in a purposeful and valuable way, that vulnerability becomes a strength because the sharing opens others up to be honest about their experiences and desire for healing and recovery.

Peer workers who have experienced significant and long-lasting mental health issues know how confronting it can be to move towards recovery. They know that this means taking on responsibilities and roles that may have been shed long ago, or never engaged with. Sharing how challenging this is helps people know that they can be honest, and that the road to recovery and reaching your optimal potential does not always feel positive or safe. However, peer workers have the credibility to say 'but I did it and I believe you can too'. Coming from one who has shared this honesty and vulnerability, helps the person feel stronger, more hopeful, braver, more capable and understood.

## Professional boundaries

It is essential for peer workers to have clear professional boundaries. Peer workers are not people's friends and they should not pretend to be. What they must be are friendly peer workers. They should feel able to proudly and honestly say 'I am not your friend but your friendly peer worker. It is my job to support you to make new and good personal friends if you would like that'.

Transparency, honesty and ethical practice are cornerstones of peer work. If, during the course of having a professional relationship with a person, it becomes obvious that there is a growing friendship or possibility of an intimate relationship, the peer worker must raise this with their manager and an alternative peer worker ought to be found for the person accessing the service. Discussions around this should include the person accessing the service so that all parties can be transparent about relationships, feelings, professional boundaries and commitments.

If boundaries are crossed and friendship and professional relationships are merged it is likely that major issues will arise. If a person believes a peer worker to be their friend, it is likely boundaries will be crossed by both parties, people will be hurt and there is a risk that the peer worker experiences burnout as they try to be all things to the person they are supporting. It is then possible that the peer worker will leave work and all contact with the person who believed the peer worker was their friend may end. This can be difficult for people, diminish the possibility of future, appropriate relationships developing with others, and should be guarded against.

**Obstacles**

It is equally important to understand potential obstacles that organisations may encounter when embarking on the development of a peer workforce. Anticipating challenges that may hamper the development and growth of a peer workforce helps guide the development of the overall strategy as well as the policies and procedures that are needed to ensure peer work delivers the intended benefits to people accessing mental health supports. Having low expectations and failing to view peer work as a profession is another misconception with serious repercussions. An organisation is more likely to attract and retain suitably qualified and experienced persons to the peer worker cohort if peer work is respected in the workplace as a specialised profession. For this to be achieved, peer work must be structured so as to provide career opportunities. Organisations run the risk of losing good employees to other organisations if they do not develop career trajectories for peer workers in their employ.

## Stigma and discrimination

It is a sad reality that stigma and discrimination exist in the community and in the workplace. However, not all stigma and discrimination are grounded in malicious intent. Inadvertent stigma and discrimination can quickly manifest in a workplace if organisations do not provide the necessary information to employees detailing the organisations peer workforce strategy and accompanying policies.

Stigma and discrimination can be based in well-meaning, misguided attempts to 'not place people with mental health issues under too much pressure', which usually accompanies an attitude of low expectations. To counter this, it is essential that organisations have a good support structure in place for all employees and that all employees are thoroughly informed of the organisation's expectations of all workers and of peer workers in particular.

Inadvertent stigma and discrimination take many forms and can prevent the development and growth of peer work. Some examples of inadvertent stigma and discrimination may include:

1. Hiring managers not following organisational selection and recruitment policies. For example, hiring managers may make selection and recruitment decisions that they would otherwise make by placing too much weight on the candidate's lived experience rather than ensuring that the candidate meets all the essential requirements for the position. These managers often offer people jobs because they 'just want to help', which potentially adds another trauma to the person's life, decreases their wellbeing and increases their feelings of being a failure if they don't succeed in the position.
2. Managers that do not support peer workers to apply for opportunities to advance their careers out of misguided concern that the advance would place extra pressure on the individual. This may be done out of concern that the peer worker is not capable of achieving in a new position not because there is any evidence of this but rather because of the knowledge that the person has lived experience.

3. Giving peer workers menial tasks that they would not give to other employees. If there are menial tasks to be done they need to be shared equally among employees.
4. Assuming employees would or would not want to do something because they have lived experience rather than asking the person if they would like to do the task at hand and whether the person is capable of carry out those duties they would ask of any other staff member.
5. Not valuing lived-experience employees' range of professional experiences and capabilities and relegating their expertise only to personal lived experience.
6. Not holding peer workers accountable for not meeting the requirements of their jobs or not meeting the code of conduct and ethics. Reasonable adjustments need to be made but these are not around poor behaviour. Codes of conduct should apply to all employees. Employees adhering to the ethics of peer work will always work within the code of conduct.
7. Managers raising matters relevant to the peer worker's personal life in their professional communications or not protecting that person's confidentiality. When any staff member does outside work, if it is not illegal it is not the business of the workplace.

**Managing the peer workforce**

In the context of running an organisation and providing high-quality services, peer work and other professions share the same expectations of maintaining professionalism in the workplace. Peer workers are no different in this from other staff. Any question managers would ask of a peer worker should be able to be asked of any staff member. If managers would not ask that question of other staff members, then they probably should not be asking it of the peer workers.

There may be times when a manager or colleague may need to respectfully check with a colleague about something they are responding to or experiencing. If respect for such things as hearing voices and deep anxiety is readily discussed at other times, understood and supported, the person will be more able to express their needs at that time. However, it is essential the manager does not treat the staff member as a 'patient'. They are a colleague.

There are many myths about people with mental health issues and peer workers. Some of these myths are related to an employee's capacity, such as people with lived experience not having resilience or not being able to work when experiencing certain difficulties such as hearing voices. Other myths pertain to more practical requirements of work, such as not being able to drive or complete shift work, not being able to work full-time, not being organised, not being able to maintain boundaries with the people receiving support, lacking training or being incapable of learning complicated tasks and concepts. These presumptions may well be false. Each potential peer worker must be given space to express their particular limitations and capacity.

It is important to reiterate that peer workers should be encouraged and supported to develop their career trajectories, and in so doing, identify appropriate training opportunities. Although some of these topics are discussed during supervision, specific peer worker supervision provided by a very experienced senior peer has a tangible benefit to the peer worker. Just as we do not expect an operational manager responsible for managing a multidisciplinary team to master concepts in psychology or occupational therapy, for example, we cannot expect a manager to also master concepts in peer work.

**Support**

It is important to plan supports that assist people to perform their jobs well. Flexibility in workplace supports is an important foundation for any peer work strategy. All staff at Flourish Australia are encouraged to have a personal situation plan. The plans are for use by any staff who have additional workplace support or flexibility needs of any sort that may require reasonable adjustments. The plan may include such things as the need for hearing loops, the need to leave work early one day per month to see a doctor, or the requirements of caring duties. The plan may also include what the staff member and others in the workplace can do should the person's mental health become compromised.

At Flourish Australia the personal situation plan is introduced on a staff member's commencement and reinforces to new staff that support is available in moments of personal challenge, family crises or psychological distress. It

## 2: Changing culture and growing peer work

highlights how the organisation will work with them to stay connected at work, with the support of managers and colleagues, wherever possible.

These approaches break down barriers, counter stigma and discrimination and help to set the organisation's culture of inclusion and respect across all staff and particularly for those who have personal lived experience of a mental health issue.

**Flourish Australia peer work journey**

Flourish Australia's journey growing the peer workforce was not straightforward. As in other organisations, there was a lack of understanding of what peer work was, how peer workers might be employed and what role they could take within teams. Common myths about peer work and peer workers were encountered and a comprehensive process to open up the conversation was required.

Debate needed to occur first of all with the senior leaders of the organisation to ensure a consistency of view and approach. Hard, challenging conversations were required, requiring deep reflection on organisational culture and values. Deep respect for each other and the conversation, and a strong commitment to the unique contribution of people with a personal lived experience of a mental health issue to services were fundamental to the success of the discussion. That provided an important foundation to future developments.

It was felt early on that hiring managers needed to be on board if the initiative was to succeed. They were the ones considering what skills and roles were required to successfully deliver services, and organised and participated on interview panels. They were fundamentally the gatekeepers.

Jackson and Fong (2017) discuss at length the importance of hiring managers having the correct information available about peer work was also an important part of growing their peer workforce. Flourish Australia developed a peer work 'myth-busting' program bringing hiring managers together and provided the opportunity to dispel some of the peer workforce myths that would otherwise have been a barrier to growing the peer workforce. Davidson et al. (2012) discuss a number of myths that Flourish Australia addressed during our peer work journey. These myths included: that peer workers are too fragile to handle the stress of the job; that peer workers may take more time off work than non-peer workers; and that peer workers may not be capable of handling the administrative demands of the job they are employed to do.

They noted that the majority of Flourish Australia's service offerings were non-clinical, but this did not prevent some clinical practitioners making requests of non-clinical staff to provide clinical functions. One such practice was to dispense medication to people accessing the service. Flourish Australia's peer workers do not engage in activities that require clinical training and experience. In fact, none of Flourish Australia's non-clinical workforce have this mandate. It soon became apparent that clinical practitioners required a better understanding of peer work and importantly what makes peer work effective as an intervention.

Furthermore, Flourish Australia believe that non-clinical staff engaging in work of a clinical nature has the effect of changing the nature of the relationship between the person in receipt of the support and the employee. This could not be allowed to take place between the peer workers and the people accessing the service. Although Flourish Australia recognise that many people are placed on medication against their wills, while others feel that medication plays an important role in their recovery, clinical practices belong to people who are clinically trained. We identified that more work needed to be done with clinical practitioners. Our position is that qualified people are responsible for dispensing, administering and supervising medication, and that it is antithetical to the peer worker role.

Jackson and Fong (2017) also cite another example of how Flourish Australia overcame resistance to peer work, which was to bring all senior managers together and provide them with the opportunity to discuss any concerns they had about growing the peer workforce. Senior managers were provided with an opportunity to seek assurances that peer work was subject to the same organisational policies and expectations that apply across the organisation. As the conversations proceeded, an echo of commonality developed. Once a common understanding had been reached with regard to employment practices, the issue of what peer workers actually do was then addressed. Copies of non-clinical frontline staff position descriptions were reviewed with senior managers. As the position description was being reviewed, the group would discuss the duty or responsibility and if there were any impediments to peer workers carrying out those duties or responsibilities. It was found that in actual fact there were no impediments to peer workers carrying out the work that another non-clinical staff were currently performing. Furthermore, the use of lived experience purposefully in every day work was recognised as adding value. The meeting was adjourned with a renewed understanding of peer work and the ability to support, manage and grow a peer workforce.

**Employment of peer workers**

(This section is adapted from Jackson and Fong, 2017.) Not everyone is ready to fulfil the role of being a peer worker and it is important to re-emphasise that peer work, like all professions, is subject to the same workplace expectations as apply to all employees. A peer worker is not appointed to a position just because they have lived experience of a mental health issue. They are appointed to roles because they meet the inherent requirements of the position and have demonstrated that they can be effective in using their lived experience and experience of recovery in their work role.

Peer workers are employed under the same conditions as all other employees and are subject to the same organisation policies, procedures and expectations. This consistency of workforce expectations cannot be overemphasised. In addition, to build an even more supportive culture, Flourish Australia have found it important for a peer worker also to be expected to build and uphold a respected culture of peer work both within and outside the organisation.

When it comes to performance and expectations, living with a mental health issue does not excuse a peer worker, or any other employee, from underperforming in their role. Whilst reasonable adjustments must be made and flexible work practices embedded for everyone, a mental health issue cannot be used as an excuse for underperformance or poor conduct.

If performance concerns arise in a workplace, consideration must be taken of the person's health or personal situation. In Australia it is a requirement for employers to explore reasonable adjustments in the workplace to provide support to people to undertake their role successfully. The emphasis is on the word 'reasonable'. Reasonable adjustment is often misunderstood or misinterpreted by organisations or individual employees. The intent of reasonable adjustment is to explore the 'reason' for the requested adjustment, whether it is possible (or we are 'able') to make an adjustment in the workplace without causing undue hardship, causing the inherent requirement of the position description to significantly change, or placing an unreasonable financial burden on a service or organisation.

In the main, there are no differences in supporting a peer workforce from supporting any other part of the workforce. Employees value highly being treated like everyone else in the team. They seek transparency in work practices, responsiveness when flexibility is needed, and equality and recognition for the work they do. They want to have the best opportunity to perform their duties to the highest standard, good training opportunities and regular opportunity to reflect on their practice with professional peers. They want the opportunity to prove that they are valuable members of the workplace and the community. They too want reasonable adjustment in the workplace if available. In Flourish Australia's experience, employees with lived experience and particularly peer workers are no different.

The task of growing the peer workforce is ongoing. Employing peer workers in teams is a major step. Continuing to develop them and provide opportunities to reflect on their practice is essential, just as it is for any other employee. If we are committed to the unique contribution of peer workers to mental health services, this commitment requires consideration of how peer workers can be supported by other peer workers. As in other health professions, sometimes that support must be provided by people from similar training and backgrounds, and not necessarily entirely from a direct line manager. Just as psychologists and nurses benefit from the support and guidance of a more senior or specialist nurse or psychologist, peer workers benefit from the support and guidance of a more senior or experienced peer worker. This does not devolve the line manager's responsibility to provide day-to-day support and guidance to the employee on behalf of the organisation, but rather recognises that the responsibility for an employee's professional development is richer if shared.

## 2: Changing culture and growing peer work

**Evaluation**

Flourish Australia are beginning an evaluation of the 'Why not a peer worker?' strategy. We are in the process of co-designing the evaluation. The results will be used in further developing our approach.

Calculating the social return on investment (SROI) is an internationally recognised methodology used to understand, measure and value the social impact of a program or organisation. It places a monetary value on the impact (the benefit) of an activity, and compares this with the cost, or investment required, to create that benefit.

An SROI evaluation of Flourish Australia's totally peer-run service, established in Hervey Bay, Queensland in 2011, was undertaken in 2014 by Social Ventures Australia (Prout, 2017). This service is unique because it is fully staffed by peers with lived experience. They deliver community-based supports. It comprises: a resource centre, where people with lived experience can attend one-on-one support sessions or group sessions and can socialise with each other; a 'warm-line' (a dedicated, non-crisis phone support service for people needing support with their mental health recovery); and a rest and recovery accommodation service, which is short-term accommodation available for people to take time out from their current living arrangements. People accessing the services do so voluntarily and can attend any or all of these services.

This evaluation showed that:
1. Our peer-operated service had a significant positive social and economic impact on its stakeholders including peers, peer volunteers, peer workers and the mental health service.
2. The SROI ratio was 3.27:1. This means that for every $1 invested in the peer-operated service, approximately $3.27 of value was created.
3. A total of 141 peers were engaged with the peer-operated service, with 40% of those engaging intensely (at least once a week). In total, activities generated approximately $2.1 million in present value for its stakeholders across a range of outcomes.
4. An investment of $700,000 (88% cash and 12% in kind) was required during this period to fund the program. This equates to approximately $5000 for each peer who participated.

5. The largest portion of value created by the peer-operated service accrued to the peers ($1.6 million). The majority (69%) of this was attributable to social recovery (developing a larger and more diverse social network) and personal recovery (development of hope, self-determination and identity).
6. The majority of the remaining value, $600,000, accrued to the mental health service, who experienced reduced pressure on their services due to lower peer admissions and readmissions and shorter lengths of stay at their health services.

## Medication

It was mentioned earlier that embarking on growth in the peer workforce led to policy change and development. Reference in this chapter has also been by some clinical practitioners requesting peer workers to engage in medication management. One policy that Flourish Australia paid particular attention to was the role of peer workers in medication support practices.

Given that peer work is a non-clinical role, Flourish Australia took the position that any staff member who is not clinically trained should limit their involvement in clinical practices such as medication administration and supervision. Great emphasis was placed on supporting each person to manage their own medications, providing reminders and encouragement when required. Where it was apparent that this was not possible, the decision was taken that non-clinical staff would work with people to build strong relationships with the local mental health team, local pharmacists, community nurses and general practitioners for them to receive appropriate clinical support.

By building people's confidence and skills to manage their own medication, new possibilities were awakened. People began to say things like: 'If I can manage my own medication, maybe there are more things about my life I can manage by myself; maybe there are other things I can achieve'. People began trying new experiences or taking part in activities and relationships they had not taken part in for some time.

People also started to connect with the community as they walked to get their medication at the same time every day. People started to feel they belonged to their community and helped their neighbours more—neighbourly interactions that most people take for granted, ordinary, empowering involvement.

2: Changing culture and growing peer work

This process exemplifies how organisations can positively influence the culture and services offered by mental health services. Peer work shines a light on what needs to be done and can be done in services to improve the life skills of people accessing services.

### Sharing our experience

Having come so far, Flourish Australia are committed to sharing our experience. We provide support to build capacity to manage mental health and wellbeing in the workplace, place peer workers into workplaces, and train staff in peer support. This has been in environments as varied as the arts, transport, health and community services. The sector is calling out for additional supports for mental health and see real value in peer-based approaches.

### Conclusion

Flourish Australia are committed to continuing to grow the peer workforce, the types and models of service in which peer work can be offered, in order to better meet the individual needs of each person accessing our services. This will have a positive effect not only on the lives of individuals in the service but also upon their families, carers, friends, other services and the broader community. The current strategy has a target of peer workers eventually making up 50% of our frontline positions.

Flourish Australia are leading the way in creating a large, professional paid peer workforce in Australia. Our experience is showing other organisations that a large peer workforce is not only achievable but is a valuable, high-quality initiative that delivers improved services and is sustainable.

We have demonstrated that peer workers build professional, compassionate relationships quickly and easily with people accessing mental health services. People respond positively to this and their lives improve as a result because their feelings and thoughts about themselves and others positively change.

The organisation's extensive experience in growing the peer workforce is showing that people with a lived experience of mental health issues and who are actively moving towards recovery can:

- and do work hard and professionally
- and do work full-time
- and do hold driver licences
- do shift work
- be relied upon
- be trusted
- go the distance
- keep confidentiality
- be strategic
- have outstanding personal skills
- be discreet and have many more qualities.

They are:
- visionary
- creative
- empathic
- resilient and strong
- reliable and honest
- dedicated
- leaders
- supportive
- brave
- efficient
- intuitive.

The work peer workers do changes lives, outcomes and futures through the purposeful sharing of their lived experience and recovery in a reciprocal way with people accessing the services. Flourish Australia intend to forge ahead with a culture of pride, acceptance, engagement and belonging for people with lived experience of mental health issues within local communities, the broader Australian community, communities in other nations, workplaces and services

If, as a service, the aim is to become redundant in someone's life as their skills and confidence grow, the outcomes achieved by people accessing services with the support of peer workers are an important added value that quickens the pace. The growth in the peer workforce improves the services that organisations offer. This in turn supports people who are accessing services to pursue their recovery, connection to family, friends and community, and their ability to lead contributing lives. They do so in ways that are strong they are living lives that are valuable and fulfilling to them, and they need less and less support over time.

The challenge for all mental health services is to open their minds to growing the peer workforce, hold the crucial conversations that break through barriers and obstacles and develop funded plans to grow a quality peer workforce.

Flourish Australia have proven it can be done.

## References

Australian Government Productivity Commission. (2017). National Disability Insurance Scheme (NDIS) costs: Productivity Commission position paper. NSW Government submission. Retrieved from https://www.pc.gov.au/inquiries/completed/ndis-costs/position

Beattie, V., Meagher, J., & Farrugia, P. (2013). *Embracing inclusion: Employment of people with lived experience* (Policy direction paper). Sydney: RichmondPRA. Retrieved from https://www.flourishaustralia.org.au/embracing-inclusion-lived-experience

Chinman, M., George, P., Dougherty, R. H., Daniels, A. S., Ghose, S. S., Swift, A., & Delphin-Rittmon, M. E. (2014). Peer support services for individuals with serious mental illnesses: Assessing the evidence. *Psychiatric Services, 65*(4), 429–441.

Davidson, L., Bellamy, C., Guy, K., & Miller, M. (2012). Peer support among persons with severe mental illnesses: A review of evidence and experience. *World Psychiatry, 11*, 123–128.

RichmondPRA. (2014). Recovery action framework. Sydney: RichmondPRA. Retrieved from https://www.flourishaustralia.org.au/recovery-action-framework

Flourish Australia. (2015). Strengths-based language guide. Available on request from Flourish Australia.

Jackson, F., & Fong, T. (2017). Why not a peer worker? *Mental Health and Social Inclusion, 21*(3), 176–183.

National Mental Health Commission. (2015). Certificate IV mental health peer work, foundations of peer work, resource book 1. National Mental Health Commission. Retrieved from http://www.mentalhealthcommission.gov.au/our-work/mental-health-peer-work-development-and-promotion.aspx

O'Hagan, M. (2011). Peer support in mental health and addictions: A background paper prepared for Kites Trust. Retrieved from http://sharc.org.au/wp-content/uploads/2016/03/Peer-Support-Overview-OHagan.pdf

Prout, K. (2017). The value of a peer operated service. Social Ventures Australia. Retrieved from www.socialventures.com.au

Trachtenberg, M., Parsonage, M., Shepherd, G., & Boardman, J. (2013). Peer support in mental health care: Is it good value for money? London: Centre for Mental Health. Retrieved from http://eprints.lse.ac.uk/60793/1/Trachtenberg_etal_Report-Peer-support-in-mental-health-care-is-it-good-value-for-money_2013.pdf

# Section 3

# The long walk

# Peer work in Mind Australia

*Erandathie Jayakody and Anthony Stratford*

*Erandathie Jayakody has been working in the mental health sector since 2011 and currently leads the consumer and carer participation team at Mind Australia. Drawing on her own lived experience of mental ill-health and recovery, Erandathie has been instrumental in the expansion of the peer workforce at Mind. With a background as a lawyer, Erandathie works from a human rights framework to support people with mental ill-health to lead a life of their own choosing. Erandathie was recently appointed to the Mental Health Tribunal and was previously a board member of the Victorian Mental Illness Awareness Council.*

*Anthony Stratford is on the executive of Mind Australia where he holds the role of senior adviser, lived experience. His work contributes to the recognition of the lived experience of mental distress and recovery informing system change both at a national and international level. His appointment at Yale University in the Program for Recovery and Community Health, working closely with Professor Larry Davidson, has enabled research on peer support to be widely disseminated in Australia.*

> The meaning of life is to find your gift.
> The purpose of life is to give it away.
>
> *Pablo Picasso*

The story of peer work at Mind Australia Ltd (Mind) is one of opportunity, struggle, learning and success, against the transitional backdrop from professional-led paternalism towards peer-led partnerships in mental health services. Mind is a leader in peer work in Australia; its leaders and peer workforce are proud of Mind's considerable achievements but also honest about their initial lack of understanding and the mistakes they made.

This chapter starts by defining peer work and outlines Mind's approach to it. The second part explores the lead-up to peer work and the third part gives a brief history of the development of peer work at Mind. This is followed by a self-assessment of how Mind has performed in developing its peer workforce. The chapter ends with people's thoughts on the future of peer work in Mind.

## 3: The long walk

This chapter was created from a range of source materials (see References), as well as interviews with 13 key people who have contributed to development and delivery of peer work within Mind over the last fourteen years.

### History, definitions and values

Peer workers include all workers in mental health services who are trained, employed and supervised to openly use their lived experience of mental distress and recovery, in a role that requires lived experience. Most provide peer support for personal recovery, in housing, in employment or for people in crisis. Some take up peer roles in learning and development, service development, research, advocacy, human resources and management. Mental health workers with lived experience of mental distress do not always openly identify their experience or occupy peer roles; they are an important and growing part of the workforce, but they are not part of the peer workforce, and are not the focus of this document. Nor are those peer workers who have a carer identity. Peer support is the most common and established peer work role. Informal peer support has always existed among people with mental distress and addiction. The earliest reference to peer support workers in mental health services was in 1793 when one of Philippe Pinel's colleagues, Jean-Baptiste Pussin, hired them. Pinel wrote at the time, 'As much as possible, all servants are chosen from the category of mental patients. They are at any rate better suited to this demanding work because they are usually more gentle, honest, and humane' (Davidson et al., 2012). However, peer work did not become embedded in mainstream mental health service delivery for another 200 years.

The twentieth century saw the development of Alcoholics Anonymous and other Twelve-Step self-help or peer support groups from the 1930s on, and a variety of mental health peer initiatives that arose from the international consumer movement from the 1970s on. In the last twenty years mainstream mental health services, mainly in western countries, have begun to employ peer workers in various roles. Peer work has also started to develop in countries like Japan, South Korea, Singapore, Hong Kong and India.

The development of peer support and other peer work roles fits with the recovery approach in mental health as well as general trends in health towards self-management of health conditions. Peer support work, for instance, has grown hugely in the United States, to over 10,000 peer support workers, since it became a billable activity under Medicaid in the 2000s. It has grown on a smaller scale in Australia over the last decade, partly in response to Commonwealth and state/territory government initiatives that have encouraged or mandated the use of this workforce.

Around the world, peer support may be funded or unfunded, use paid staff or volunteers, operate out of peer-led organisations, peer-led teams within mainstream organisations or individual peers in teams of non-peer workers. Peer support can take place in any service or community setting.

Peer workers can provide many of the same kinds of services that non-peer workers and other professionals provide. The essence of peer work is not so much what kind of service is provided but who provides it and how. The 'who' must be a person with an openly identified lived experience of mental distress and recovery, in a designated peer work role. The 'how' must be built on the lived experience values of peer support, derived from the consumer movement and the recovery movement. All peer work must facilitate:

- self-determination: the right for people to direct their own lives
- equality: the right to equal treatment and opportunities with other citizens
- mutuality: a two-way helping relationship
- experiential knowledge: the use of lived experience as a knowledge base
- hope: belief in people's ability to recover and live the life they want.

The values of mutuality and experiential knowledge are unique to peer work; mutuality is particularly important in peer work. Peer work values have many implications for how all types of peer workers do their work, including the difference in boundaries exercised by peer workers and traditional professionals.

## Evidence for peer support

There is a far larger evidence base for peer support work than for other forms of peer work. The evidence for peer support shows high satisfaction as well as the same or better personal outcomes than traditional services (Davidson et al., 2012; Doughty & Tse, 2011; Grey & O'Hagan, 2015; Janzen et al., 2006; Nesta and National Voices, 2015; Rogers et al., 2007):

- reduced distress and or substance use
- reduced use of health services, including hospitals

3: The long walk

- improvements in practical outcomes, e.g. employment, housing and finances
- increased sense of self-efficacy
- increased social support, networks and functioning
- increased ability to cope with stress
- improved quality of life
- increased ability to communicate with mainstream providers
- reduced mortality rates, particularly for suicide in people with addiction.

**Mind's approach to peer work**

Peer work is a broad landscape in terms of job roles, service settings, remuneration, professional development and adherence to peer values. Every organisation must make choices about where they position themselves in this landscape. Mind believes in equity for the peer workforce and recognises its unique contribution:

- All peer workers have the same minimum educational requirements as other workers.
- All peer workers are paid on an equal basis with other staff doing similar jobs.
- All interviewees for peer positions are asked about what they have learnt from their mental distress and recovery as part of their employment interview.
- All peer workers are trained in peer work and are offered peer-led supervision.
- Peer workers either work in mixed teams or in peer-led teams.
- Peer workers have the same opportunities for career advancement as other workers.
- Mind Australia are working towards employing peer workers in all relevant functions across the organisation.
- Mind Australia understand there is a diversity of emerging peer roles that will require different skill sets.
- No peer workers take part in clinically focused or coercive practices.

The current peer workforce in Mind includes the following roles, with the expectation that more diverse roles will be added in the future:

- Peer practitioners provide peer support to clients and lived experience-based advice to their teams.
- Peer project worker in the Learning and Development team.
- Peer trainers deliver training for all Mind staff.
- Learning and development consultants design and deliver courses for students at the Mind Recovery College.
- Consumer consultants provide consumer feedback to the organisation and contribute to service development.
- Peer educators and coaches support the peer workforce in Mind.
- Senior adviser lived experience is a senior position providing advice to the executive on the integration of lived experience in all activities and processes across the organization.
- Peer researchers in the Research and Advocacy Division.

## The lead-up to peer work at Mind

Contemporary mental health services have inherited a mixed 200-year legacy from mental health services. The dominant strand has been one of paternalism, neglect and abuse through institutionalisation, harmful treatments and coercion. The other strand has advocated freedom and recovery and can be seen in moral therapy, therapeutic communities, deinstitutionalisation, the consumer movement, the recovery movement and peer work.

The lead-up to the peer workforce in Mind started when the newly formed Richmond Fellowship of Victoria opened Edith Pardy House in Melbourne in 1977. At the time, the numbers of people in the old psychiatric hospitals were shrinking; progressive professionals, concerned citizens, and families responded to the need for home-like accommodation for people beyond the hospital walls, where they could start their reintegration into society. Edith Pardy House was a therapeutic community, modelled on a 'more democratic, user-led environment, avoiding the authoritarian and demeaning practices of many psychiatric establishments of the time. The central philosophy of a therapeutic community is that clients are active participants in their own and each other's mental health treatment and that responsibility for the daily running of the community is shared among the clients and the staff'

(Wikipedia, n.d.). This philosophy laid some of the groundwork for the development of peer work in Mind over thirty years later.

Further developments occurred in the 1980s and 1990s with the emergence of the consumer movement and the recovery approach in mental health services. There had long been some individual consumer advocates and small consumer networks in Australia prior to that, but the movement, with its focus on human rights and social inclusion, really began to grow and be noticed in the 1980s. For instance, the Victorian Mental Illness Awareness Council (the peak body for mental health consumers in Victoria) was founded in 1982 (Pinches, 2014).

During the 1990s Victoria embarked on a decade-long process of de-institutionalisation, which heralded the steady growth of the community mental health support services. In the early 1990s the Commonwealth Government introduced a policy of consumer participation (Australian Health Ministers, 1992) and a similar Victorian policy followed (Aged Community and Mental Health Division, 1996). Consumer consultants began to be employed in Victoria's public mental health services in 1996 (Meadows and Singh, 2003).

The new community mental health services in Victoria, including Richmond Fellowship, were influenced by the recovery approach, coming out of some American universities that were working in partnership with the consumer movement. Unlike the pessimistic paternalism of the institutional era, recovery highlighted hope, self-agency, respect for lived experience and social inclusion (Anthony, 1993). According to an early consumer leader in Victoria, who later became a Mind board member, the new recovery approach 'convey[ed] a sense of empowerment, renewed hope, a rekindling of one's aspirations or dreams, gaining more control over our lives and choices, having greater access to needed knowledge and resources, to achieve more positive self-esteem, and to see oneself as a worthwhile human being' (Pinches, 2014). By the early 2000s, recovery was a centrepiece of Commonwealth mental health policy (Australian Health Ministers, 2003).

In the meantime, Richmond Fellowship changed its name to Mind in 2007, thirty years after the opening of Edith Pardy House. By its forty-year celebration in 2017, Mind had grown from a single-facility service to one of the leading community managed mental health service providers in Australia with revenue of $68 million and approximately 900 staff serving 20,000 clients through a broad range of services and supports in four states (Mind Australia, 2017).

There is nothing new about people with lived experience working in community mental health services. Many people with experience as family members have openly identified this expertise in their work. It has been riskier, however, to identify as having personal lived experience of mental distress; up until the last decade there were very few designated lived-experience positions where people could use their lived experience of mental distress and recovery to inform their work.

## A brief history of peer work at Mind

### Accelerating development

While the consumer movement, community-based services, the recovery approach and research evidence laid the theoretical foundations for the peer workforce, it was the Australian Government that initiated the growth of the workforce, through its consumer participation policy in the 1990s which facilitated the development of the role of consumer consultants, and the requirement for a peer mentor role in the Personal Helpers and Mentors Service (PHaMS) teams from 2007.

Mind (then Richmond Fellowship) created its first lived experience role in in 1991 when Alan Pinches, a local consumer activist, joined the board. It took another thirteen years for the organisation to employ two consumer consultants in 2004. The pace picked up in the mid-2000s, and the development of the peer workforce has accelerated since then to fifty-nine positions in 2018. The numbers have increased, the roles have diversified, an infrastructure for peer recruitment, training and supervision has been developed and non-peer staff have been educated on recovery and the peer workforce.

Robyn Callaghan joined Mind as a lived experience project worker in 2010. Reflecting on the accelerating pace of development, she said,

> 'There was an alignment of people and events that encouraged culture change. There was a sense that the organisation needed more than just a name change when it went from Richmond Fellowship to Mind. By 2013, both the Commonwealth and state governments had published their

**Mind peer workforce development timeline**

1991     First person with openly acknowledged lived experience joins the board.

2003     Establishment of Consumer Consultants Advisory Group.

2004     First consumer consultants employed.

2007     First peer practitioners employed to work in PHaMS teams.

2010     Consumer, Carer, Family and Peer Engagement Unit established.

          Peer worker training course established.

2012     Anthony Stratford is appointed the board of the International Association of Peer Supporters based in the USA.

2013     Mind creates the executive level position of senior adviser lived experience, filled by Anthony Stratford.

          Mind wins TheMHS Silver Achievement Award for the peer worker training course.

          Mind Recovery College established.

2014     Peer refresher days, later peer communities of practice established.

          Recovery Learning Experience training developed for all staff.

          Mind signs a memorandum of understanding for joint work with Yale University Program for Recovery and Community Health.

          Mind takes on the auspicing and funding of the Centre for Excellence in Peer Support.

2015     Peer workforce development project reviews and makes recommendations.

          Recovery College awarded the National Disability Award for Excellence in Choice and Control in Service Delivery in 2015.

          Recovery College wins the silver TheMHS Achievement Award in 2016.

2016     The National Disability Insurance Scheme goes live in Victoria.

mental health recovery frameworks. PHaMS required a peer worker in every team. From the start of his appointment in 2009, Gerry Naughtin, the new chief executive, was very keen to move the organisation towards a recovery-oriented culture and a lot was initiated through his close working relationship with Anthony Stratford.'

Anthony is now the senior adviser lived experience on the Mind executive.

## Consumer consultants

The first paid role requiring lived experience of mental distress and recovery came with the consumer consultant roles. In 2003 Mind established a Consumer Consultants Advisory Group to create a formal structure for consumer participation within the organisation. This would later become part of the National Consumer Reference Group which still exists today. In 2004, Mind became one of the first community managed mental health services in Victoria to employ consumer consultants, a decade after they were introduced into public mental health services. The role of the consumer consultants is to engage with consumers, provide consumer feedback to the organisation and work collaboratively with staff and management in planning, delivery, evaluation and quality improvement of the service.

Judy Hamann was in a senior management role in Mind at the time:

> 'I pushed for Mind to have consumer consultants. I'd come from the clinical system where we had them and the people using Mind were the same as the people using the clinical service. We brought on the first two consumer consultants in part-time roles. I remember people asking me— how can we employ these people? What do we do if they get sick? I said, treat them the same as anyone else and the consultants said the same. It was my job to make sure they had a useful role, or if the job got too big. They were able to coordinate other consumers to be on policy committees and on interview panels. Some of my most cherished memories are working with the consumer reference group. All our policies were much better because of asking consumers. I would never do anything without asking them.'

## 3: The long walk

'Consumer consultants have fulfilled an important purpose in the last twenty years', according to executive director research and advocacy, Sarah Pollock, 'but we need to reimagine the role. How can centrally located workers drive consumer participation across four different states? How does Mind spread the voice of lived experience into every corner while ensuring those voices are not isolated from each other? Do consumer consultants still have a role with a growing peer workforce at different levels and branches of the organisation, all of whom will have some affinity with consumer participation?'

However, Robyn Callaghan said that hearing the voices of people who use the Mind services is a constant challenge. 'We need someone with lived experience on every committee. We need to meet the challenges of working together. We need to be tenacious, resilient and persistent.'

### Personal Helpers and Mentors Service (PHaMS)

In 2006, the Commonwealth Government announced and funded PHaMS, 'to increase opportunities for recovery for people whose lives are severely affected by mental illness' (Department of Social Services, n.d.). Mind won tenders for six PHaMS teams on the first round of funding and a further four teams on the second round.

Judy Hamann recalled, 'PHaMS really kicked off the development of the peer workforce in Mind, because we had to have at least one person with lived experience on each PHaMS team. We at Mind welcomed this. We thought, why didn't we think of having a peer worker in every team across our programs. Someone in a government department thought of it before us!' Many community mental health services around Australia developed peer work initially to get PHaMS tenders—they were not necessarily invested in peer work or understood how to be a good employer to them.

Steve Morton, who was initially responsible for the development of the Mind PHaMS programs, said, 'Suddenly we had six peer workers, then four more. They were isolated, there was no formalised support for them and people thought anyone with a lived experience could do the job. The federal funder didn't write any guidelines for peer workers in PHaMS and so every organisation did it differently.'

Robyn Callaghan was a project worker both in the Learning and Development Team and the newly formed Consumer, Carer, Family and Peer Engagement Unit. She soon noticed that, 'Mind advertised for people with experience of mental ill-health when recruiting peer workers in the PHaMS teams. I suggested they add 'and recovery' because they were recruiting anyone with a lived experience and then not offering them training or support. There were some real disasters at the start—people falling over and becoming unwell. It really showed the need for clearer recruitment, training, supervision and support for the peer workers. We also needed clearer position descriptions that included peer skills and values.'

### Anthony Stratford

Anthony had headed a multinational organisation in Australia and parts of Asia before changing his career to mental health in 2000. He applied for three positions at Mind before he was appointed as a peer support worker in 2007. Despite his impressive career in marketing, Mind was nervous about taking on someone with significant experience of mental distress. Since 2013, Anthony has been on the Mind Executive. Anthony is now a visiting scholar at Yale University and facilitates joint work between Yale and Mind. Anthony holds an honorary fellowship in the Global and Cultural Mental Health Unit, Melbourne School of Population and Global Health. He also holds an honorary fellowship in the Department of Psychiatry at the University of Melbourne, where he teaches recovery for the Master of Psychiatry degree. Anthony also has representative and advisory 'lived experience' roles for the state and Australian governments. His numerous national and international contacts, as well as his commitment to lived experience, have enlarged Mind's horizons and helped to build their reputation for innovation and collaboration. Anthony's career and peer leadership demonstrates how misinformed Mind's initial caution was. At the same time, his story illustrates some of the early challenges peers faced in trying to demonstrate their suitability for these emerging roles.

## 3: The long walk

### The Consumer, Carer, Family and Peer Engagement Unit

Gerry Naughtin and the senior management team recognised some of the early difficulties in implementing peer work and understood its system-changing significance. Mind established the Consumer, Carer, Family and Peer Engagement Unit in 2010 to drive policy and practice development in this area. Steve Morton, despite not identifying as having lived experience of mental distress, was appointed the first manager of the Engagement Unit. He said of the Unit, 'It helped to build momentum for peer work and lived experience perspectives in Mind. It was great to have a dedicated team'. The team initially included Anthony Stratford and the consumer and carer consultants, but it soon grew, and it became the focal point for recovery and peer work development in Mind. Erandathie Jayakody joined in 2012 and became the team leader in 2014. Erandathie said, 'When I came to Mind we didn't have good structures or supports for peer workers. Everyone was talking about it but there were no systems set up to enable a thriving peer workforce. Part of my role was to bring structure.'

The Engagement Unit forged ahead with the development of the peer worker training course, the Peer Communities of Practice, and the recovery and peer work training open to all staff within Mind. It demonstrated good practice and enabled the development of the lived experience workforce within the organisation. The Engagement Unit became the 'go to' place in the organisation to learn about recovery-oriented practice and peer work.

Sarah Pollock recalled, 'The Engagement Unit was a big success. It was vibrant and had a strong identity and a visible presence within the organisation. In the early days the peers supported each other and generated a lot of ideas and energy. I used to love going in there for a yarn—I would always come out understanding something in a new way.'

The role, size and organisational position of the Engagement Unit has changed over the years. Sarah said. 'There were eight people working in the Engagement Unit in its heyday. When it was in the Research, Development and Advocacy division it had a whole-of-organisation function. It gave lived experience a prominence it wouldn't have had otherwise. Now it sits in the Quality and Practice team where it is more narrowly focused on practice and service improvement.'

Sarah added, 'Our big challenge now is how do we embed and sustain peer roles across a national organisation and in multiple functions. It's increasingly hard to meet the needs of the organisation from a centralised unit. How do we generate new ideas if people are dispersed?'

## Peer worker training course

The five-day peer worker training course was the first of its kind in Australia, developed by Anthony Stratford and Robyn Callaghan in 2009 and delivered by them from 2010 on. Anthony described it as, 'An intense course—much of it is focused on "who am I" and the domains of recovery.' According to Robyn, 'The way we developed the course was as much about the process as about the content. It had a strong focus on interaction and story-telling and on how to lead your own story instead of having others, like professionals, lead it for you. We also explored how to utilise our own experience with people, when it was appropriate and not appropriate to share. The values that we embraced in the peer training were reflected in the way we delivered the training itself.'

The peer worker training course is popular. It is offered to all new Mind peer workers, aspiring peer workers in the community and peer workers employed in other organisations. It has also been delivered in Singapore and Indonesia. Mind won the Mental Health Services (TheMHS) Silver Achievement Award for the training course in 2013. The Engagement Unit further developed the training in response to participant feedback and emerging thinking on the peer worker curriculum. Robyn believes the Certificate IV in Mental Health Peer Work course, released in 2013 and delivered in 2015, does not have the same focus on exploring identity and the core importance of utilising your lived experience in peer work.

Robyn also said that Margaret Grigg, then the deputy chief executive, encouraged her in her Learning and Development role to bring the values inherent in peer work training into the training offered across the organisation.

## Peer Communities of Practice

After completing the peer work course, Mind peer workers attend peer refresher days, now known as Peer Communities of Practice, which meet for half a day six times a year—either remotely or in person.

## 3: The long walk

'It is important to stress that the communities of practice are not a form of peer support. It is group peer supervision—a forum for peer workers to come together and reflect on their practice. The day allows peer workers to feel part of a community, which is important as most of the peer workers are on their own in teams', said Erandathie Jayakody.

Until recently the communities of practice were co-facilitated by Bianca Childs, peer practice coach, and Erandathie. Bianca explained how they work:

> 'At the start of the year we ask the peer workers for the topics they want to discuss. We also send them the latest peer work papers and research throughout the year. At the community of practice days, we discuss the topic and the papers, then do a reflective exercise where a peer worker discusses a challenging aspect of their job and the group asks exploratory questions. We finish with a discussion on self-care.'

Erandathie Jayakody reflected on the importance of including a facilitator from an operations background:

> 'We found it difficult to find a peer facilitator with operational experience as there were no peer workers in team leader or other management roles, or who had supervision skills. Recently one of our peer workers became a team leader. We approached her to be a co-facilitator. This has worked well and has improved the quality of the Peer Communities of Practice. It ensures that there is a connection between theory and practice. All other Mind communities of practice have a facilitator from operations. A person in operations is always going to bring the conversation back to practice in a way that a coach doesn't.'

According to Erandathie, in the early days managers would not always release peer staff to come to the community of practice. 'They asked what was going on in the meetings and said other staff don't get the same opportunity. We had to raise their awareness. Now the managers understand and value the peer supervision and most are proactive in supporting peer workers to attend them.'

Anthony Stratford said the impact of the peer communities of practice has been major—a hugely constructive way of approaching supervision for peer workers by senior peers. Robyn Callaghan said of them, 'They are really important for people because they create a confidential environment for people to talk about the challenges they face in their practice without them being pathologised as part of their mental health condition.'

> **Robyn Callaghan**
>
> Robyn's contact with Mind started as a client of the PHaMS. She was writing a thesis on mental health recovery for her psychology degree when some organisational change jobs came up at Mind. Her PHaMS worker, who happened to be Anthony Stratford, encouraged her to apply. At the time Mind was undergoing a major recovery-oriented culture change. In addition to the peer work training and communities of practice, Robyn developed and helped deliver the Recovery Learning Experience training, Mind's recovery-oriented practice framework, orientation for new workers and the concept paper for the Mind Recovery College. Being at the forefront of organisational change wasn't easy. 'Some people told me we were elevating people with lived experience above everyone else. They thought recovery could never work in practice. They thought they knew best and that their good intentions meant they were ethical. It was brutal.' Robyn was well informed about recovery and wellbeing and she soon learned to have agile conversations with people that helped to move them along without alienating them. Some staff left Mind because they didn't like the changes. Robyn feels very optimistic about future developments in Mind as people with lived experience collaborate with others to create healing environments.

## Recovery and peer work training for non-peer staff

By the late 2000s Mind was undergoing a transition from a benevolent charity approach to an empowering recovery approach. The new chief executive, Gerry Naughtin, and the senior management team wanted to accelerate the transition. Change was imperative to deliver a good service into the twenty-first century, and peer work was intrinsic to this. Robyn Callaghan explained, 'Some of the old guard at Mind didn't understand lived experience at all—it wasn't safe for the peer workers. I said to Gerry, "We're only taking baby steps here." He said, "No, I want big strides, big strides!"' One of the big strides was to put all the staff through the Recovery Learning Experience training and to offer them the Understanding Peer Work training.

## 3: The long walk

The Recovery Learning Experience training was very timely and there was great enthusiasm in Mind for it at the time, Erandathie Jayakody reflected. 'During the design phase we did a lot of consultation with the staff about their understanding of recovery. Two of the big themes that came through were questions about what is lived experience and what is peer work. We addressed these themes in the training which laid some important foundational work for the development of the peer workforce.'

The Recovery Learning Experience training was designed and delivered by Robyn and Erandathie. All the staff in Mind was offered the training, including administration, senior management and the board. It is now incorporated into the orientation program which is mandatory for all new Mind staff. The training enabled difficult conversations and, according to Anthony Stratford, 'It helped to change the culture in Mind. We've come a long way in ten years, and Professor Larry Davidson at Yale University say it takes a minimum of twenty-five years to have a major impact on a system.'

The Understanding Peer Work training has been offered to non-peer staff since 2017. The training helps staff understand the rationale for peer workers, the benefits of lived experience work and how they can best harness the knowledge and experience of peer workers to inform the work of the team. Feedback from staff has been consistently positive.

**Mind Recovery College**

The Recovery College created a new structure and peer roles with Mind. Margaret Grigg and Judy Hamann visited a recovery college in Nottingham, England, and were impressed with its educational focus and the participants' role as students rather than clients. Margaret then employed Sarah Pollock to develop the concept and business case for the Mind Recovery College, based on her dual experience in education and in participatory service design. Sarah and Robyn Callaghan worked together on the development of the Recovery College so that everything was co-produced right from the start. The implementation was funded by grants from two philanthropic foundations, the Ian Potter Foundation and the Lord Mayor's Charitable Foundation. In mid-2013 Mind employed Dianne Hardy and Graham Panther to lead the implementation of the Mind Recovery College. Dianne said, 'We were given a lot of freedom to create a model we thought would work best. Margaret ensured we weren't hampered by internal blockages because all the systems at Mind are created for a community mental health service model, not an education one.'

Dianne explained that there are significant differences between the Mind Recovery College model and most recovery colleges in the United Kingdom, which are housed in clinical settings and co-produced by people with lived experience and clinicians:

> 'We co-produce using lived experience, learning and development expertise and subject matter expertise … . It's a powerful combination. All our teachers have lived experience. Very few courses are co-designed or delivered with clinicians. Also, people can dip in and out of Mind Recovery College, instead of being eligible for just one year after discharge. Mind Recovery College also role models (both to the learners for staff and students and the rest of Mind) non-hierarchical relationships. We have no separate toilets or kitchens, and we don't have secure offices or facilities that only staff can access.'

There are approximately ten full-time Learning and Development Consultants who deliver courses in ten sites throughout Victoria and South Australia on topics as varied as hearing voices, coping with Christmas, smart spending, sexuality, sleep and journaling for recovery. According to Dianne, 'The Learning and Development consultants share their lived experience very actively in the job. They are great role models for the learners. They shake the learners' ideas about and blow the small size of their worlds out of the water—because they see the teachers doing things they assumed they would never do. It's very transformative.'

Erandathie Jayakody reflected that the Recovery College created a fundamental shift in Mind's thinking about how mental health services are provided. 'We now think about education as a platform for supporting recovery. It creates a much more empowering relationship where students are acquiring skills as opposed to being supported by staff.'

Anthony Stratford said the Mind Recovery College has been a 'massive achievement' for the organisation. It was awarded the National Disability Award for Excellence in Choice and Control in Service Delivery in 2015 and the Mental Health Services (TheMHS) Achievement Award in 2016.

## 3: The long walk

Despite its success, the Mind Recovery College is still struggling to become sustainable, in part due to delays in the introduction of the National Disability Insurance Scheme. Sarah said the Recovery College faces some big challenges. 'It's been an ongoing challenge is to secure sufficient income for the College without weakening the co-production model that is at the core of its success. A second challenge is how to use the co-produced service delivery at the College to create culture change in the broader organisation. Whilst this was one of the original intentions of the Recovery College, it has not been able to drive culture change as much as we hoped.'

---

**Paul Judd**

At sixty-three years old, Paul Judd thought he was destined to spend the rest of his life bouncing around the mental health system, but thanks to the support he received at Mind he has found a new lease on life, rediscovered his passion for learning, and landed a new job! Education has proven to be both a powerful and empowering tool for recovery. Learning and development improves confidence, independence, social skills and community involvement. Actively involving consumers and their families, friends and carers in the design and delivery of the courses is what makes the Recovery College so unique and effective. Paul agrees. He pinpoints his time at the Mind Recovery College as the real turning point in his recovery journey. 'I thought I was done with my career. My working days were over. When you're in a mental health clinical setting you sometimes feel that this is your lot in life. I felt trapped in the mental health system. It would be a miracle for me to get out of it.' (adapted from *MindView*, Autumn 2017, p. 8).

---

### The Centre of Excellence in Peer Support

The Centre of Excellence in Peer Support was established in 2011, by seven consumer and carer agencies and networks in Victoria, to provide a clearing-house and online resource centre for mental health peer support. It also provided in-house training and mentoring to individuals or services wanting to implement new peer support projects or enhance existing ones. The Centre received philanthropic funding for its first for three years and was housed at the Association for the Relatives and Family of the Emotionally and Mentally Ill

Victoria (ARAFEMI Victoria). It has been under the auspices of Mind and funded by it since 2014, when ARAFEMI Victoria merged with Mind. The organisation is currently reviewing funding models to ensure the Centre's long-term sustainability.

*Peer workforce development project*

The peer workforce development project was a significant piece of work undertaken in 2014, when Mind commissioned a project worker to 'strengthen the framework surrounding the recruitment, training, support and professional development of the peer workers at Mind' (Mind Australia, 2015).

The project drew on the plentiful and consistent literature that establishes both the efficacy of peer work and good practice in employing peer workers. However, the literature added that peer work was a young profession with 'poorly defined roles, myths and misconceptions surrounding peer work, limited opportunity to embed practice and supervision processes and ineffective integration or utilisation within the team.'

Erandathie Jayakody echoed this observation:

> 'Through years of experience we knew what needed to be done. We knew what was in the literature and we knew what others were doing both inside and outside Australia. However, we needed to look at how these theories and practices apply to Mind. First, the project took stock of what was happening at Mind in relation to the peer workforce. This included online anonymous surveys, one-on-one in-depth interviews with the external consultant, and workshops with staff at all levels of the organisation.'

The project developed a best-practice toolkit for managers that mirrored the curriculum for the manager peer work training. The toolkit includes a definition of peer support work and advice on effective advertising, recruiting, inducting and supervising of peer practitioners, including the necessity for Peer Communities of Practice. The toolkit also outlines the importance of a team culture that understands and values peer work.

The project included recommendations to promote and raise awareness of peer work within Mind, to extend and enhance the peer work training for non-

## 3: The long walk

peer Mind managers and team leaders, to formalise the Peer Communities of Practice, and to create avenues for career progression.

Steve Morton said much has come out of that report, including the introduction of a peer practice coach role to coordinate the recommendations, facilitate communities of practice, support line managers, and develop training for non-peer staff and orientation for peer workers.

---

**Erandathie Jayakody**

Erandathie migrated to Australia from Sri Lanka at the age of 12. 'I first became unwell at 16. There was and still is a lot of stigma about mental illness in my community.' She said if a peer had been around when she first became unwell her journey would have been much easier. 'I just needed someone to say—you will be OK, this isn't the end of your world.' Erandathie completed a law degree and worked at the Supreme Court of Victoria, the Legal Services Board and the Victorian Government, where she came across a peer network for public servants called Open Minds. 'The first time I went to a meeting I thought, oh my god, I've met my people! I was in awe.' Anthony Stratford was a guest speaker, and he arranged for Erandathie to meet with Margaret Grigg. 'I had a lot of internalised stigma, but Margaret told me the sector needed my skill set combined with my lived experience. That conversation changed my life.' Six months later Erandathie started working at Mind. 'I get great satisfaction from of my work here, and I want to see more people from diverse backgrounds in the peer workforce.'

---

### Peer work and the National Disability Insurance Scheme

The new National Disability Insurance Scheme (NDIS) provides Australians under the age of sixty-five who have a permanent and significant disability with the reasonable and necessary supports they need to enjoy ordinary and fulfilling lives. The scheme aims to help people with disability to achieve their goals, which may include greater independence, community involvement, employment and improved wellbeing. The NDIS also provides people with disability, their family and carers with information and referrals to existing services in the community. As an insurance scheme the NDIS adopts a lifetime approach, investing in people with disability early to improve their outcomes across their life course.

When fully rolled out, the scheme will support 460,000 Australians with disability, 64,000 of whom will have psychosocial disability. Disability arising from mental health issues (psychosocial disability) was included late in the scheme's planning. NDIS has been disruptive to the community mental health sector because it involves a massive reorganisation from block-funded programs and mental health support services to individually funded services for a proportion of the clients of our services. Advocates for peer work hoped that NDIS would open opportunities for this workforce, but the achievement of this as a reality has not been so straightforward.

The National Disability Insurance Agency (NDIA) is an independent statutory agency whose role is to implement the National Disability Insurance Scheme. The Independent Advisory Council was established under the *National Disability Insurance Scheme Act 2013*. Two members of the Council, Janet Meagher, an internationally recognised peer leader, and Gerry Naughtin, wrote a discussion paper on peer work for NDIA. The paper proposed that the NDIS adopt strategic goals and policies to enable the employment of appropriately skilled people living with a disability to offer expertise, support and leadership to participants in the scheme with similar life or participation challenges. The paper envisaged that peer workers, by their professionalism, intent and status as lived experience experts, would model recovery and community participation. The paper remains a guiding document for the NDIA.

Gerry Naughtin, who resigned from his position as chief executive of Mind in early 2018 to accept the position as senior adviser, mental health to the NDIA, stated, 'There is a lot of interest in peer work in the National Disability Insurance Agency, but the take-up has been lower than anticipated. One reason is that peer work is not as well recognised in other parts of the disability sector and some planners don't understand peer work and don't promote it. In the emerging choice-based market, we need to understand why participants are and aren't choosing to buy peer work'.

In theory, NDIS should provide a great opportunity for peer work. However, the NDIA lacks a clear understanding about peer work in mental health and its evidence base. In the broader disability sector, peer work is understood more in terms of advocacy or aligned to notions of mutual support and self-help. There is not a strong discipline of support built around trained and qualified peer workers. As it stands, the only form of peer support participants can engage with relates to life transition planning, and support for participants to establish volunteer networks. The notion of a peer who can coach, motivate and empower individuals to rebuild hope and a positive sense of self so that they can pursue their goals that is at the heart of mental health peer work is currently lacking.

There is a concern that current policy thinking views people with a lived experience as cheap labour. Margaret Grigg said, 'I've always seen the NDIS, not as much as a financial risk but as a values risk. Will we create a cheap workforce out of peer workers in response to the NDIS financial pressures?' Sarah Pollock also expressed concerns about losing the voice of lived experience in the midst of the NDIS disruption. 'How do we access and hear the lived experience voice at a time when the NDIS is creating extreme financial and strategic pressures for the organisation?'

## The executive

Mind has a senior executive group made up of the chief executive and four executive directors and a larger executive team sitting under it. Sarah Pollock, who is on the senior executive group, said this leaves a gap. 'There is no-one with declared lived experience or a designated peer role on the senior executive group, so we don't talk about how things look from the other side as much as we should. Lived experience is a way of knowing that challenges the dominant ways of knowing, that social workers or nurses might hold. Alternate ways of knowing lead to alternate solutions.'

However, in 2013 Mind created the executive level position of senior adviser lived experience, which has been filled by Anthony Stratford. 'Being on the executive team means that when I raise matters they are listened to and considered at the highest level of the organisation,' Judy Hamann added, 'Anthony's role has made a huge difference. He gets authority from being at a senior level. And he asks awkward questions like "What about the consumers?" ' Anthony has used this position to embed lived experience and peer work as an integral part of Mind's policy and practice across the organisation.

Robyn Callaghan enthused about Anthony's role at the executive level, 'He had hot coals on his tongue, a burning passion in his heart to see people with lived experience in the organisation at every level, from the executive level all the way down. He was a game-changer. He had ambition. Without Anthony's mission to promote lived experience, things might have worked out very differently. Once he and Gerry were working together, there was no stopping it—the gates were open'.

Sarah said that while there had been a lot of enthusiasm for lived experience leadership in Mind, 'It has been really hard to turn this into action and create change on the ground.'

## The board

Mind's board has included people with openly acknowledged lived experience since 1991. For a number of years, there was a nominated board position for a director with lived experience of mental distress. More recently the board has moved away from a nominated position in order to include lived experience as one of the preferred attributes of some directors and to ensure that all directors are highly attuned to the wishes of the people who use Mind's services. Bernie McCormack brings his lived experience of mental illness and his many other skills to his role as a director. 'In the new marketplace', Gerry Naughtin said, 'being grounded in what people find helpful is a responsibility of all board directors and not the sole responsibility of one board member. We've come a long way in our inclusion of lived experience in our governance of the organisation.' Sarah Pollock expressed the view that lived experience perspectives at board level need to go beyond communicating what is helpful or tweaking mainstream service delivery. 'It's about hearing alternative ways of knowing and acting on them.'

## External partnerships

Mind has entered into local and international partnerships that have brought benefits to the peer workforce and the profile of lived experience in the organisation.

Anthony Stratford first developed a relationship with the Yale University Program for Recovery and Community Health during a brief exchange visit in

## 3: The long walk

2011. Professor Larry Davidson invited him back to Yale as a visiting scholar for three months. Mind Australia and the Yale School of Medicine then signed a memorandum of understanding in 2014 which has resulted in several jointly written papers (Stratford et al., 2017; Byrne, Stratford, & Davidson, 2018). The Yale University Program for Recovery and Community Health is an international leader in research on recovery and peer support.

Anthony was appointed to the US-based International Association of Peer Supporters as a board director in 2012 and holds the position of chair of the International Committee. His role in the Association has linked Mind to a wider international community of peer workers.

Anthony, in his role as an expert adviser to the World Health Organization in Geneva, was a member of an international team that reviewed and contributed to the QualityRights psychosocial training for mental health services. This training includes some sections on the peer workforce.

Prevention and Recovery Communities (PARCs) are step-up, step-down facilities for people leaving inpatient units or as an alternative to a hospital admission. Mind is the largest provider of PARC services in Australia and delivers the services in partnership with local clinical services. Each PARC has a peer worker as part of the Mind team. This has brought about culture change in many of Mind's clinical partnerships because the influence of peer workers has enriched their practices.

Mind funds a senior research fellow, currently held by Associate Professor Lisa Brophy, in the Centre for Mental Health, Melbourne School of Population and Global Health, at the University of Melbourne. Lisa has trained several Mind employees as peer researchers in specific research projects. At the time of writing, Mind is employing one of the original peer researchers to work on a major smoking cessation research project.

Mind also part funds a lived experience teaching position in the School of Mental Health Nursing at the University of South Australia.

Gerry Naughtin was a member of the NDIA Independent Advisory Council until his resignation as chief executive of Mind in 2018. The function of the Advisory Council is to provide the NDIA with independent advice, which the board must consider when performing its duties as governing body of the NDIS. Gerry and his Council colleague Janet Meagher promoted the potential of the peer workforce for the NDIS.

## A snapshot of the Mind peer workforce in 2018

Mind has continued to expand and diversify its peer workforce in line with service user demand and funding. It now employs a peer worker in nearly all of its service delivery teams. There is also a pool of peer workers, with the Certificate IV in Training and Assessment, who are released from their peer work positions from time to time, to deliver training for Learning and Development across the organisation.

Mind has positions that require lived experience for their role:
- forty-one peer practitioners who provide peer support to clients and advice to their teams
- ten learning and development consultants in the Recovery College
- three consumer consultant positions
- two peer educators and/or coaches within the Engagement Unit
- one lived-experience project worker in the Learning and Development team
- one peer researcher
- one senior adviser lived experience on the Mind executive.

This equals 6.5% of the total Mind workforce of around 900. This is a huge increase since the first two part-time consumer consultants were employed fourteen years ago, but there is plenty of room for growth. Around 34% of Mind staff have lived experience of mental distress; those in generic roles often do not share their experience with their colleagues or the clients (Mind Australia, 2016).

## A review and reflection of peer work at Mind

Mind went on a steep learning curve when the organisation began to employ peer workers. When the organisation started building its peer workforce it had no blueprint to follow. The Mind leadership soon learnt, through some significant challenges, that they had to create a strategy and plan to develop a thriving peer workforce relevant to Mind's culture. Progress has been made

## 3: The long walk

> **Damian Outtrim**
>
> Damian Outtrim has been a peer worker with the Mind PHaMS team in South Australia since 2011. He says the biggest reward of the role is working with clients, so they feel respected and there isn't a power imbalance. 'It's a privilege when people share their lives with me. I try to put clients in the seat of a teacher by finding areas where they have skills and knowledge, especially in areas I don't. That way they feel more self-worth and realise their skills and knowledge are valuable.' Damian tailors his own story in response to what the clients need. 'I never tell exactly the same story twice.' He added that peer work has also helped him on a personal level. 'I've been able to use my dark experience and shed light on it. Peer work is like being a tracker in the outback. We know the hazards and can guide people who are new to the territory.' Damian and his co-worker Lyndia Vaselli were recognised for their pioneering work when they won the Mind Australia Award for Best Service Achievement in 2015.

through leadership and culture change and improved employment conditions for peer workers. Work continues to seek opportunities to grow the peer workforce and to clarify peer work roles and the roles of lived experience generally within the organisation. Mind's experience confirms the evidence (Grey & O'Hagan, 2015) that the best organisational conditions for the peer workforce include organisational commitment and positive attitudes as well as good supports and conditions for peer workers. It also takes time to clarify definitions, roles and the best ways to use lived experience.

### Organisational commitment and positive attitudes

Organisational change cannot be sustained without the leadership driving culture change and the willingness of people within the organisation to change. When Gerry Naughtin arrived in 2009, he recognised that Mind's approach to lived experience had a way to go. He said he is immensely proud of how the organisation has grown and matured in its approach. Anthony Stratford added, 'There has been a cultural change from seeing staff with lived experience as separate to seeing them as part of the workforce and respecting their unique contribution'.

Margaret Grigg was a senior executive in Mind from 2011 to 2016, when she developed a great appreciation for the unique contribution of peers. She said it was not just an organisational journey but a personal journey as well. 'I feel lucky that I learnt so much from the peers in Mind. I first went into mental health in Victoria in the 1980s. I remember discovering that people don't have to live in institutions. There was such a great sense of hope in those days. Then I went to work in another state and I remember coming back to Victoria and thinking, how did community care become so institutionalised? It was wearing and exhausting. The peers in Mind re-ignited hope in me that our services and systems can deliver to people.'

The commitment of the board and the executive was crucial, as was their ability to listen and respond to the voice of lived experience. Gerry reflected, 'Anthony was good at telling me—this is what is going on, this is hopeless or why weren't peers involved in that. It was really valuable. The board and the senior management had a strong commitment to lived experience too. How well we've done it is another issue, but the commitment was there.'

According to Robyn Callaghan, 'Some of the managers' responses to the peer workforce are complex. Sometimes managers promoted the role of people with lived experience, but the same people also blocked it. Managers were looking for more input from people with lived experience, but they didn't have a great idea of what they wanted it to look like, and they wanted to be able to control it.'

In Erandathie Jayakody's experience, 'People say they value lived experience and they genuinely believe that. However, this doesn't always translate into practice. Often, when there are competing financial, operational and time constraints, the peer workforce is not a priority. This indicates to me that there is still a lot of work to be done in changing the mindset so that the peer workforce becomes an essential part of how we deliver services and not just a value-add'. She suggested that lived experience might get more traction if there were more peers working in operational management, 'Currently our more senior positions are at a policy, systems or advisory level. The actual

## 3: The long walk

implementation happens in operations, so having lived experience voices in operations might go some way in addressing this.'

Erandathie added, 'This work takes a long time and we need resilience to keep going. Sometimes I think "We had this conversation six years ago and we're having it again." If there is a change of guard at the top you have to start all over again. This is because the stewardship is held by a few key individuals. We need to saturate the organisation with an understanding of the peer workforce so that everyone has stewardship for the growth of the peer workforce and plays their part in it.'

Sarah Pollock reflected, 'Wouldn't it be good if more people in operational management declared their own experience of mental distress and recovery? Then we could develop a training course for managers on how to use their own experience in their work. It would be great for everyone's resilience and health at work if we all felt safe to be vulnerable.'

### Chris Murphy

Chris co-manages two residential services and a post-discharge peer support program with Austin Health. 'Our four peer workers hold the teams accountable and keep us conscious of the humanity of our clients. They change the whole discussion and have really influenced decision-making, especially in the clinical setting. The peer workers also connect with the clients with a sense of equality—it's a different, lovely dynamic. We get the highest attendance in groups run by peer workers because the clients feel more heard and feel it's their own space. One challenge has been supporting the other team members to treat peer workers as colleagues and not view them through a clinical lens. Another challenge has been supporting peer workers to manage their own boundaries. 'One of the peer workers had used the service he is now working in and he knew some of the clients from that time. It took him about a year to feel comfortable in his new role, but it was powerful for the residents to see him move from being on the ward with them to being on the other side of the desk.'

Culture change happens at all levels of the organisation and peer workers themselves can be powerful change agents. Bianca Childs, a peer practice coach, has seen how the introduction of peer workers can create culture change within teams. 'Peer workers can call out language within the team that doesn't respect or acknowledge lived experience. Other team members often go to them for advice on how they can help clients. Peer workers are a role model for recovery for the other team members. They also role-model self-care and through their sharing and create a culture where is OK for other team members to talk about their problems.'

Sustaining momentum in organisational change is always a challenge. Anthony, using his role on the executive, has led, defined and shaped a whole range of processes. However, he believes the NDIS has diverted attention from this new workforce. 'All community mental health services are really challenged by the Scheme.'

## Supports and conditions for peer workers

In addition to working on broad organisational and attitude change, Mind had to learn how to be a good employer to a new workforce. Anthony Stratford observed, 'Mind was unsure how to support them. The most important learning is that people with lived experience don't always make good peer workers.' Margaret Grigg said that like other organisations, Mind experienced problems early on with poorly integrated and unsupported peer workers. 'The peer workers felt their jobs were unclear. I thought: this is a new workforce— we need a methodology. We had to deal with the underlying issues such as human resource management, culture change and education for the non-peer staff'.

Because of the development work of the last several years, Mind now provides ongoing relevant training and support for peer workers. 'There has been a lot of progress', said Erandathie. 'We have peer communities of practice, orientations, training on working with peer workers, and a peer worker in every team. We've also improved our interview practices with applicants for peer roles. Panellists used to skirt around applicants' lived experience and they were at risk of hiring someone who didn't have lived experience or experience of recovery. Now they know what do and what to ask because we cover it in our peer work training for managers'.

## Clarifying roles

Mind has a developed variety of peer worker positions, such as peer practitioners (those who work in work in frontline services), project workers (those who work on specific projects), learning and development consultants (those who develop and deliver training), consumer consultants, senior advisers and so on. All these roles required different skill sets. However, there is an unresolved debate within Mind about the value of merging aspects these roles, for instance the engagement and participation aspects of the consumer consultant role with the peer practitioner role.

Finding ways for the consumer consultants to reach scattered consumer groups in several states has been an ongoing challenge. In response to this, Mind is trialling peer practitioners in Queensland to do some consumer consultancy work. Steve Morton said, 'We have developed the Your Voice Matters pilot program for people to give their feedback on the service. We use the peer practitioners to promote the program and to encourage people to fill out feedback cards. The peer practitioners meet with management monthly to discuss the feedback.'

Erandathie Jayakody has another perspective. 'Sometimes when people talk about the peer workforce, they bundle it all together. There is still a belief among some, that peer practitioners should be able to do consumer consultant work.' There is also a potential conflict when a person in a service delivery role also gathers feedback from people using the service; an independent person may elicit more honest and open comments from clients.

## Defining and using lived experience

How do we define lived experience? Who can use their lived experience in their work? These are some of the questions that Mind is debating. Erandathie Jayakody suggested, 'After the work that we have done in the last ten years to raise awareness of peer work and lived experience, we now have a fertile environment to explore the more nuanced answers to these questions.' These answers will shape the contribution of lived experience and peer work into the future.

'At the moment people with lived experience in non-peer roles don't talk about it because they worry that their colleagues will think they are weird', commented Sarah Pollock. She said some people think that, while others wonder why they would want to share their lived experience at work. Or they believe their colleagues will think they are claiming their experience is equivalent to that of Mind's clients, who often have the additional experience of terrible mental health services and social exclusion. Sarah added, 'We need to have more sophisticated conversations about this and a language to help us share our lived experience. At the same time, we need to retain what is distinct about peer designated roles and protect them.'

Bianca Childs talked about the situations that can cause confusion within teams. 'A peer worker position was advertised and a person with lived experience in the team applied for it and didn't get it. The unsuccessful person then asked if they were allowed to share their lived experience in their work, so we offered the peer support training to them. That would allow them to use their lived experience safely in their generic support worker role, but unlike a peer worker, they would be able to control when and to whom they disclose their lived experience. Steve Morton believes Mind could broaden the definition and use of lived experience. 'There's the question of how we give support to people with lived experience who aren't in peer roles. Peer workers have permission to talk about themselves. Some non-peer workers would like to do that too, but they need training and support and a framework for doing this.'

Bianca shared another situation where, 'A peer worker said they wanted to share their lived experience with clients but not with team members—because they were worried they would be viewed as less professional by the staff. They didn't understand that using their lived experience in the team, which is part of the job, may just mean using that lens, not necessarily sharing your story.'

There is also the question of whether peer work should be seen as a role or a set of skills and capabilities that can be used in a number of non-peer roles. Margaret Grigg said, 'As a nurse I can be in a nurse role on a ward, for instance, or I can use my nursing skills and capabilities in management or bureaucrat roles, sometimes explicitly. It's similar with lived experience—you can use it in any role.' When asked if that meant we could see a future with no specific peer roles but a lot of people with lived experience using it actively in generic roles, Margaret responded, 'Possibly, but it's probably good to do both. We may want to name some roles peer roles for a reason, but we should also extend those peer-related skills and capabilities to other people with lived experience in the workforce. Erandathie Jayakody is clear that Mind needs to retain and further develop roles that require lived experience. 'This is more than just about having lived experience. These lived experience disciplines have developed ways of knowing and thinking that have a unique contribution to make.'

> **Gayle Clifford**
>
> Gayle experienced family violence and alcohol and drug issues as a young person. She married a man with severe depression who also had alcohol and drug issues. Gayle couldn't find any services or supports for her husband but several people she knew were in a similar position, so they supported each other. In 2007 Gayle saw an advertisement for a PHaMS peer worker at Mind. She did the Intentional Peer Support and Mind peer work training. 'That training really stuck with me', said Gayle. 'Everyone has lived experience of some sort. Peer training would help them to use more mutuality in their work'. People often worry that peer work doesn't lead to career progression, but Gayle disproves this. She now manages the new Mind residential step-up step-down service in MacKay. 'My lived experience keeps me really grounded as a manager. It allows me not to make too many judgements and to treat everyone equally. I find the sharing of all kinds of lived experience builds team cohesion. So, yes I can still use my lived experience in a management role.'

## If we did it again

People in leadership roles in Mind over the last decade reflected on how they would develop the peer workforce differently if they had the opportunity to do it again. Margaret Grigg said, 'I learnt that the change to a peer workforce is hard and it takes time. If we did it again I would be more ambitious. We could have done it faster and been just as effective. We could have set targets for the numbers of peer workers or workers with lived experience, and we'd have a less ambivalent organisational strategy, so we could hold ourselves to account.'

'If I did it over again', said Gerry Naughtin, 'I would have employed a much larger group of peer workers and given them a stronger mandate. I would have tried out some peer-run services and got them evaluated. And I would have done more market testing to understand who wants peer work and who doesn't.'

Anthony Stratford agreed. 'Mind is an innovative leader in many areas. The Equality Centre for LGBTIQ community is a great example. However, I think we could be more innovative with the peer workforce and peer-run services. We could be opening peer-run crisis and respite centres, for instance.'

## Thoughts about the future

Mind has learnt a great deal from its successes, mistakes and missed opportunities in the development of peer work over the last fourteen years. Staff and managers continue to debate peer work and the nature and use of lived experience against the backdrop of a challenging external environment that sometimes makes it hard to innovate.

A review of consumer and carer involvement in Mind is underway. This will focus on people with lived experience as recipients of services rather than as providers and it will consider how peer work in Mind complements consumer and carer engagement in the organisation's structure, functions and activities. This review on its own will not create an organisational vision for the future of peer work. Sarah Pollock reflected, 'We don't have a vision for peer work at the moment - that's part of the problem. Our challenge is to find the next big idea.'

However, the story of peer work in Mind will not stand still and the people who were interviewed for this chapter shared their thoughts about the future.

Several people shared their personal ideas on the future of peer work at Mind. Some agreed that Mind needs to set a target to increase its peer workforce

from around 6% of the total workforce to nearer 50%. This will get a critical mass going and would allow for:
- a greater diversity of peer roles
- at least two peer workers in every team
- more lived-experience roles in administration, human resources, learning and development, information systems, research and advocacy, operational management and executive level positions
- the creation of stand-alone peer-run services, such as crisis or respite services
- the development of new models of peer work, such as informal community networks and peer-led services for distinct demographic groups
- further development in defining a capability framework for peer practitioners and to link this with Mind's industrial relations agreements
- an organisational culture that fully embeds peer work as part of 'the way we do things around here'.

At the same time, the future could see a large majority of Mind's workforce with lived experience. The organisation also needs to attract people with lived experience into generic non-peer roles and support them to use their lived experience, both implicitly and explicitly, in whatever role they fill. Mind needs to continue to celebrate lived experience, so people will feel safe enough to be open about it and to support them to use it for the benefit of others.

**Conclusion**

The people who opened the Edith Pardy House in 1977 would have probably found the peer workforce a far-fetched idea, as hard to grasp as gay marriage or the smartphone. However, the seeds for the peer workforce were already being sown by the international consumer movement which would spread to Australia over the following decade. While the consumer movement developed the initial expertise in peer support, it was the recovery movement that enabled people to imagine that peer workers could be part of mainstream service delivery. Commonwealth and state/territory governments followed the lead of both movements by creating the policy and funding levers for the peer workforce to develop at scale. However, there are external pressures at play, such as the replacing of bulk funding from both Commonwealth and state/territory governments with the individualised funding of the NDIS for a small but significant number of clients.

Clinical services, through their partnerships with organisations like Mind, now recognise the evidence base and contribution of peer work to a person's recovery. It is a matter of time until this knowledge informs the NDIA. In this challenging and uncertain world of NDIS, it is difficult to predict how this workforce will grow in this part of the service spectrum. If the scheme aims to assist people to achieve their goals, the discipline that most naturally supports this approach is the peer workforce, which has a more robust evidence base for good outcomes than other disciplines in mental health or disability support.

Therefore, we cannot confidently predict in what areas or how Mind's peer workforce will grow over the next five to ten years. Much of this depends on how the dust will settle from the various disruptions to the community mental health sector (i.e. combined impacts of National Mental Health Reform (Public Health Networks), state and territory service cutbacks, redesign and restructure processes as well as the rollout of the NDIS) and on how the sector adapts and matures. That said, the various disruptions of reforms together with the NDIS can also offer the largest opportunity for the growth and rollout of this workforce in more diverse and imaginative niches. Mind will then be well placed to make informed business decisions as to how to continue to support the growth of its peer workforce. In spite of these challenges, Mind is still very committed to the growth of the peer workforce and attracting people with lived experience into non-peer roles.

Mind is on a sound footing to continue the climb towards a large, diverse and leading peer workforce. The organisation is still in the foothills of peer workforce development, in constantly changing conditions that sometimes reveal, and at other times obscure, the pathways towards the elusive peak.

The words of Nelson Mandela evoke the long walk Mind is on:

> I have walked that long road to freedom. I have tried not to falter; I have made missteps along the way. But I have discovered the secret that after climbing a great hill, one only finds that there are many more hills to climb. I have taken a moment here to rest, to steal a view of the glorious vista that surrounds me, to look back on the distance I have come. But I can only rest for a moment, for with freedom come responsibilities, and I dare not linger, for my long walk is not yet ended (Mandela, 1994, p. 751).

3: The long walk

## References

Aged Community and Mental Health Division. (1996). *In partnership: Families, other carers and public mental health services*. Melbourne: Victorian Government Department of Human Services.

Anthony, W. (1993). Recovery from mental illness: The guiding vision of the mental health service system in the 1990s. *Psychosocial Rehabilitation Journal, 16*(4): 11–23.

Australian Health Ministers. (2003). *National Mental Health Plan 2003–2008*. Canberra: Australian Government.

Australian Health Ministers Advisory Council. (1992). *National Mental Health Plan*. Canberra: Australian Government Publishing Service.

Byrne, L., Stratford, A., & Davidson, L. (2018). the global need for lived experience leadership. *Psychiatric Rehabilitation Journal, 41*(1), 76–79.

Davidson, L., Bellamy, C., Guy, K., & Miller, R. (2012). Peer support among persons with severe mental illnesses: A review of the evidence and experience. *World Psychiatry, 11*, 123–128.

Department of Social Services. (n.d.). Personal helpers and mentors. Retrieved 18 March 2018 from https://www.dss.gov.au/our-responsibilities/mental-health/programs-services/personal-helpers-and-mentors-phams

Doughty, C., & Tse, S. (2011). Can consumer-led mental health services be equally effective? An integrative review of CLMH services in high income countries. *Community Mental Health Journal, 47*(3), 252–266.

Grey, F., & O'Hagan, M. (2015). *The effectiveness of services led or run by consumers in mental health*. Sydney: Sax Institute. Retrieved from https://www.saxinstitute.org.au/publications/evidence-check-library/the-effectiveness-of-services-led-or-run-by-consumers-in-mental-health/

Janzen, R., Nelson, G., Trainor, J., & Ochocka, J. (2006). A longitudinal study of mental health consumer/survivor initiatives: Part IV—Benefits beyond the self? A quantitative and qualitative study of system-level activities and impacts. *Journal of Community Psychology, 34*, 285–303.

Mandela, N., (1994). *Long walk to freedom: The autobiography of Nelson Mandela*. Boston, MA: Little, Brown.

Meadows, G., & Singh, B. (2003). 'Victoria on the move': Mental health services in a decade of transition 1992–2002. *Australasian Psychiatry, 11*(1), 62–67.

Mind Australia. (2015). *Peer workforce development project 2015: Final report*. Melbourne: Mind Australia.

Mind Australia. (2016). *Employee engagement survey 2016 full report*. Melbourne: Mind Australia.

Mind Australia. (2017). *Annual report 2016–2017*. Melbourne: Mind Australia.

Nesta & National Voices. (2015). Peer support: What is it and does it work? London: Nesta & National Voices. Retrieved from https://www.nationalvoices.org.uk/publications/our-publications/peer-support

Pinches, A. (2014). What the consumer movement says about recovery (Brochure). Retrieved from http://www.ourcommunity.com.au/files/OCP/PinchesRecovery.pdf

Rogers, E., Teague, G., Lichenstein, C., Campbell, J., Lyass, A., Chen, R., & Banks, S. (2007). Effects of participation in consumer-operated service programs on both personal and organizationally mediated empowerment: Results of multisite study. *Journal of Rehabilitation Research and Development, 44*(6), 785–800.

Stratford, A., Halpin, M., Phillips, K., Skerritt, F., Beales, A., Cheng, V., …. Davidson, L. (2017). The growth of peer support: An international charter. *Journal of Mental Health.* Online 6 July 2017. doi: 10.1080/09638237.2017.1340593

Wikipedia (n.d.). Therapeutic community. Retrieved 16 March 2018 from https://en.wikipedia.org/wiki/Therapeutic_community

# Section 4

# Examples of involvement in peer work by states and territories

# Research promoting and supporting the peer workforce: how to use it, how to create it

*Louise Byrne*

*Dr Louise Byrne has a personal experience of mental health diagnosis, accessing services, periods of healing and working in peer support roles. Her PhD and subsequent research focus on supporting the peer workforce. Louise commenced a Vice Chancellor's research fellowship with RMIT University in August 2017 and was also awarded a Fulbright postdoctoral scholarship in 2017 to explore issues relating to the peer workforce in the United States, while based at Yale University.*

## Introduction

For those of us who are familiar with peer work, the benefits for service users are obvious and include mutuality, empathy, belonging, hope and increased quality of life (Davies, Gray, & Butcher, 2014; Jackson & Fong, 2017). However, the sector as a whole is largely still grappling with understanding and embracing peer work, and much of what we know about the benefits of peer work is at times discounted as 'anecdotal'.

This chapter outlines how to influence the wider research environment to ensure greater peer presence and perspectives, describes how to access and utilise research in the development of a peer workforce, explains what is counted as formal evidence, and will summarise how formal evidence can be produced.

## Influencing research: peer involvement in research

Co-production has become a buzzword in recent times, but is also an essential way of doing business. True co-production involves partnership and collaboration at all stages, including co-planning, co-design, co-delivery and co-evaluation (Roper, Grey, & Cadogan, 2018). Co-production allows peers, service users and colleagues in traditional roles the opportunity to share knowledge and power (Baldwin & Sadd, 2006) ultimately creating more relevant, effective and responsive initiatives.

## 4: Examples of peer work in states and territories

Increasingly over the past few years, concerns have been expressed about research into peer work being conducted without the meaningful partnership and involvement of peers. As with research into any unique community, gender, ethnicity or culture, peer research is made credible, and pertinent questions are asked, when peers provide leadership in the design, delivery and reporting of research (Callard & Rose, 2012).

What I didn't realise until I undertook formal research training was how deeply the worldview, beliefs or 'lens' of each individual influences the research we lead. I had always imagined research to be somehow unbiased, and certainly efforts are made to recognise and reduce bias. Some schools of thought still maintain there are absolute truths to be uncovered. However, the research 'philosophy' I subscribe to acknowledges the subjectivity of all things and how the mind of the researcher interacts with the area or object of study, influencing the results. It soon became apparent to me that the degree of understanding I had and my own default ways of viewing the world were impacting on my choices in terms of what I wanted to investigate, the questions I thought would be useful to ask and even the type of answers I was seeking. Every part of the research design impacts on the quality and type of data we end up with—from the choice of methodology, type of data collection, the way data is analysed, the view that is brought to that analysis and ultimately the results that are presented to the world. In this time of rapid change and development for peers, it is increasingly urgent that our views and ways of understanding are meaningfully utilised in the research that is conducted on and about peers. More peers are becoming involved in research, but the number of designated academic positions for peers in this country is very small, with most still short-term casual positions, which often limits the degree of influence peers have on the choice of research priorities, design and delivery. Utilising people who are currently working in peer roles as part of the research team is a potential growth area, as are additional peer research roles within both industry and academia. It is important that peers with current industry experience are actively involved in research. Equally, it is important that some peers have training in and understand the complexities of research, to better influence the direction and design. Some organisations have started to ensure greater co-production by insisting on minimum standards of peer involvement for any research team that wishes to access service users and staff. Increasingly, the idea of minimum standards of peer involvement is being raised as an issue. The design of organisational, district, state and/or national policy on minimum levels of peer and service user involvement could be of great benefit in ensuring the fidelity and quality of future peer research.

The Statement on Consumer and Community Involvement in Health and Medical Research (2016) further validates service user and peer involvement and may be of assistance in advocating for higher standards of co-production (NHMRC & Consumers Health Forum of Australia, 2016).

As well as becoming involved in producing research, some peers are influencing research in a range of other ways, including research governance.

## Research governance, research funding and minimum standards for peer involvement

Some peers sit on research committees and subsequently contribute at a governance level to decisions on research.

Largely driven by a number of notorious human rights abuses, including experiments by Nazi scientists during World War II, the Nuremberg Code, and later the World Medical Association's Declaration of Helsinki were instituted internationally for the protection of human research participants. The development of human research ethics committees further ensured that balances and checks were placed on the design of research, the behaviour of researchers and the outcomes or potential impacts for participants (Orb, Eisenhauer, & Wynaden, 2001).

The Australian Code for the Responsible Conduct of Research, published by the National Health and Medical Research Council (NHMRC), provides guidelines for the ethical practice of research (NHMRC, Australian Research Council, & Universities Australia, 2007). Utilising these guidelines, each university in Australia (and some public and private organisations including government hospitals) have their own NHMRC-certified human research ethics committees.

Human research ethics committees assess applications for ethical approval to conduct research and ensure the national code is followed in the design and delivery of research. For research to be published or counted as evidence it will usually require ethics committee approval. The committee can influence the design of research and frequently send back detailed feedback that requires additions or modifications to the research design. Peer involvement on ethics committees can provide another opportunity to guide research.

Additionally, peers have been part of assessing and awarding funding, which can have a significant impact on the type of research that gets off the ground.

A few years ago, I was invited to be part of a team assessing applications for a large grant. It was a lengthy process involving several rounds of group assessment as well as individual 'scoring' of each application. Of interest, my view of what was valuable knowledge and skills was at times quite different from the members of the panel who had clinical or management backgrounds. There was a great deal of mutual respect demonstrated in this process, but also considerable head-scratching as we tried to understand each other's priorities and ultimately reach consensus. The inclusion of a peer on the panel definitely raised some possibilities that would otherwise not have been explored.

**Using research: How can I use research to inform peer workforce development?**

Not all that encompasses good practice is contained in published research. However, there are many critical areas of peer work that are increasingly understood and represented in the literature, including the benefits of peer work (Crane, Lepicki, & Knudsen, 2016; Swarbrick, Gill, & Pratt, 2016), the barriers for peer workers (Bennetts et al., 2013; Davidson, 2015), the impacts of the work on peers (Byrne, Happell, & Reid-Searl, 2017; Salzer et al., 2013) and factors that promote success for peer roles (Byrne, Stratford, & Davidson, 2018; Gillard, Edwards, et al., 2013).

Research findings can be distributed and shared in a variety of ways to improve the perceived value of peers in the workplace, to enhance understanding of peer work practice and the contribution it can make to the wider sector, and to encourage organisational practices that support peers. However, the key for many busy industry-based people is often first how to find the research that is relevant to them and their organisation.

## How can I find the research I need?

Research is often not readily accessible unless we have institutional access, i.e. through a university student or staff account. The evidence for peer work is spread across various journals in different discipline areas, and the sheer number of scientific journals now available precludes the average individual from affording the fees associated with access. Time is also a factor for many people working in industry, so unless research is a feature or component of the job role it can be difficult to trawl through the numerous publications or to learn strategies for searching that would allow research results to be filtered. These barriers limit the accessibility of research to many people in key roles within industry who might otherwise use the research to improve or hone their own practice, advocate effectively for peer work, and/or assist and encourage the development of effective workplace supports and structures.

## If you have institutional access

For people who have institutional access through a university account, database searches using key words and Scopus alerts are the best way to narrow down the research that's interesting to you. If you're not already familiar with these terms or strategies, the research librarians at your university will be the best source of advice and guidance. There will likely also be tutorials accessible via your university webpage.

## If you don't have institutional access

For the majority who do not have institutional access, a great source of free access to wide-ranging research is the social media platform ResearchGate. ResearchGate is free to join, and researchers from all over the world have profiles which include their publications. Many publications are freely available to download at the click of a button, and many more can be requested privately from the authors—again at the click of a button. Go into the article you wish to access and if it's not freely available to download, select 'Request full text'. Many researchers will be happy to provide a copy.

If you have read any research you found interesting in the past, start by searching for the authors of that work. Some may not be on ResearchGate but many will, particularly with recent publications. You can 'follow' the researchers and receive notifications when they publish new work. By looking at the people *they* follow you can also discover other authors in that area. It is likely that other works referenced in publications you find interesting will also be interesting and credible and provide a useful source of additional authors and publications. There is still a time commitment getting started with this process but once you've identified key authors and subscribed to (followed) their work, you will receive updates automatically.

Some workplaces have regular research meetings and/or events throughout the year; this is a great opportunity to share pertinent publications. Attendance at relevant conferences and symposiums also provides a great opportunity to hear from researchers about their work and potentially create networks and explore partnership opportunities.

**How can I use the research findings to be impactful?**

If the author hasn't already provided a succinct, plain English version of results, the first step is to create a punchy summary of the most relevant points to your organisation or situation. Even if a summary exists, it may not focus on the results you find most relevant. Create your own bullet point list or one-pager to distribute to the most applicable people. The best information to have up front is a 'hook', something catchy that gains people's attention, e.g. 'Peer workers sink or swim: how to provide lifeboats'.

Working out who is most relevant to approach and how they are likely to receive information is half the task. People learn in a variety of ways and different groups are more likely to give credibility to diverse presentation styles. You may find members of your face-to-face delivery team prefer information shared in an informal manner, while members of the executive board may prefer an item tabled at a governance meeting, accompanied by a short PowerPoint presentation. A lot will depend on the personalities of individuals and the work culture within your organisation. Using your insider knowledge will assist in effectively delivering your message.

Formal advocacy at an organisational, district, state and national level can also be impactful. In a contemporary example, peers in positions of industry influence came together to discuss recent relevant research, identified their top priorities from the findings and provided recommendations to their state

Mental Health Commission. Meeting to discuss research findings has the added benefit of collectively exploring how the results specifically relate to your context.

Industry-based research seeks to improve and inform practice, so the golden rule in creating impact is to find a variety of ways to get people informed and talking about research results, with the aim of facilitating action.

**Doing research: where to start?**

All research starts with a problem or issue that requires deeper understanding. The first step in deciding *what* to research is by clearly identifying the issue that needs to be explored. Once the problem is clear, the *how* starts to emerge.

In 2004 I worked in a peer-designated position at a child and youth mental health service, followed by systemic advocacy and training positions within clinical services, and peer support roles in the not-for-profit sector. What I found interesting was the variety of ways my role was received. Even within the same organisation there were often people who felt peer work was a missing link in the chain of support, and others who felt peers were just there to criticise their work without understanding or valuing their practice. I could see from my own experiences that if people were enthusiastic and wanted to collaborate, I had an opportunity to be effective in my role. Conversely, when people were defensive or uninterested it was more difficult to work effectively and certainly not as part of the team. To me this became a burning question: were others in peer roles experiencing similar things? Were the impacts similar? How might peer roles be viewed and supported within organisations to allow for best practice outcomes?

Once the central problem or issue of interest is identified, it's important to consider what is feasible in terms of available time and physical resources— what's doable. We may wish to explore the impacts of peer work on peer workers themselves, service users, organisations, colleagues in traditional roles and the general community, but often we need to pick a small component of the larger issue to ensure we can do an adequate job. So, identifying the time and resources available, sourcing more when possible, and enlisting others to be part of the project is important preparation for the research. There is often

4: Examples of peer work in states and territories

a bit of to and fro at this point—if we apply for funding and are successful that will impact the project differently than if we aren't. If our supervisor allows dedicated time to work on the project, it will impact how long it takes us to complete. The scope, length and breadth of the project may have to be renegotiated a number of times.

**How do you know what sort of questions to ask?**

The key to what questions to ask in your research is in the initial problem or issue that informs the research aim. This is the component of the wider issue or problem *we* have the capacity and drive to investigate. The aim is useful for letting other people know what we're intending to achieve. It's also a great signpost in the development of the research design as it reminds *us* what we're trying to achieve and assists in deciding the methods. An example of a research aim is:

> Understand the perspectives of senior managers of mental health services regarding the barriers and enablers for lived experience (peer) workers within the mental health sector

The aim should be both clear and as comprehensive as possible. It can take some time to really pin down but will add a lot of clarity. It's a good idea to test your aim by asking people who don't know about the research area if they understand what you're trying to achieve. All the questions you ask within your research should seek to directly answer and serve the aim. It's useful to keep referring back to in the development of research questions and ask—does this directly assist in answering the aim of the research? What else is needed to answer the aim as completely as possible?

**Get the basics right and the rest will follow**

The overall design of research does take time and involves consideration of multiple factors. Early in the design process it's useful to create a one-pager with seven to ten dot points that summarise the project.
- Consider the significance of the research—what is the wider context: why does this matter, not just to 'us' but to the community, locally, state-wide, nationally or internationally?
- Make clear the scale of the issue or problem.

- Briefly explain the focus of the research—what are peer workers, what does that mean and why are they important?
- Outline the key findings of existing research—what is already known that's relevant to this project?
- Identify the 'gap' in understanding you will explore and establish why that's an important contribution.
- Explain *how* you are going to address that gap in knowledge and why that's a relevant and credible approach.
- Identify why you/your team is appropriate to address this task. If you're clear on the skills and experience your research team possesses, others will be as well.

**Collecting data to help make a difference**

For all our progress towards a recovery-orientated system emphasising individual outcomes, the sector and systems we work within are still largely traditional and often clinical in their perspectives (Boutillier et al., 2015). Consequently, what is counted as evidence is still predominantly based on traditional ideas of knowledge and strongly favours scientific, peer-reviewed research. As most of us are well aware, the formal evidence in favour of peer work is still considered emergent and often discounted as not robust or conclusive enough. We work in an increasingly evidence-based and audited system, and data collection is largely used as a way of demonstrating program outcomes. For those of us interested in the evolving peer workforce, there is a need to be strategic in data collection and consider the role of formal evidence and advocacy in the ongoing development of the peer workforce. In the longer term, what is deemed 'most credible' may be worth critical consideration to ensure the outcomes and experiences of service users are best represented (Bellamy, Schmutte, & Davidson, 2017; Gillard, Foster, et al., 2017). For the moment, however, this is the reality and there is consequently a need for more data to be collected, and collected in such a way that it may be counted as formal evidence.

4: Examples of peer work in states and territories

## How do you make sure the data you're collecting can be counted as 'evidence'?

A number of factors influence the way data is assessed. The easiest way to measure if something counts as formal evidence is whether it could be published in a scientific journal or book. The research will need to have a design that demonstrates a system or evidenced strategy of enquiry: a way of 'doing' research that is recognised as credible (Stenhouse, 1981). The design must be consistent with recognised ethical guidelines and legal requirements (NHMRC, Australian Research Council, & Australian Vice-Chancellors' Committee, 2007). The results or findings of the research should aim to have a degree of generalisability: be useful across a range of settings, and undertake an original contribution to the broader knowledge on a topic (Higher Education Funding Council for England, et al., 2005).

Evaluations of service delivery are one of the more common research priorities for industry researchers. To utilise evaluations as formal evidence, the same steps apply as with other forms of research.

## Grey literature

The information we need is not always available in peer-reviewed published work. Peer sources are often not published, but provide essential perspectives. Industry and government reports also provide a valuable source of information. These publications are classified as 'grey literature'. Grey literature can certainly be used to support your research argument as long as the majority of sources are peer-reviewed. Grey literature is not weighted as heavily since it was not required to undergo the scrutiny of ethics committees and the peer-review process.

## Creating evidence: quality or quantity?

Choosing a research methodology can provide a good reason to collaborate with people who work in research roles, have research training and/or research higher degrees, as they will have familiarity with selecting a methodology, qualifying the use of that methodology and, of course, using the methods. There are many different methodologies and methods to choose from, and while they sound similar, methodology provides the theoretical context and justifies the use of methods, while methods are simply the tools we use to get the research done (Crotty, 1998). How deeply we delve into methodology will depend on circumstance, including whether we're applying for research funding and what type of funding scheme it is.

There are two main research philosophies, each offering different benefits and approaches. Qualitative research focuses on in-depth exploration of a limited number of participants and aims to understand the thoughts, feelings and/or experiences of participants (Corbin & Strauss, 2015). Qualitative research often seeks to uncover what is unknown, typically acknowledging that 'reality' may be perceived and experienced differently by people and is not fixed (Rubin & Rubin, 2012).

Quantitative research, as the name suggests, involves much larger participant groups and uses statistics to measure overall patterns and provide more generalisable (widely applicable) findings (Morgan, 2007). Quantitative research often seeks to prove a theory, confirming what is thought to be true and usually assumes there is a set reality to uncover (Rubin & Rubin, 2012).

The type of methods used in a project will be dictated by whether it is qualitative or quantitative, with qualitative research utilising in-depth interview, focus groups and/or participant observation and quantitative research mostly using surveys or interviews with set answers to choose from.

For my first substantive research project, once I'd identified my 'burning questions', I referred back to the aim to identify who my participants should be and how the data would be collected. In that case, I wanted to know what others like me were experiencing across the sector, and if it was different in certain types of roles or organisations. So I needed to talk to peers in a range of roles across the country and in different types of organisations. I wanted to learn about a relatively unknown subject area and dig deeply into people's experiences. This helped me identify the methodology—a form of qualitative inquiry called 'grounded theory' which is often used when little is known about an area. The best method for what I wanted to achieve was in-depth interviews, to allow exploration of the participants' experiences, feelings and views. For analysis I used a grounded theory method that was easy for a student researcher to learn and check, and provided a thorough analysis of the data while focusing on accurately representing the participants' experiences.

## 4: Examples of peer work in states and territories

Depending on the question and aims of *your* research, the methodology, data collection and analysis methods may be quite different from mine. However, the process of selection—to serve the research aim—remains the same.

When you have designed your research and are ready to start 'doing', it's time to seek ethical approval.

**What's involved in ethical approval?**

Some human research ethics committees provide rolling review, which means applications can be submitted and assessed at any time. Others have monthly submission dates and set monthly meetings. A few now offer both. It's wise to look at the meeting and submission dates for the relevant committee at the beginning of your research process to gain an idea of when you will need to have ethics ready for submission. The degree of complexity in the research significantly impacts the length of time it takes to receive final approval.

I conducted a study involving 24 organisations, including both government and not-for-profit. Some of the not-for-profit and all the government organisations had their own ethics committees or research approval processes. So, in addition to my usual institutional ethical approval process, I then had to submit another ten applications, each with differences. I had allowed three months for ethics clearance, but I soon realised that would not be sufficient. Ultimately the project was finalised six months after it was originally due to finish. The moral of the story for me has been to think carefully about how the design of the project affects the ethical approval, simplify where possible, and always allow more time than I think I'll need!

Collaborating with an experienced researcher can assist in this process but how important the timelines are will vary. If it's something you are personally interested in but are not required to finalise by a certain time, it can be beneficial to dive in and learn a lot through the ethical approval process.

**Categories of risk**

Different research is classified as 'no more than low' or 'greater than low' risk and consequently involves different levels of scrutiny and different forms or processes (NHMRC, Australian Research Council, & Australian Vice-Chancellors'

Committee, 2007). Low-risk research typically has non-identifiable participants, often taking the form of anonymous surveys, and may be exempt from ethical review. When participants are identified in some way, as interview or focus group participants or as members of a site under study, the risk is often deemed to be 'greater than low' and will usually require a more thorough approval process. As with most things in research, how the level of risk is determined depends on multiple factors including the type of participants (age, perceived vulnerability and ability to provide informed consent). As a general rule, the less intrusive and less sensitive the topics, the lower the risk is perceived to be. For research to be approved, potential benefits to the participants and wider community must be considered by the committee to outweigh potential risks.

Regardless of what type of research we're doing, except in a few rare cases, the participants will need to provide informed consent. This will usually involve an informed consent form and information sheet that provides details about the research itself, what participation will involve, any potential risks and benefits in participation, and how the results will be used. The consent process and form must also make clear that any participation is voluntary, participants can withdraw without consequence at any time, and provide contact details for both the research team and relevant research ethics committee. Confidentiality is extremely important in research, and ensuring all precautions are taken to protect the confidentiality of participants is a primary concern in the design and must also be clearly communicated to participants as part of the consent process (NHMRC, Australian Research Council, & Universities Australia, 2007).

## What else is possible?

If you do dip your toe in the research pool and find it's something you want to develop further, comprehensive research training is most easily accessed by completing a research higher degree. A research masters (rather than a masters by coursework) will provide many new insights and allow focused time and feedback on a research project. If you feel you would like to include research as a significant component of your future career, a PhD provides deeper understanding of research processes, philosophies and methods and can be viewed as a type of 'research apprenticeship'.

## 4: Examples of peer work in states and territories

If you decide to pursue a research higher degree or wish to collaborate with established researchers, ResearchGate and Google will be handy tools in finding appropriate people. People whose publications you're interested in are a good point of contact. All university-employed researchers will have a profile on their university website providing information about their research interests and experience. Once you have an idea of some people you may wish to partner with, a cold-canvas email giving a brief explanation of your research interests and requesting a time to chat is quite usual.

With research higher degrees, the student should always be recognised as the principal author of the work. Supervisors will often be included on publications depending on what is negotiated within the supervisory team.

In the case of research partnerships or collaborations, the research design and any contracts should stipulate the roles each party will play. It's a good idea to establish author guidelines as early as possible, including what order the names will be in and what constitutes enough involvement in the write-up to warrant inclusion as an author.

**Practical resources and important sites**

- ResearchGate: www.researchgate.net
- Statement on Consumer and Community Involvement in Health and Medical Research (2016) www.nhmrc.gov.au/guidelines-publications/s01
- National Statement on Ethical Conduct in Human Research: www.nhmrc.gov.au/guidelines-publications/e72
- Australian Code for the Responsible Conduct of Research: www.nhmrc.gov.au/guidelines-publications/r39
- To apply for ethical approval in Australia there are two main sites to access. For most research participants and sites, you can create an account to access the NHMRC ethics application form at hrea.gov.au
- If your study involves participants or research sites that include Australian public hospitals participating in the National Mutual Acceptance scheme, you will likely need to access the online forms site at au.ethicsform.org/Home.aspx. A phone call to the research governance officer at the relevant hospital or health service will provide further guidance.

## References

Baldwin, M., & Sadd, J. (2006). Allies with attitude! Service users, academics and social service agency staff learning how to share power in running social work education courses. *Social Work Education, 25*, 348–359.

Bellamy, C., Schmutte, T., & Davidson, L. (2017). An update on the growing evidence base for peer support. *Mental Health and Social Inclusion, 21*(3), 161–167.

Bennetts, W., Pinches, A., Paluch, T., & Fossey, E. (2013). Real lives, real jobs: Sustaining consumer perspective work in the mental health sector. *Advances in Mental Health, 11*(3), 313–326.

Boutillier, C. L., Slade, M., Lawrence, V., Bird, V. J., Chandler, R., Farkas, M., ... Leamy, M. (2015). Competing priorities: Staff perspectives on supporting recovery. *Administration and Policy in Mental Health, 42*, 429–438.

Byrne, L., Happell, B., & Reid-Searl, K. (2017). Risky business: Lived experience mental health practice, nurses as potential allies. *International Journal of Mental Health Nursing, 26*(3), 285–292.

Byrne, L., Stratford, A., & Davidson, L. (2018). The global need for lived experience leadership. *Psychiatric Rehabilitation Journal, 41*(1), 76–79.

Callard, F., & Rose, D. (2012). The mental health strategy for Europe: Why service user leadership in research is indispensable. *Journal of Mental Health, 21*(3), 219–226.

Corbin, J., & Strauss, A. (2015). *Basics of qualitative research: Techniques and procedures for developing grounded theory* (4th ed.). Newbury Park, CA: Sage.

Crane, D. A., Lepicki, T., & Knudsen, K. (2016). Unique and common elements of the role of peer support in the context of traditional mental health services. *Psychiatric Rehabilitation Journal, 39*(3), 282–288.

Crotty, M. (1998). *The foundations of social research: Meaning and perspective in the research process.* Crows Nest, NSW: Allen & Unwin.

Davidson, L. (2015). Peer support: Coming of age of and/or miles to go before we sleep? An introduction. *Journal of Behavioral Health Services & Research, 42*(1), 96–99.

Davies, K., Gray, M., & Butcher, L. (2014). Lean on me: The potential for peer support in a non-government Australian mental health service. *Asia Pacific Journal of Social Work & Development, 24*(1/2), 109–121.

Gillard, S., Foster, R., Gibson, S., Goldsmith, L., Marks, J., & White, S. (2017). Describing a principles-based approach to developing and evaluating peer worker roles as peer support moves into mainstream mental health services. *Mental Health and Social Inclusion, 21*(3), 133–143.

Gillard, S. G., Edwards, C., Gibson, S. L., Owen, K., & Wright, C. (2013). Introducing peer worker roles into UK mental health service teams: A qualitative analysis of the organisational benefits and challenges. *BMC Health Services Research, 13*(1), 1–13.

Higher Education Funding Council for England, Scottish Higher Education Funding Council, Higher Education Funding Council for Wales, & Department for Employment and Learning Northern Ireland. (2005). RAE 2008: Guidance to Panels. Retrieved from http://www.rae.ac.uk/pubs/2005/01/rae0105.doc

4: Examples of peer work in states and territories

Jackson, F., & Fong, T. (2017). Why not a peer worker. *Mental Health and Social Inclusion, 21*(3), 176–183.

Morgan, D. L. (2007). Paradigms lost and pragmatism regained: Methodological Implications of combining qualitative and quantitative methods. *Journal of Mixed Methods Research, 1*(1), 48–66.

NHMRC, Australian Research Council, & Australian Vice-Chancellors' Committee. (2007). *National statement on ethical conduct in human research 2007*. Canberra: National Health and Medical Research Council. Retrieved from https://www.nhmrc.gov.au/guidelines-publications/e72

NHMRC, Australian Research Council, & Universities Australia. (2007). Australian code for the responsible conduct of research. Canberra: National Health and Medical Research Council Retrieved from https://www.nhmrc.gov.au/guidelines-publications/r39.

NHMRC & Consumers Health Forum of Australia. (2016). Statement on consumer and community involvement in health and medical research. Canberra: Commonwealth of Australia. Retrieved from https://www.nhmrc.gov.au/guidelines-publications/s01

Orb, A., Eisenhauer, L., & Wynaden, D. (2001). Ethics in qualitative research. *Journal of Nursing Scholarship, 33*(1), 93–96.

Roper, C., Grey, F., & Cadogan, E. (2018). Co-production—putting principles into practice in mental health contexts. Retrieved from https://recoverylibrary.unimelb.edu.au/__data/assets/pdf_file/0010/2659969/Coproduction_putting-principles-into-practice.pdf

Rubin, H. J., & Rubin, I. S. (2012). Research philosophy and qualitative interviews. In *Qualitative interviewing: The art of hearing data* (3rd ed.). Los Angeles: CA: Sage.

Salzer, M. S., Darr, N., Calhoun, G., Boyer, W., Loss, R. E., Goessel, J., … Brusilovskiy, E. (2013). Benefits of working as a certified peer specialist: Results from a statewide survey. *Psychiatric Rehabilitation Journal, 36*(3), 219–221.

Stenhouse, L. (1981). What counts as research? *British Journal of Educational Studies, 29*(2), 103–114.

Swarbrick, M., Gill, K. J., & Pratt, C. W. (2016). Impact of peer delivered wellness coaching. *Psychiatric Rehabilitation Journal, 39*(3), 234–238.

# The lived experience workforce in Central Adelaide Local Health Network: a South Australian experience of developing a peer workforce in clinical mental health services

*Matthew Halpin*

Matthew Halpin has worked in mental health since 2005 and has been a leader in the peer work movement within South Australia. Matthew's current role is the lived experience workforce coordinator for Central Adelaide Local Health Network (LHN) and he has worked in a variety of senior lived experience leadership roles across South Australia, including recently as consumer consultant to the Chief Psychiatrist. Matthew is also an adjunct lecturer in the School of Nursing at the University of South Australia and regularly teaches across all three South Australian universities. He has published in the areas of recovery-based practice, peer work and trauma-informed care.

Being diagnosed with a mental illness and receiving treatment from a mental health service can be a daunting experience for many. It often comes with many unanswered questions such as: 'What does this mean for me?' 'How long will this last?' 'Why me?' and 'Can I get better?' The experience is often life-changing, with people at times feeling a loss of identity and fundamentally questioning who they are and what their future may look like. Mental Illness is still today one of the most stigmatised of all illnesses in the community, often due to a lack of understanding and negative portrayal of what a 'mad' person is through the media. Stigma doesn't just come from others; self-stigmatisation is also experienced by many people living with mental health issues, which often relates to unanswered questions associated with the illness, treatment and future along with questions this may raise internally about their identity (Watson et al., 2007). Both these external and internal forms of stigma can have a negative impact on the person including avoidance of treatment or the lack of motivation for the person to engage in varying treatment options. Stigma can also impact on the individual's ability to engage in social networks and employment due to loss of self-esteem and/or poor self-image leading to increased isolation and lower socioeconomic status (Wrigley et al., 2005).

## 4: Examples of peer work in states and territories

Consequently, the impact of stigma can increase the negative impacts of already existing symptoms of the illness itself.

Peer work by its nature challenges stigma by providing positive examples of people living with mental health issues who have also been able to live meaningful and rewarding lives, therefore providing hope and empowerment to consumers and their families that recovery and living well with an illness is achievable (Slade et al., 2014). Peer support here is defined as support from a person who has either experienced mental illness or provided a caring role for someone with a mental illness who subsequently provides support to other consumers or carers (Mead & MacNeil, 2006). The support provided by peer workers differs from traditional support as it is mutual, reciprocal and based on equality and can enhance a person's understanding or self-awareness of what they are experiencing while promoting hope and self-responsibility (Davidson et al., 2012).

Central Adelaide Local Health Network's mental health service has invested in developing the roles of peer workers (peer specialists) for a number of years. In South Australia, peer worker roles were initially piloted in Adelaide in 1998 across a range of community services. These initial roles worked as part of the mental health teams, providing group-based education to consumers and the families on mental health recovery from the personal lived-experience perspective. The introduction of peer work roles in South Australia has greatly assisted consumers in their own personal journeys and assisted carers to better understand and support their loved ones. Peer workers also provided one-on-one support through home visits with mental health clinicians (Kling, Dawes, & Nestor, 2008; Gallagher & Halpin, 2014).

In 2006 a significant investment was made to further develop the peer support workforce or, as it was later called, the lived experience workforce, across central and northern regions of Adelaide under the leadership of the Mental Health Executive. The goal of this project was to establish a peer support workforce across South Australian Health's adult mental health services with the long-term aim of peer work being an established, funded and well-supported staffing group across all services. This program recruited the first peer workers and carer consultants to work in adult inpatient mental health services including acute care, inpatient rehabilitation and forensic mental health services.

Peer workers and carer consultants were recruited and provided with on-the-job training. This training included a detailed orientation program, an education program on recovery-based practice delivered by Helen Glover (a leading Australian trainer in the area of recovery-based practice and consumer engagement) as well as participants being supported to complete the Certificate III in Mental Health through TAFE South Australia in their first year of employment. In the second year of employment, the peer workers were supported to complete the Certificate IV in Training and Assessment to further assist them to develop their presentation and group facilitation skills. The education provided to peer workers greatly assisted the development and delivery of psychosocial education groups to consumers and assisted in the improvement of education programs on recovery and lived experience to clinical staff. In the following years, peer workers were also recruited to psychosocial day programs in the community, intermediate care centres, community rehabilitation centres and some community mental health teams (Gallagher & Halpin, 2014).

To ensure the continual growth and long-term success of the peer workforce in Central Adelaide LHN, leadership roles were established to provide program support and oversight and to manage the day-to-day coordination of the workforce. Originally, two positions oversaw the program: a peer specialist coordinator (lived experience role) and a carer connect coordinator (non-lived-experience allied health role). These roles worked with unit managers to provide supervision, manage recruitment, assist with human resource management, develop policy and procedures for the workforce and provide ongoing training and development. In 2012 the two roles were combined into a single lived-experience leadership role which required a person with both a lived experience and experience as a peer worker. This role was rebadged as 'coordinator, lived experience workforce'.

The redeveloped role reported directly to the executive director of Central Adelaide's mental health services and was part of the mental health executive team. As part of the executive team, the role was involved in the operational and strategic decisions relating to mental health services operations. Initially

## 4: Examples of peer work in states and territories

the scope of the coordinator lived experience workforce was to provide strategic leadership and management of the lived experience workforce across Central Adelaide LHN as well as being an adviser to other LHNs on the advancement and support of the lived experience workforce. In 2014, the scope of the role expanded to also become the strategic lead for wider consumer and carer engagement portfolio across Central Adelaide's mental health services.

Today Central Adelaide's lived experience workforce is a vital component of service delivery across mental health services. As much as 81% of clinical services in this health service, including bedded inpatient services and community services, have at least one lived experience worker as part of the team, with a range of services having both peer workers and carer consultants. Central Adelaide is a leading South Australian LHN in relation to the progress of the peer workforce, with the highest numbers and most developed program management, and is also the only South Australian LHN with a dedicated lived experience workforce management role to coordinate the workforce.

In 2014 Central Adelaide LHN published a research-based evaluation of the lived experience workforce examining perceptions, attitude and value of the workforce from a staff, consumer, carer and managerial perspective (Gallagher & Halpin, 2014). This evaluation demonstrated positive results showing the peer workforce was highly valued by staff and managers and was very beneficial in inspiring hope, role-modelling recovery, increasing linkages to community services and assisting consumers with their individual recovery journey. Staff found that lived experience workers benefited the wider mental health teams by role-modelling positive coping strategies and reducing consumer distress. The evaluation of the lived experience workforce also highlighted some challenges and priority areas for future development. These included:

- role clarity
- recruitment and retention
- training
- supervision and line management
- resourcing and funding.

The recommendations from this evaluation have provided a blueprint to guide the ongoing growth of the peer workforce in Central Adelaide.

One of the priority areas for development was role clarity, highlighting a need for improvement across services to increase understanding of the roles and more clearly identifying the core duties of the workforce. In response to this lack of clarity, training on the peer worker role in a multidisciplinary team was introduced and expanded to increase the understanding of staff that enter mental health services. This has included allied health intern training programs, nursing graduate education, the South Australian Psychiatric Training Branch program, and general staff programs.

Additionally, the opportunity was taken to work with all South Australian universities to provide guest lectures on consumer experience and the lived experience roles. The relationship developed in the university sectors also provided a greater opportunity for lived experience involvement in research and education. An example of this is the contribution that the lived experience lecturer in the University of South Australia School of Nursing has made to a range of mental health research projects and the development of training in the lived experience area across the health sector. This partnership has also provided an opportunity for peer work staff to assist the university with a range of projects, training and research. The coordinator of the lived experience workforce at Central Adelaide LHN was also appointed as an adjunct lecturer within this school and continues to work closely with the university on a range of research projects.

To influence sufficient cultural change, a range of strategic supports need to be in place to assist the growth of the workforce (Davidson et al., 2012). In South Australia education has been an important contributor to cultural change, improving role clarity and embedding the work of the lived experience workforce within the health system. To achieve effective longitudinal change and ensure the workforce continues to grow and develop and that the roles are clearly defined across the whole service, other key work has needed to happen. This has included an improved communication strategy to provide updates and share the work of the peer workforce. The need for clear communication about the work of the peer workforce has highlighted research as an effective and important strategy in improving role clarity and support for the workforce across health services (Kemp & Henderson, 2012).

To achieve this, key relationships have needed to be developed with the communication and the business operations teams to ensure peer work is seen as core business by all involved. This has included the development of fact sheets and posters to assist in role clarity for consumers, carers and staff. A dedicated web page on the Central Adelaide LHN Mental Health Directorate intranet has also been introduced.

In the early years of the program at times when vacancies existed, the recruitment of new staff was not prioritised, leading to a range of vacant positions at times for extended periods. Over the last five years there has been a dramatic shift in managerial and clinical staff buy-in and support for the workforce, with many vacancies now being advertised as soon as possible and both local management staff and clinical staff on the ground stating 'our team and consumers are missing out by leaving these positions vacant'. Services are also strongly advocating for increased numbers of peer workers in all areas. This has been a significant cultural shift compared to when peer work program was first introduced in 2006 (Kling et al., 2008; Gallagher & Halpin, 2014).

The lived experience workforce is still a relatively new and emerging workforce in many areas. Introducing any new workforce can come with a range of challenges that need to be addressed if long-term success is going to be achieved. The peer workforce is part of a movement based on human rights that often challenges the perceptions and traditional beliefs of mental healthcare. It moves the consumer from patient to person to partner in their own care and provides them with the skills, motivation, hope and empowerment. It emphasises that this is their life and their healthcare and that they should play a major role in their own personal recovery (Repper & Carter, 2011).

Some of the barriers that the workforce's pioneers have needed to confront have included: stigma towards mental health and the roles themselves; fear from other disciplines that peer workers are going to take their jobs (Bromley et al., 2013); and a lack of understanding of peer worker roles from managers, human resources, finance and other areas. This often impacts on recruitment and funding. The peer workforce is also often made up of small numbers of staff meaning peer workers are working in isolation, with often as few as one staff member per team (Vandewalle et al., 2016). To change this, strong leadership from executive and the motivation to deliver a recovery-orientated culture is crucial (Vandewalle et al., 2016; Byrne, Roennfeldt, & O'Shea, 2017).

The involvement of a range of non-peer staff as well as leaders and consumers in the development of the program and senior level staff who champion the role of the peer workforce within the organisation is also vital (Davidson et al., 2012). For Central Adelaide this has meant that managers of the workforce have needed to truly be embedded in core business and as part of the executive team ensuring that when workforce and service planning is discussed the peer workforce is always a core component. At the ground level, lived-experience staff have needed to be influencers of change and have required highly developed communications skills and a strong team focus so they can embed their role in each team. This has required hard work, highly motivated and passionate staff and at times sheer grit to work In a role where they are consistently contributing and influencing mental health services to move closer to the goal of true person-centred care (Bradstreet & Pratt, 2010).

Effective training for the peer workers themselves as well as non-peer staff and leaders is a key priority in supporting the growth of the peer workforce (Repper & Carter, 2011; Bradsheet & Pratt, 2010, Gallagher & Halpin, 2014; Davidson et al., 2012). The Evaluation of the Lived Experience Workforce in South Australia's Public Mental Health Services (Gallagher & Halpin, 2014) highlighted this as a key recommendation in the development of the workforce across Central Adelaide LHN. At the state level, there was a need for specific peer work training to be introduced to new staff and to build on existing knowledge of more senior lived experience staff.

To achieve this, Central Adelaide LHN took the lead by approaching Mind Australian and entering into discussions about how they could partner to deliver the peer work training developed by Mind Australia to South Australia Health's lived-experience staff across all LHNs. This collaboration resulted in Mind being funded to deliver training to lived-experience staff and was co-facilitated by the coordinator of the lived experience workforce. This program greatly assisted peer staff to better understand their role and further develop their skills in working with consumers. This project was a key initiator and an

## 4: Examples of peer work in states and territories

example to organisational leaders of the importance of developing a continual lived-experience workforce professional development program.

The Lived Experience Workforce Project coordinated by the Mental Health Coalition of South Australia also found in a 2015 training needs analysis that managers and peers across the non-government sector highlighted lived-experience professional development as a key improvement area. This professional development need for peer workers included further training on sharing their story effectively, supporting consumers in crisis, working as part of a multidisciplinary team, and better understanding of community and support services for consumers and carers. There was also interest in raising understanding in specific areas such as different therapies (mindfulness, cognitive behavioural therapy etc.) and working with consumers with co-morbidities such as substance abuse. For managers this has been more focused training on developing role and job descriptions, recruitment of peer workers, supervision and supporting the worker in the workplace. This highlighted that both sectors were facing the same challenge. To address this a partnership was formed initially between Central Adelaide LHN Mental Health Directorate and the Lived Experience Workforce Project to explore developing a joint training program offered state-wide to peer work staff across both government and non- government services. This partnership led to the introduction of the Statewide Lived Experience Workforce Professional Development program which is run quarterly and offered to all lived-experience staff. The design of these training days followed a co-production model which included peer leaders, service leaders, project leads and peer workers working together to best support the training needs of the workforce. The aim of this training was not to focus on the day-to-day professional that could be accessed through general staff training but to specifically focus on core skills of the peer workforce.

Training topics have included trauma informed care, advocacy, the Hearing Voices Movement, understanding drug and alcohol services and support, mindfulness and a range of other topics. Each day has also included group work, cross-sector networking and opportunities for organisations and peer workers to showcase key work and projects they are involved with. As the program quickly developed and gained popularity across both sectors, room size became a problem as did the increasing workload for a small number of people. To address these growing requirements additional key representatives joined the program including the lived experience lecturer at the University of South Australia School of Nursing and the consumer and carer consultant from the Office of the Chief Psychiatrist in South Australia Health, additional leaders and staff from both the LHNs and the non-government sector. The number of attendees to the program often exceeded eighty peer workers from both consumer and carer backgrounds. This program has moved from being seen as an add-on to many professional development plans to become a core component of many peer workers' development.

The next goal of the Lived Experience Professional Development Program was to look at management training. This was initiated by the Mental Health Coalition of South Australia and initially planned to only be delivered to the non-government sector. However, due to the success in this partnership it was decided to trial another cross-sector training collaboration. This was piloted in 2016–2017 delivering four targeted leadership training programs to managers who directly manage peer workers. Through a co-production process it was decided that specific topics would be introduced at each training session building on managers' knowledge. These topics could be delivered as solo sessions but would also work side by side for managers who were able to attend multiple or all training sessions. The delivery of this training included managers from both the lived experience workforce and non-lived-experience managers providing specific skill training through a combination of presentations and group work. All sessions also included senior lived experience staff sharing their experiences of working in the roles. The training topics included developing the role, recruiting to the role, supervision and support and supporting the peer workers in the workplace. This program has also been highly successful and will continue in 2018.

In addition to the lived experience workforce training the Lived Experience Workforce Project has hosted an annual lived experience workforce conference that has highlighted best practice, provided networking opportunities across the lived experience sector and provided another opportunity for lived experience workforce and leaders from both sectors to come together. Furthermore, there have been international keynote speakers and workshops for further skills knowledge across the workforce. This cross-sectional partnership project has highlighted that there is a range of significant variations across the sectors, in the environment, in service delivery, in staffing profiles, and at times in client profile. There is also the variation between the traditional views of clinical services versus non-clinical services. By cross-sector collaboration and an effective co-production process this project has shown benefits. It can be universal and also forge closer working relationships, strengthen networks and increase understanding of the variety of mental health services available to the community.

Effective supervision and support has been identified as a key priority in the growth of peer workforces (Salzer, 2010) at the day-to-day service level and more widely across the organisation. Being a peer worker comes with some unique challenges which differ from other workers, including the fundamental experience that many peer workers work within a system where they have received treatment and may have varied personal experiences. Some of these experience may have included involuntary mental health treatment, seclusion and restraint, and negative impacts on their physical health from side effects of some medications, all of which can affect how a person may view mental healthcare. These experiences along with living through the often traumatic experience of mental illness can influence how a person perceives themselves and the role of health services. On the positive side, this shared understanding is a real benefit to the work of peer workers and the empathic care they can provide, but such experiences may also have been quite traumatic for peer workers, with some unavoidable triggers or reminders of their own personal experience. Because of this, working in a service were they have been treated can be challenging for peer workers.

For many peer workers one of the driving motivations for working in the mental health area is to assist other consumers to have a more positive experience as well as to contribute to cultural change in the mental healthcare system (Stratford et al., 2017). To effectively support the peer workforce, a critical component is an effective supervision model that focuses on support and skill, not merely the person's mental health status (Davidson et al., 2012). Central Adelaide LHN's evaluation of the lived experience workforce (Gallagher & Halpin, 2014) led to a review of supervision structures and improvements to better supports offered to peer support workers. Peer workers, like other staff, require regular operational supervision at the services level which involves the day-to-day management of staff including sign-off of timesheets, leave requests, providing direction on work when needed and being the first point of call for debriefing when required at the service level.

This provides an opportunity for peer workers to meet regularly with the manager to discuss their day-to-day work and their work with individual clients. It would be an opportunity to debrief and to discuss day-to-day human resource needs. In addition to this, research has highlighted that the peer workforce also benefits from specific lived experience supervision with someone in a senior role who has had experience working in a peer worker role (Repper et al., 2013; Gallagher & Halpin, 2014; Davidson et al., 2012). This lived experience supervision provides an opportunity to discuss specific challenges within the role, to debrief on specific work challenges and to talk to someone who also has a lived experience and understands the unique nature and personal challenges of working within a peer role. Career progression and planning is also another key area that lived experience supervision can provide a unique and valuable perspective to and assist by providing advice on specific professional, mentoring or coaching and provide a gateway for greater involvement in the wider peer work movement at a state, national and at times international level.

Finally, peer-to-peer supervision has also been identified (Repper & Curtis, 2001) as a key driver of success for peer workers. This is where peers can meet regularly with other peer workers and discuss similar experiences they may have had, seek advice on working with clients in a range of settings, refer clients between services, and seek advice on how they may approach a range of challenges in their roles such as working as part of a clinical team, group work, engaging different discipline etc. Important factors in the peer-to-peer support groups have been mutuality and equality, where no individual is seen as an expert, providing a forum for group discussion and learning. By implementing the three different levels of supervision—operational, lived-experience-specific and peer-to-peer—the workforce has felt more supported, there has been less turnover in staff and a greater team focus across the service. This has also greatly assisted in moving individual peer workers from feeling isolated as a solo peer worker in a team to feeling part of something much bigger as a member of the lived experience workforce.

## 4: Examples of peer work in states and territories

Resourcing has been a continual challenge for the lived experience workforce in mental healthcare services and is a common problem across health services internationally (Mead, Hilton, & Curtis, 2001). Although in some areas in South Australia there has been growth, in other areas there has been reduction in staffing numbers often due to changes in funding and recruitment and retention planning. Byrne et al. (2017) write that leadership support and buy-in are significant contributors to the success of the peer workforce, and ineffective support can be a barrier to change. Since implementation of the lived experience workforce in South Australia there has been a number of organisational and leadership changes across the sector, bringing changes in policy, funding and at times focus on specific areas. The lived experience workforce in Central Adelaide LHN has been fortunate that all leaders have embraced the value of the workforce and continue to support its growth. Influential lived experience roles at a senior level have been recognised as a positive influence on ensuring the peer workforce is at the forefront of mental health service strategic planning (Byrne et al., 2017). It has also been crucial that these roles are involved in the continual strategic development of the services. Locally this has included lived experience leads also leading Standard 2 in the National Health and Safety Quality Standards and associated National Mental Health Standards in health service accreditation. This has assisted in demonstrating that lived experience workforce and effective partnerships with consumers and carers are not just core to local operations but are significant components of national standards.

With limited availability of additional funding for peer services, networking, influencing and ensuring that the peer workforce is always part of the mental health service reform agenda have been key. This has required executives and key decision makers including politicians seeing the value of the workforce. Evidence-based evaluations, effective business cases to justify increases in funding and utilising innovative funding sourced outside of the traditional health funding budget have provided key opportunities. An example of this was receiving funding through an innovation grant for a specific project. Effective resourcing and utilisation of current roles has also been a key requirement and has involved the review of peer work roles and funding to ensure the best utilisation of the positions. This has included moving some positions from inpatient to community services or changing working times of staff to ensure they are available when needed most. An example of this has been carer consultants being available outside the traditional nine-to-five Monday-to-Friday pattern to better meet the needs of carers and family members within the services.

Funding for lived experience roles is a continual challenge that is clearly identified in peer work research (Mead et al., 2001; Vandewalle et al., 2016; Byrne et al., 2017). To ensure continual service growth of the workforce, workforce planning has needed to effectively address the range of areas discussed earlier, including improvement of role clarity, better supervision, improved training and executive support. Development across all of these areas has assisted in Central Adelaide LHN's peer workforce to recruit quality staff, increase influence, increase numbers and become a vital component of the mental health workforce.

Establishing and growing a peer workforce based in traditional mental health services has come with many challenges and has required support, commitment, investment and most of all passion from a variety of people at all levels of services. Most importantly consumers have had the biggest influence by continuing to advocate for person-centred recovery-based care. The peer workforce continues to face a number of obstacles and will require advocacy and support from a range of areas. Within South Australia the peer workforce aims to continue to develop as an effective support for consumers and carers while positively impacting on mental health culture, most importantly the care provided on a daily basis to people living with mental illness.

### Reference list

Bradstreet, S., & Pratt, R. (2010). Developing peer support worker roles: Reflecting on experiences in Scotland. *Mental Health and Social Inclusion, 14*(3), 36–41.

Bromley, E., Gabrielian, S., Brekke, B., Pahwa, R., Daly, K. A., Brekke, J. S., & Braslow, J. T. (2013). Experiencing community: Perspectives of individuals diagnosed as having serious mental illness. *Psychiatric Services, 64*(7), 672–679.

Byrne, L., Roennfeldt, H., & O'Shea, P. (2017). Identifying barriers to change: The lived experience worker as a valued member of the mental health team: Final report. Brisbane: Queensland Mental Health Commission. Retrieved from https://www.qmhc.qld.gov.au/sites/default/files/identifying_barriers_to_change_final_report.pdf

4: Examples of peer work in states and territories

Davidson, L., Bellamy, C., Guy, K., & Miller, R. (2012). Peer support among persons with severe mental illnesses: A review of evidence and experience. *World Psychiatry, 11*(2), 123–128.

Gallagher, C., & Halpin, M. (2014). *Lived experience workforce in South Australian public mental health service: What we have learned, what we have achieved and future directions.* Adelaide: Central Adelaide Local Health Network Mental Health Directorate, SA Health. Retrieved from https://www.researchgate.net/profile/Matthew_Halpin/publication/305986473_Lived_Experience_Workforce_in_SA_Public_Mental_Health_Services/links/57a8665908aed76703f4f7a1/Lived-Experience-Workforce-in-SA-Public-Mental-Health-Services.pdf

Kemp, V., & Henderson, A. R. (2012). Challenges faced by mental health peer support workers: Peer support from the peer supporter's point of view. *Psychiatric Rehabilitation Journal, 35*(4), 337.

Kling, L. W., Dawes, F. J., & Nestor, P. (2008). Peer specialists and carer consultants working in acute mental health units: An initial evaluation of consumers, carers and staff perspectives. *International Journal of Psychosocial Rehabilitation, 12*(2), 81–89.

Mead, S., Hilton, D., & Curtis, L. (2001). Peer support: A theoretical perspective. *Psychiatric Rehabilitation Journal, 25*(2), 134.

Mead, S., & MacNeil, C. (2006). Peer support: What makes it unique. *International Journal of Psychosocial Rehabilitation, 10*(2), 29–37.

Repper, J., Aldridge, B., Gilfoyle, S., Gillard, S., Perkins, R., & Rennison, J. (2013). *Peer support workers: Theory and practice.* London: Centre for Mental Health.

Repper, J., & Carter, T. (2011). A review of the literature on peer support in mental health services. *Journal of Mental Health, 20*(4), 392–411.

Salzer, M. S. (2010). Certified peer specialists in the United States behavioral health system: An emerging workforce. In L. D. Brown & S. Wituk (Eds.), *Mental health self-help: Consumer and family initiatives* (pp. 169–191). New York, NY: Springer.

Slade, M., Amering, M., Farkas, M., Hamilton, B., O'Hagan, M., Panther, G., ... Whitley, R. (2014). Uses and abuses of recovery: Implementing recovery-oriented practices in mental health systems. *World Psychiatry, 13*(1), 12–20.

Stratford, A. C., Halpin, M., Phillips, K., Skerritt, F., Beales, A., Cheng, V., ... Kobe, B. (2017). The growth of peer support: An international charter. *Journal of Mental Health*. Online 6 July 2017. doi: 10.1080/09638237.2017.1340593

Vandewalle, J., Debyser, B., Beeckman, D., Vandecasteele, T., Van Hecke, A., & Verhaeghe, S. (2016). Peer workers' perceptions and experiences of barriers to implementation of peer worker roles in mental health services: A literature review. *International Journal of Nursing Studies, 60*, 234–250.

Wrigley, S., Jackson, H., Judd, F., & Komiti, A. (2005). Role of stigma and attitudes toward help-seeking from a general practitioner for mental health problems in a rural town. *Australian & New Zealand Journal of Psychiatry, 39*(6), 514–521.

# Western Australia's peer workforce: principles, practice and opportunities

*Rhianwen Beresford and Vivien Kemp*

*Rhianwen Beresford, BA (Hons) Gender and Cultural Studies, Graduate Diploma Management, is convener of the Western Australian Peer Supporters' Network and co-hosts the Peer Workforce Champions' Community of Practice. She has ten years experience in consumer advocacy, mental health peer support work and peer work roles, including seven years experience in supervision and coordination of peer workforce initiatives and peer-led projects.*

*Vivien Kemp, BA (Hons) Psychology, was involved in the first paid peer support trial in Western Australia. She has twelve years experience in training peer support workers and consulting organisations about implementing peer work programs.*

*In writing this article the authors seek to add to contemporary perspectives and debates on the value of peer work and the ethics of peer workforce practice, through reference to the unique context, challenges and achievements of the Western Australian peer workforce.*

> Inclusion and citizenship are not about 'becoming normal', but about creating inclusive communities that can accommodate all of us (Slade et al., 2014).

## Introduction

The Western Australian Peer Supporters' Network was established in 2014 to advance peer support and peer work and to act as an interim peer workforce association. The Network is a collaborative news sharing, learning and networking forum to connect people who are practising, or aspire to practise, peer support in formal roles (peer support workers) and informal roles (peer supporters). Auspiced by the state's mental health consumer association, Consumers of Mental Health WA, the Network works in partnership with Consumers of Mental Health WA and other carer, family and service champions to promote and advocate for peer workforce growth and development.

Peer support was defined by the Network's founding members as 'a relationship of respect, support and reciprocity between people who identify a significant shared identity and/or experience', and as a process of valuing and holistically supporting each other on the human journey. Emerging from that basic understanding of peer support were two founding principles: firstly, of an inclusive network established for people involved in peer support from all sectors and walks of life; and secondly, of a network that understands peer work as expressing the equal rights and wellbeing of people (a principle we shall define and explore in this chapter on peer work as a process of human development). These two principles of inclusion and the recognition of peer support as a human development process are distinctive features of the peer leadership movement in Western Australia.

It is the task of this brief chapter to illuminate within the Western Australian context the importance of these principles to peer workforce development. We outline how they are being incorporated in practice and utilised to enhance workforce development. Our hope in highlighting the operation of these principles with reference to the Western Australian landscape is to invite further ideas and conversations about their value to peer work and their potential for helping to grow peer work as a social asset harnessed in a range of sectors and community contexts in Australia. Within and beyond the mental health sector, peer workers represent a new and distinct workforce of potential value wherever empathic connection and mutually empowering supports have a role to play in enhancing people's lives.

**Embedding inclusion in peer workforce development**

Peer work is a practice grounded in equality and mutuality of relationships and action (such as peer support and peer advocacy). The forging of spontaneous and voluntary connections through empathic relating between individuals cannot easily be confined by, or grown from, single externally imposed or siloed understandings of identity. By appreciating and drawing on intersectionality theories of diversity, peer work might achieve greater equality and mutuality through an openness to points of both commonality and difference of experiences.

Few of us carry a sense of having only one salient identity or experience that we could say has determinatively shaped our lives. Rather, each person carries multiple significant diversities with respect to culture, gender, sexuality, age, class, orientation, distress, ability, our social roles, unique relationships, and transformative life events. This cross-cutting and blending of diversity within each individual, particularly those diversities that position us as complexly located in relation to inequalities of class, gender, ethnicity, disability, mental health, sexuality and age, is known as intersectionality.

Intersectionality theory critically examines the relationships, hierarchies, meaning and credence attributed to these identities with the aim of supporting more equal and inclusive social relations. In this way, intersectionality and inclusivity are interrelated, aspirational principles against a backdrop of uneven and unequal relationships of social difference.

The Western Australian peer workforce is maturing to the point where it is better to ask, rather than assume, who a peer worker is 'peer' to in their role, on account of the diverse identities and experiences of those working in and undertaking qualifications in the sector. This includes peer workers who are employed to work alongside people with lived experience of particular diagnoses or experiences (such as peers in hearing voices and eating disorders programs) as well as those working alongside people on the basis of a shared lived experience of emotional distress, alcohol and other drug use and/or criminal justice involvement.

As more Western Australians become peer work leaders, many are drawing upon their diversity of experiences to inform strategies for community acceptance, social justice and empowering change. Some are also practising as leaders across multiple sectors, in the process undercutting traditional sector silos and encouraging all sectors in which they participate to be more inclusive and reflective of people's diversity. Peer work is thus also a developing and productive space for growing awareness of intersectionality and using this to foster inclusivity in the design and delivery of formal services and supports.

The diversity of peer workers is advantageous to growing peer work within new specialities and new sectors, and to enabling consideration of paid workforce opportunities in contexts where peer support is predominantly used informally or implicitly. Historically, however, research, policy and discussion have focused on mental health peer work with less attention to considering the value and implications of the range of cultural and experiential diversity of people with lived experience, and to the exclusion of learning from other communities practising mutual support for self-determination and wellbeing,

## 4: Examples of peer work in states and territories

such as people overcoming addictions, sex- and gender-diverse people, Aboriginal and diverse cultural communities, young people, seniors and people with disability. The result is a significant gap in awareness, policy interest, evidence base, guidance and development readiness for intersectional and inclusive peer work practice, a gap that we feel impacts nationally and internationally, as well as in the Western Australian context. Defining peer work with a sole focus on mental health as the basis of peer identity risks marginalising diverse consumer experiences and identities in discussions of peer work in the mental health context, and in the process, may also discourage exploration of peer work among other communities.

Where new sectors which support other communities are discovering and exploring peer work and peer support, the fidelity of peer approaches to the identity and experiences of the specific communities relies on putting members of these communities at the centre of defining, designing and taking up peer support and peer roles. Centralising service user and citizen voices in peer work development requires overcoming barriers to inclusion, voice and decision-making, such as power imbalances, disparities in knowledge, and fear of stigma, coercion or reprisal from speaking up. This means that actions to develop peer work may need to occur alongside actions to grow service user and citizen participation and empowerment to contribute their experiential leadership in decision-making with services and government. In Western Australia, this is occurring within the alcohol and other drug sector, where consumers of alcohol and other drug services are simultaneously working to strengthen consumer participation, through participation projects and the development of a consumer association, while they are also growing peer workforce roles, models and training opportunities.

The principle of inclusion has fundamentally influenced our structure and approach in Western Australia to peer support development by the Western Australian Peer Supporters' Network. The Network functions as a resource for people offering peer support on a formal, paid basis (peer support workers) but also as a resource for community members practising similar activities on an informal, grassroots basis (peer supporters). Our vision is to be a resource for peer supporters who are offering peer approaches in the broader sense (shared identity and/or experiences), and in diverse contexts where people might not have, or might not aspire to have, paid peer work roles in their community approach to peer support.

The Peer Supporters' Network works in partnership with Consumers of Mental Health WA to contribute lived experience leadership to peer workforce development in the mental health sector, as the sector in which substantial peer workforce activity has historically occurred. Due to resource limitations, it has been a major challenge to balance the Network's contribution to mental health peer workforce development with actions to forge alliances in the broad community and across sectors for more inclusive peer support and peer workforce development. Over time, we hope that by sustaining a commitment to peer support in its broadest understanding (as shared identity and/or experience), and strengthening these alliances over time, the Network will grow as a meeting ground and a space for shared learning and action of a vibrant, diverse peer support network in Western Australia.

In late 2017 a new forum, the Peer Workforce Champions' Community of Practice, was established by the Western Australian Peer Supporters' Network in partnership with Consumers of Mental Health WA to support those involved in peer workforce development within their agency or sector to share best practice learning and foster collaborations. Community of Practice members have similarly embraced an inclusive understanding of peer work for group membership, welcoming people involved in peer work development from a range of sectors and community contexts. As the group is a collaborative learning network broadly aimed at those involved in peer workforce development, including lived experience leaders, policy makers, funders, service providers and trainers, our hope is that the Community of Practice will increase cross-sectoral awareness, interest, capability, collaborative action and investment in both peer work and peer support.

### Realising peer work as a process of human development

We have discussed the importance of ensuring that where peer work is established in new contexts that it is designed by and for, and maintains fidelity to, the values and priorities of diverse communities. In this next section we focus on the context of mental health peer work. We argue that understanding mental health peer work as a process of human development

## 4: Examples of peer work in states and territories

can help ensure the fidelity of peer work to the values and priorities of people with lived experience and can help to advance peer workforce growth.

The vision for the Western Australian Peer Supporters' Network established by its members was for peer support to be 'accepted … and utilised as a key role in society at the heart of humanity', so that each person has the opportunity to be valued and supported. In doing so, the founders envisioned peer support as a key community asset and as an expression of our humanity, those universal qualities that are expressed globally as human rights and freedoms. Peer work enhances people's wellbeing, but it is also a social action that practises and advances empowerment through reciprocal and equal relationships. This dual focus on empowerment and wellbeing in mental health peer work has its focus in the consumer movement and the movement's founding concept of recovery.

Recovery is different from the attainment of health, even when health is understood holistically, as it is by the World Health Organization, as a 'state of complete physical, mental and social well-being and not merely the absence of disease or infirmity'. Recovery has a range of definitions but involves a process of personally regaining and reclaiming of meaning, freedom and participation, irrespective of whether distress or illness persists over time. Human rights and freedoms sit at the forefront of the mental health consumer movement's development and use of the recovery concept, and particularly the right to human self-determination—for individuals 'to have full power over their own lives … including freedom of choice, civil rights, independence and self-direction'. Consumer movement founders recognised that lived experience and the freedom to self-determine the meaning of these experiences is the primary resource for personal resilience, growth and sustained wellbeing, regardless of the treatments and/or supports we may access.

As the value of lived experience and the right to live a self-determining life has been traditionally neglected or harmed in service approaches as a common experience across our individual journeys, individual (self-)empowerment is deeply connected to working together as peers to address the human rights challenges we face. The consumer movement uses mutual support and collective advocacy as core methods for advancing our empowerment and wellbeing together. Mental health peer worker roles vary and may focus more on mutual support or collective advocacy, but all roles share this dual focus on advancing our empowerment and wellbeing. In this way, while each person is the greatest resource for their own recovery, peer work is the greatest resource for our recovery.

However, mental health peer work tends to be established under health policy and funding arrangements that do not capture this dual focus of peer work. Even within funded programs with a recovery focus, peer work is often positioned as an intervention for wellbeing that addresses illness outcomes (such as reduced reliance on treatments, improved functioning and enhanced coping).

Limiting mental health peer work's value to wellbeing, but not empowerment, compromises the fidelity of the occupation to peer workers' aspirations, diminishes its potential to transform lives, and undermines its relevance for and alignment with the needs of people with lived experience. Approaching mental health peer work as a process of human development provides an opportunity to counter this tendency, through offering a way to express the dual value of peer work in advancing empowerment and wellbeing.

The concept of human development emerged as a new global understanding of how to measure the development of nations, and as a contrasting viewpoint to earlier discourses that limited the measurement of progress to the extent of a population's total economic wealth, or a population's met needs for services and commodities. Deeply informed by Nobel laureate Amartya Sen's philosophies, human development recognises progress as the expansion of people's capabilities (freedom and ability to achieve life aspirations) as well as their level of wellbeing. While key capabilities include access to knowledge, health and resources for a 'decent standard of living', it also includes key capabilities of 'political, economic and social freedom, opportunities for being creative and productive, and enjoying self-respect and guaranteed human rights'. Human development thus takes the holistic aspects of wellbeing (such as physical health, housing and income) together with human rights and freedoms (both freedom from and freedom to), as equally important aspects of human flourishing. This aligns with and captures the dual value and focus of mental health peer work on empowerment as well as wellbeing.

## 4: Examples of peer work in states and territories

Through its focus on the importance of freedom and agency to flourishing, human development also significantly redefines the role of people in development. People cannot merely benefit from development but must also be 'the agents of the progress and change that bring it about' and in a way that 'must benefit all individuals equitably and build on the participation of each of them'. If development requires people traditionally seen as service recipients to be instead recognised as 'the agents of the progress and change', then human development resonates with recovery as a self-directed journey. It also indicates the greater value of mental health peer work—as reciprocal and equal participation in support of each person's recovery—than of recovery programs that bring various types of service expertise to and for (from a place of distance from) an individual's personal recovery.

When mental health peer work is only understood in terms of contribution to wellbeing outcomes, its growth is also stifled because it is only valued to the extent it achieve these outcomes, often competing at disadvantage to proving its worth against more established occupations. When its worth is only measured against part of what it does, it retains a contingent (conditional and precarious) rather than intrinsic (enduring) value at a sectoral and service level. The enduring value of established occupations has already been earned by establishing legitimacy (unique and indispensable value) and power (such as through vocational and union representation, lobbying and self-regulation of their occupations). Achieving an enduring value for mental health peer work starts with consensus on peer work's unique and indispensable contribution as an occupation. By providing a way to capture what is unique about this work, the concept of human development offers ideas for advocating for and achieving sustained peer workforce growth and inclusion.

The contingent value of mental health peer work can be seen by cyclical interest by government, according to the legitimacy offered by a favourable review of evidence, or its promise to governments to deliver comparable outcomes at lower cost. Although peer work research, awareness, concepts and leadership have certainly developed, peer work grows at an inadequate pace and with often limited uptake by services. The contingent value of peer work also occurs at significant human cost, contributing to peer worker experiences of job insecurity, marginalisation, co-optation and stigma and exclusion in the workplace. Both the history and current issues faced by peer workers and peer employers in Western Australia highlight how peer worker wellbeing, status and opportunities are limited by the contingent value of peer work.

Mental health peer workers were hired in Western Australia from the mid-1990s as consumer workers responsible for establishing mental health consumer participation projects. The first paid peer support work was established to address poor physical health outcomes laid bare by the state's *Duty to care* report (Coghlan et al., 2001). The Peer Advocacy and Support Service pilot (2007–2008) successfully trained and supported peer support workers to assist consumers to improve their physical health. As a result of the trial Peer Advocacy Services, funding was made available by the Division of Mental Health (a former state government agency) for three years from 2009 to further develop peer support in Western Australia through two full-time peer support worker positions. Funding to include peer workers within teams delivering the new Commonwealth Personal Helpers and Mentors programs and Carer Respite programs from 2007 provided a boost to peer work numbers and contributed to growth in awareness of and interest in peer work within the mental health sector.

Various sector development activities have occurred over the past ten years in parallel with peer worker uptake by services in order to advance understanding, capability and structures for peer work. These have included: delivery of the first Introduction to Peer Work course, originally developed by Baptist Care and Mental Illness Fellowship South Australia (2009); the first provision of mental health funding to Western Australia's consumer association, Consumers of Mental Health WA, to advance peer support and peer work (2011); multi-stakeholder work supported by the Western Australian Mental Health Commission to contribute to national curricular development of the Certificate IV in Mental Health Peer Work (2013–2014); the first state-based piloting of the qualification (2014); the development of a peer workforce framework for the mental health and alcohol and other drug sectors (2014); workforce readiness training for managers (2014); and the establishment of the Western Australian Peer Supporters' Network (2014).

These are significant achievements over a decade. At the same time, development activities have had limited success in achieving peer workforce

## 4: Examples of peer work in states and territories

growth and inclusion. Peer work positions have grown over the past ten years, but available data indicates negligible growth in state-funded community mental health peer work positions over the past three years. Western Australia's peer workforce in public mental health services remains significantly below the national average, and peer workforce growth has not yet been well supported within primary care settings. The priority accorded peer work by a number of community mental health providers is under threat as a result of Commonwealth program changes associated with the National Disability Insurance Scheme. Overall, the value of peer work does not appear to be sufficiently understood for sustained commitment to investment and growth. While there are Western Australian examples of successful transition of peer workers from a precarious occupation to a core, distinct and valued occupation within specific organisations, peer workers in Western Australia are often brought on as an adjunct to existing programs and to achieve similar outcomes to other workers on those programs. There is a need to better articulate how the unique value of peer work transforms lives in ways that communities would not otherwise be able to achieve, and that require reviewing service models, peer roles, service cultures and funding streams to harness that unique value.

Making a case in Western Australia for our distinct value is about the lives of people who want but cannot access peer support. It is also about the lives of peer workers who are harmed by being conditionally valued in workplaces and in many cases appraised not on their actual role but as auxiliaries for, and on the terms of managers from, other occupations. Prior research has highlighted peer workers' frequent exposure to role stress and strain related to isolation in the workplace, including role strain and role conflict associated with workplace requirements at odds with peer values and practices, and cultures resistant to the critique of dominant paradigms necessary to bringing about peer-inclusive workplaces. In a 2017 survey of Western Australia's mental health and alcohol and other drug peer workforce, 42% were dissatisfied with levels of stigma and discrimination in the workplace and 57% had taken sick leave or resigned for work-related reasons, including bullying, lack of supervision, and workplace stigma and discrimination. These figures will change when peer workers are employed and supported as peer workers (when roles, workplaces and supervision arrangements fit the requirements of the vocation they practice).

## The way forwards

A starting point to advocating for the unique value of our vocation and ensuring employers understand the requirements of our vocation is to have meeting spaces as peer workers that are ours. This is important for having opportunities to talk about the roles and relationships that we need as peer workers and also for having collegial relationships with one another in order to sustain wellbeing as we navigate the gap between what we need and what exists in workplaces. Where formal, broader scale vocational establishment work is undertaken, these local peer worker spaces must be linked to and able to partner in this work so that peer work development, like human development, benefits peer workers 'equitably and builds on the participation of each of them'.

The Western Australian Peer Supporters' Network offers one example of a meeting space that has been designed to address both the empowerment and wellbeing aspects of peer workers. While the Network is not a mental health peer workers' forum, because of its focus on both peer supporters and peer workers, it is led by and for peer workers and has both empowerment and wellbeing aims in its approach.

We have remained an unincorporated association to allow flexible, self-paced development of voice, leadership and development by and for peer supporters and peer support workers. The Network holds six events a year and in doing so provides a space for developing new collegial connections of support and development. The Network meetings blend formal learning, knowledge sharing, networking and peer group supervision as tools for both empowerment and wellbeing. Reflecting the values and strengths of peer support workers, there is a strong spirit of equality and reciprocity of learning and support at our meetings. Giving and receiving mutual support at the meeting as peer supporters and peer support workers strengthens our confidence and capacity in our roles to articulate and speak up for the unique values of peer work, to negotiate challenges, to achieve desired changes within our workplaces and to sustain wellbeing across these learning curves and challenges.

Collaborations between the Network and Consumers of Mental Health WA enable peer workforce development to align to peer work voices, consumer voices and the consumer movement. Both the Network and Consumers of

## 4: Examples of peer work in states and territories

Mental Health WA are peer-led and consultative organisations to support peer workers' to lead development of their occupation, mutually coordinate activities for peer workforce advocacy and development, and advance partnerships between peer work representatives, employers and other industry stakeholders.

Lastly, the Peer Workforce Champions' Community of Practice provides a forum for bringing various stakeholders together to understand and advance the value of peer work at a sectoral level through conversation and co-production, including peer workers, consumer leaders, employers, funders, researchers and educators. Co-hosting of the Community of Practice by the Western Australian Peer Supporters' Network and Consumers of Mental Health WA supports fidelity of peer work to the voices of consumers and peer workers while supporting employers and governments to benefit from peer worker advice to support change, development and uptake at a service and sectoral level. In these ways we hope to achieve shared understanding of the distinctive contribution peer workers make and to support collaborative action by all stakeholders that shifts peer work from nominal uptake and conditional value, to broad availability and enduring value.

## Conclusion

In addressing critical health and social issues through mutual empowerment as well as support to enhance wellbeing, peer work offers potentially greater impact for addressing social and health inequalities than interventions focused only on improving wellbeing. Consequently, promoting and advocating for peer work as an inclusive practice and a process of human development will remain priorities for the Western Australian Peer Supporters' Network in its discussion and development of peer work in Western Australia. The Network will continue to take up the challenge of making peer work and peer support accessible and available to a diversity of community members who might wish to use life experiences of social identities for mutual support, connection and empowerment, and to advocate for the unique value of peer work. Peer Work is perhaps Western Australia's most exciting opportunity to strengthen communities through shining an overdue spotlight on and support for community practices that are often already happening informally, and in diverse contexts, with a significant impact. While perhaps too often discounted and under-valued for its difference from traditional service delivery models, mutual support and empowerment action sit at the heart of humanity, and enable us to develop more equal, contributing, and supporting lives.

## Further reading

Alberta, A. J., & Ploski, R. R. (2014). Cooptation of peer support staff: Quantitative evidence. *Rehabilitation Process and Outcome, 3*, 25–29.

Alberta, A. J., Ploski, R. R., Carlson, S. L. (2012). Addressing challenges to providing peer-based recovery support. *Journal of Behavioral Health Services & Research, 39*, 481–491.

Alkire, S. (2010). Human development: Definitions, critiques, and related concepts. Human Development Reports Research Paper 2010/01. United Nations Development Programme. Retrieved from http://hdr.undp.org/sites/default/files/hdrp_2010_01.pdf

Balogun-Mwangi, O., Rogers, E, S., Maru, M., & Magee, C. (2017). Vocational peer support: Results of a qualitative study. *Journal of Behavioral Health Services & Research.* Online 28 December. doi: 10.1007/s11414-017-9583-6

Baptist Care (SA) Inc. & MIFSA Peer Work Project. (2009). Employer toolkit: Employing peer workers in your organisation. Adelaide: Baptist Care (SA) Inc. & MIFSA Peer Work Project.

Bates, A., Kemp, V., & and M. Isaac, M. (2008). Peer support shows promise in helping persons living with mental illness address their physical health needs. *Canadian Journal of Community Mental Health, 27*(2), 21–36.

Bowleg, L. (2012). The problem with the phrase women and minorities: Intersectionality—an important theoretical framework for public health. *American Journal of Public Health, 102*(7), 1267–1273.

Carastathis, A. (2014). The concept of intersectionality in feminist theory. *Philosophical Compass, 9*(5), 304–314.

Dennis, C. L. (2003). Peer support within a health care context: A concept analysis. *International Journal of Nursing Studies, 40*, 21–33.

Fukuda-Parr, S. (2003). The human development paradigm: Operationalizing Sen's ideas on capabilities. *Feminist Economics, 9*(2–3), 301–317.

Happell, B. (2008). Polarisation and political correctness: Subtle barriers to consumer participation in mental health services. *Australian e-Journal for the Advancement of Mental Health, 7*(3), 84.

Kumar, S. (2000). Client empowerment in psychiatry and the professional abuse of clients: Where do we stand? *International Journal of Psychiatry in Medicine, 30*(1), 61–70.

Lawrence, D., Holman, C. D. J., & Jablensky, A. V. (2001). Duty to care: Preventable physical illness in people with mental illness. Perth: University of Western Australia. Retrieved from http://research-repository.uwa.edu.au/files/9062569/Binder1.pdf

Mead, S., & MacNeil, C. (2006). Peer support: What makes it unique? *International Journal of Psychosocial Rehabilitation, 10* (2), 29–37.

O'Hagan, M. (2015). The alien test: The outsider view of human responses to mental distress. *Canadian Journal of Community Mental Health, 34*(4), 151–158.

4: Examples of peer work in states and territories

Simpson, A., Ostler, C., & Muir-Cochrane, E. (2017). Liminality in the occupational identity of mental health peer support workers: A qualitative study. *International Journal of Mental Health Nursing, 27*(2), 662–671.

Slade, M., Amering, M., Farkas, M., Hamilton, B., O'Hagan, M., Panther, G., … Whitley, R. (2014). Uses and abuses of recovery: Implementing recovery-oriented practices in mental health systems. *World Psychiatry, 13*: 12–20.

WA Association for Mental Health. 2014. Peer work strategic framework. Retrieved from https://waamh.org.au/assets/documents/projects/peer-work-strategic-framework-report-final-october-2014.pdf

Walby, S., Armstrong, J., & Strid, S. (2012). Intersectionality: Multiple inequalities in social theory. *Sociology, 46*(2), 224–240.

Western Australian Peer Supporters' Network. (2018). The peer workforce report: Mental health and alcohol and other drug services. Retrieved from http://www.comhwa.org.au/wp-content/uploads/2017/06/The-Peer-Workforce-Report-2018.pdf

World Health Organization. (1946). Constitution of World Health Organization: Principles. Retrieved from http://www.who.int/about/mission/en/

# Honouring, developing and growing Victoria's lived experience workforce

*Vrinda Edan and Emma Cadogan*

*Vrinda is an experienced consumer worker with nearly twenty years work in the consumer field. She has a background as a health professional, has worked in strategic leadership positions for twelve years and has recently gained experience in education, research and evaluation. Vrinda principally uses a human rights framework, supporting consumers to regain choice and control in their lives. This approach is sustained by her roles as chair of the board of the Victorian Mental Illness Awareness Council and as a member of the Speaking from Experience group (Victorian Legal Aid), the Ministerial Taskforce for the 10-year mental health plan and the Lived Experience Leadership Expert Reference Group (Department of Health and Human Services Victoria). Vrinda is currently undertaking a PhD at the University of Melbourne, exploring consumers' experiences of advance statements under the Mental Health Act 2014.*

*Emma is a social worker who has always been drawn to roles that promote human rights and social justice. An early career role at a mental health community support service back in 2002 sparked a long-term goal to work in mental health policy. Emma has had the privilege of working alongside and learning from experienced and knowledgeable consumers and carers in her role as a policy adviser in the Workforce Branch of the Department of Health and Human Services Victoria. Through collaborative projects, including experiments with co-production, Emma's appreciation for and understanding of the unique attributes and skills of the lived experience workforce continues to grow.*

## Introduction

This chapter seeks to detail the history, current situation and vision for the lived experience workforce employed within Victorian mental health services. The scope of the workforce discussed in this chapter is paid consumer and family/carer lived experience specific roles in public mental health services in Victoria. The authors would like to acknowledge and thank the contributions of many lived experience workers and many other key informants in contributing to this information, much of which has been collected through the Workforce Branch of the Department of Health and Human Services.

## 4: Examples of peer work in states and territories

**Historical context of the consumer workforce in Victoria**

People with lived experience were first employed in Victorian mental health services in 1996. Four roles were created as a pilot project at Royal Melbourne Hospital following the completion of the Understanding and Involvement Project (Epstein & Wadsworth, 1994). These roles, originally called consumer staff collaboration consultants, were initiated to lead quality improvement projects in each area mental health service. Within a short time, the funding for the positions became ongoing and the title shortened to consumer consultants. These roles were often isolated and evolved in unique ways, influenced by the management of the service, the consumers' needs within the service, and the individuals filling the roles. The timeline shows some of major development milestones for the consumer lived experience workforce in Victoria (Figure 1).

|  |  |
| --- | --- |
| 1996 | First consumer workers employed |
| 1997 | Ongoing funding secured for consumer consultant positions |
| 2001 | Consumer academic position established |
| 2002 | First consumer on mental health service executive |
| 2003 | First paid lived experience roles in Psychiatric Disability Rehabilitation and Support Services (now Mental Health Community Support Services) |
| | First Consumer Consultant Conference (Victorian Mental Illness Awareness Council) |
| 2005 | Director, consumer and carer relations employed at a metropolitan health service |
| 2007 | Pilots of peer support in inpatient units undertaken |
| 2008 | First strategy developed for the growth of lived experience workforce in a mental health service |
| 2010 | Lived experience coordinators employed at two metropolitan mental health services |
| 2011 | Centre of Excellence in Peer Support founded |

| | |
|---|---|
| 2012 | Lived experience workers included in Victorian Public Mental Health Services Enterprise Agreement |
| 2013 | National Mental Health Council funded the development of training resources for Certificate IV in Mental Health Peer Work |
| 2014 | Peer support roles introduced in secure extended care units |
| 2015 | Expanding Post-Discharge Support Initiative pilots commenced |
| | Certificate IV in Mental Health Peer Work developed for delivery in Victoria |
| | Consumer Workforce Development Group established |
| 2016 | Expanding Post-Discharge Support Initiative funded |
| | Consumer and carer statewide workforce development positions established |
| | Workforce development program for Expanding Post-Discharge Support Initiative developed and commenced (including Intentional Peer Support training) |
| 2017 | Lived Experience Workforce Census Survey undertaken |
| | Consumer Perspective Supervision project commences |
| 2018 | Consumer-led workforce innovation grants funded |

**Figure 1: Milestone developments for the consumer lived experience workforce in Victoria**

### What does the lived experience workforce look like now?

There have been significant changes to the size and composition of the lived experience workforce in Victoria since the establishment of the first roles twenty years ago. A census survey, undertaken by the Department of Health and Human Services Workforce Branch, requested data from thirty-eight state-funded mental health services, asking for information about each dedicated lived experience position at the service including whether it was currently vacant or filled. Information was provided about position titles and perspective (consumer or family/carer, the full-time equivalent level, functions of the position, location and whether the person in the position was providing any supervision as a line manager or discipline leader.

## 4: Examples of peer work in states and territories

Thirty-one services provided responses, including all clinical mental health services. Data collection closed in October 2017. It showed that there were 341 positions that amounted to 187 equivalent full-time positions. Thirty-two positions were vacant at the time of reporting. It is not clear how many workers are filling these positions, but data collected in a recent Victorian lived experience workforce needs survey indicates that approximately 40% of 109 lived experience workers worked in more than one position. It is assumed that some of the workforce in Victoria were holding more than one lived experience role.

Of the 341 positions, 238 were located within clinical mental health services and 103 were employed within mental health community support services. The number of lived experience positions in clinical mental health services has increased recently due to a Department of Health and Human Services funded initiative (the Expanding Post-Discharge Support initiative) that sees peer support workers employed at all area mental health services.

Many more lived experience workers were employed to bring a consumer perspective than to bring a family/carer perspective. Less than a third (102) of the lived experience workers in Victoria were in family/carer-specific roles, with more than two-thirds (239) working from a consumer perspective.

A significant proportion of lived experience work involves peer support, with 211 peer support positions identified. A lower proportion of family/carer workers (52) were providing peer support when compared with the number of consumer peer support workers (159). There was a relatively even number of both consumer and carer consultant roles across the state, with thirty-eight consumer consultants and thirty-six carer consultant positions. There were eighteen educator positions (with only two of those from a family/carer perspective), and also a small number of manager roles (eleven in total, ten of whom worked from a consumer perspective). 'Other' positions identified were described as advisory roles, group facilitation, and National Disability Insurance Scheme (NDIS) transition roles.

The vast majority of positions are part-time, with only forty-one full-time positions; 203 of the positions are three days a week or less.

Of the 341 reported positions, twenty-six provided lived experience supervision to other lived experienced workers, and eleven were managers.

This demonstrates that there are limited career progression opportunities in the current lived experience workforce environment.

## Current reforms impacting lived experience workforce

The implementation of the NDIS sees many mental health community support services re-orientating to provide NDIS services instead of mental health support. Many organisations in this sector are currently exploring how to utilise dedicated lived experience roles for psychosocial disability supports, however the demand for, and capacity of organisations to provide these specialist supports in the NDIS environment are not yet fully understood. Information from the sector is that there is a move to replace existing lived experience positions with generic support worker roles to better suit the NDIS funding model, thereby reducing the complement of dedicated lived experience workers. Lived experience workforce positions within mental health community support services are not likely to remain stable.

> 'The rollout of the NDIS has seen a sharp decline in the number of peer support workers in the Grampians region. Membership of the once vibrant Grampians Peer Workers Network has dwindled to the point of non-existence with no formal meeting since 2016.' Rick Corney, peer support worker

## Workforce development approach in Victoria

The Department of Health and Human Services is taking steps towards co-production and co-design, with several workforce initiatives underway that apply and test co-production principles and/or a co-design methodology. One example of this approach is the Consumer Workforce Development Group, established in 2015, where consumer workers from a variety of backgrounds and experience have partnered with the Department to provide direction and advice for consumer workforce initiatives.

The Consumer Workforce Development Group applies the following co-production principles to their work as far as is possible (seen in Roper, Grey, & Cadogan, 2018, p. 6):

## 4: Examples of peer work in states and territories

1. Consumers are partners from the outset: Consumers are involved in setting the priorities and agenda from the very beginning. Consumers are engaged for their thought leadership, experience and expertise and then throughout the enterprise. Consumers can also be engaged to lead projects.

> 'Co-production starts with what's important to the people who are most affected by the problem, or the service, and works backwards. What do you think the problem is, how should we proceed? What resources would we need? Who should be at the table?' Cath Roper, consumer academic

2. Power differentials are acknowledged, explored and addressed: In any partnership some partners are 'more equal' than others. Co-production means that the more powerful partners relinquish power and support empowering environments for others.

3. Consumer leadership and capacity are developed: The utilisation and development of consumer leadership are a feature of co-production methods in mental health. Consumers are thinkers and doers, not passive recipients of care, and they are holders of wisdom and knowledge no-one else has.

### Developing and expanding the lived experience workforce in Victoria

Current government policy articulates an intent to support and grow the lived experience workforce. *Victoria's 10-year mental health plan* (DHHS, 2015) and the *Mental Health Workforce Strategy* (DHHS, 2016) set out high-level directions in relation to the further development and expansion of the lived experience workforce. The directives in the Strategy have opened up new opportunities for education, training and practice supports for Victoria's growing lived experience workforce.

*Consumer and family/carer workforce development positions*

Soon after the establishment of the Consumer Workforce Development Group it was apparent that there was much work to be done if the workforce and their employing organisations were to receive adequate guidance and support. Without the structures typically available to other professions, such as a professional body, there was no organisation or person that had capacity to undertake the required work without additional resourcing. In late 2016, two department-funded, dedicated lived experience positions were established to drive and support lived experience workforce development in Victoria. One position brought consumer perspective and the other brought family/carer perspective, with both working closely together to support the development of the lived experience workforce. Each role began as 0.6 full-time equivalent (three days per week) and increased to 0.8 full-time equivalent (four days per week) the following year. These roles have been instrumental in progressing the groundwork needed to create further foundations for the lived experience workforce in Victoria.

The two lived experience workforce development workers (the Consumer and Carer Workforce Development Team) and a senior policy adviser within the Department of Health and Human Services closely collaborate to respond to workforce needs. They offer support and leadership to further establish and strengthen the Victorian mental health consumer and family/carer workforce through consultation and advice to health services, and development of training, resources and practice supports. Through having these positions, some important foundational work can now be taken forward, including articulating the different roles within the lived experience work, and how they relate to one another.

One of the main goals of the Consumer and Carer Workforce Development Team is to assist people to understand lived experience work and the different specialities within that and what they bring to the mental health service system and to the people that use services. The roles support lived experience work to be recognised and valued for the unique perspective and contribution that it brings.

### Consumer workforce strategies

As at April 2018, a strategy for the development of the consumer workforce is in progress. This strategy is a partnership between members of the consumer workforce, the Department of Health and Human Services, and the peak body for mental health consumers, the Victorian Mental Illness Awareness Council. The Consumer Workforce Strategy is an important document that set out the future vision for the consumer workforce and what needs to be done to reach that vision. Priorities for the consumer workforce can be grouped into main themes: defining; promoting; supporting; and growing.

4: Examples of peer work in states and territories

Priority actions around defining the workforce include the need to articulate the values, principles and key tasks of the workforce to strengthen the identity of the discipline of consumer work.

**The Expanding Post-Discharge Support initiative—a new setting for the lived experience workforce**

In 2016, the Department of Health and Human Services funded a new program, the Expanding Post-Discharge Support Initiative, which has seen a rapid expansion of peer support roles in clinical mental health services. The initiative seeks to reduce readmission rates to acute adult inpatient units within the first twenty-eight days after discharge through the provision of peer support and an increase in community connections. Almost all peer support workers in clinical mental health services are employed as part of this initiative, with a steady increase in recruitment activity at clinical services since mid-2016.

All twenty-one area adult mental health services in Victoria and one youth service (Orygen Youth Health) are implementing peer support services through the Expanding Post-Discharge Support Initiative. All services have implemented the initiative using different models—some services have employed family/carer peer support workers, while some have chosen to employ consumer peer support workers only. Some services have models with several peer support workers, while the smaller regional services might only have a peer support worker. Consistent with similar programs nationally and internationally most have grappled with the challenges of role clarity and integrating peer support into clinical teams/environments (Gallagher & Halpin, 2014; Australian Healthcare Associates, 2013; Kling, Dawes, & Nestor, 2008; Lawn, Smith, & Hunter, 2009; McLean et al., 2009).

> 'There were initially some barriers to overcome when introducing the peer support program ... concerns were expressed by some staff about "ex-clients" being part of the treating team. One of the challenges for staff who work on an inpatient unit is that they support people when they are acutely unwell and don't have the opportunity to see a person change their life circumstances and recover from their illness.' FB, manager, Peer Support Program

The Expanding Post-Discharge Support Initiative created a sense of urgency that we needed to invest more towards developing peer support capabilities among our lived experience workforce. A program of workforce development activity was developed in partnership with experienced lived experience workers, some of whom had been employed into services in consultant roles twenty years earlier. It was with their sage advice that Intentional Peer Support from the USA were engaged to train workers in the Intentional Peer Support framework. Peer support workers, their managers and other colleagues working as part of the Expanding Post-Discharge Support Initiative were all offered training through Intentional Peer Support. In addition to Intentional Peer Support training, the Department of Health and Human Services, through a centralised program of workforce development, has offered:

- co-reflection groups to support peer support practice development
- tailored support for health services provided by the Consumer and Carer Workforce Development team
- a guide, 'Preparing your organisation for the Expanding Post-Discharge Support Initiative'
- online communities of practice for both coordinators or supervisors of peer support workers and peer support workers, to support connection and sharing of knowledge and resources
- reflective space specifically for coordinators and supervisors of peer support workers
- a one-day forum for coordinators and peer support workers.

The rollout of the centralised workforce development plan has not been without its challenges—communication and reaching workers have been difficult with workers dispersed so widely across the state and within services. The online connection point (Basecamp) has helped to some extent, but not all workers are registered for, or use, the portal. The different implementation timelines of each service have created challenges for the rolling out of training—as soon as one training course was completed, more workers would be recruited, resulting in some training courses running with only small numbers of attendees, and/or at times a long delay between access to training and workers starting in roles. Due to the small number of workers employed at regional services, most of the training and development activity needed to be

## 4: Examples of peer work in states and territories

delivered in locations in the central business district. This created a burden for the regional staff, with limited access to connection with other workers in similar roles day to day in their service.

From a workforce development implementation perspective, the experience of program implementation is easier for other professions, because they have a larger critical mass of workers, established communication channels, connection points and multiple training providers to draw from.

A research project is being undertaken through the Department of Health and Human Services Centre for Evaluation and Research that will look at the Expanding Post-Discharge Support Initiative through a workforce lens to understand the impact for health services, teams, peer support workers, colleagues and for service users.

### Access to discipline-specific supervision

Access to specific supervision for lived experience workers has been highlighted as an urgent need. There is not yet an obvious pool of experienced and skilled supervisors that can provide supervision in a sustainable way, as there is in many other professions. Whilst access to supervision to support practice development is challenging across all health workforce professions, the challenges are more pronounced for lived experience workers due to the smaller size of the workforce, the poor understanding by other professions about lived experience work, and the differences between the medical model used by many mental health professions and the relational model that lived experience workers apply. The lived experience workforce census data indicates that there are currently twenty-six workers providing supervision. With a total of 341 positions currently identified, it demonstrates that not all workers will have access to lived experience supervision.

> 'Peer workers have the same entitlement to supervision that other professions have. Supervision is an opportunity for peer workers to strengthen their practice and their understanding of the role.' CB, manager, lived experience workforce

## Consumer perspective supervision project

With the increase in lived experience roles in mental health services there has been a recent drive to acknowledge consumer perspective as a unique discipline within the mental health workforce. Understanding consumer perspective as a discipline leads to questions about what might comprise the discipline, what makes it unique and how critically important it is for workers to be able to access members of their own discipline for supervision. Understanding consumer perspective as a discipline allows the articulation of the unique tensions and challenges that are part of the work.

A workshop at the 2016 Victorian Mental Illness Awareness Council consumer workforce conference facilitated a discussion among more than fifty consumer workers where it was emphasised that the lack of expert consumer-perspective, discipline-specific supervision was a significant risk to the workforce. In partnership with the Centre for Psychiatric Nursing, University of Melbourne, the Council approached the Department of Health and Human services to support a co-produced project to develop the discipline of consumer perspective supervision.

This project, undertaken in 2017–2018, has developed a framework for consumer perspective supervision and aims to develop a platform for consumer lived experience workers and services to find potential supervisors for the consumer lived experience workforce.

During the consultations for the framework it was repeatedly reported that services had difficulty understanding the importance of lived experience supervision for the workers. Line management was often mistaken as supervision, or was the only model offered. Line management should be distinguished from professional supervision where participants are able to deepen their knowledge and skills, and navigate challenges that relate to their specific discipline. Line managers of peer workers are responsible for activities such as the allocation of workloads and overseeing their completion, providing advice about immediate problems, assuring compliance with policies, performance development (Mental Health Commission NSW, 2016).

> Ideally, peer workers should be line-managed by other peer workers. Alternatively, their managers should have either a formal relationship or an informal arrangement with a peer worker leader or a peer-run provider of training and

## 4: Examples of peer work in states and territories

> supervision. This will give them the opportunity to discuss and understand peer values, peer roles, and peer practice issues and tensions (Mental Health Commission NSW, 2016, p. 21).

Like many other disciplines, consumer workers need access to a space where they can explore ideas with another lived experience worker who, through their own work experience, can assist in bringing clarity to the work. This can be uncomfortable if they are talking to somebody who can then take action on what has been discussed and who has institutional power over the worker.

The framework articulates values and principles for consumer work and, using examples from consultations discusses the functions of supervision, describes the unique properties of the consumer perspective supervision relationship, highly valued practices and approaches, and includes a section written for organisations that describes how to support the growth and development of the lived experience workforce through the provision of expert supervision.

### What's working well?

The continued growth of the lived experience workforce in Victoria signifies the important place this workforce has in mental health services. As stated earlier, the ten-year strategy for mental health in Victoria supports the development of the peer workforce and principles of co-production in improving the delivery of services.

In the context of the rapid growth of peer support programs, a number of services have found innovative ways to utilise the expertise of this new workforce. Some examples include running groups in inpatient units, and exploring, both with the service and consumers, alternative ways of addressing risk. These initiatives are testing new ways of working as mental health services and support the exploration of alternative worldviews to experiences that are diagnosed as mental illnesses.

Examples of growth in the Victorian lived experience workforce outside public mental health services include the expansion of the consumer academic program at University of Melbourne, supporting co-production of workforce training packages and research, Department of Health and Human Services funded activities supporting the provision of training specific to the discipline of consumer perspective work, the expansion of lived experience expertise in research activities in the mental health community support services sector, the growth of lived experience positions in the justice system, and the inclusion of lived experience expertise in the development of advocacy services through Victoria Legal Aid.

The move towards co-production with developing strategy and implementing lived experience workforce initiatives has created depth of understanding about lived experience work for non-lived experience worker partners. This has created a network of 'champions' within services and within government that can help influence the conditions and cultures that need to change.

## Challenges

As discussed previously, access to discipline-specific supervision is a key issue for the lived experience workforce and will remain a challenge until there is a sustainable, appropriately experienced and skilled pool of lived experience workers that can support the increasing number of the workforce. Access to supervision will support lived experience workers with some of the common challenges they experience such as professional isolation, exposure to ethical tensions, and working from a disclosed mental health perspective.

Culture and attitudes continue to create challenges for lived experience workers. There is still a significant cultural change to achieve in the perception and understanding of lived experience work, and in particular how this can complement the work of other professions. As an example, when a new service or program is being funded, organisations could be looking to see how lived experience roles could improve the mix of skills available, rather than thinking only in terms of familiar established professions. There are also ongoing experiences of tokenism by consumer workers, for example, being asked to undertake work not relevant to their role, being brought into a project after most of the important decisions have been made, and not being paid adequately (or paid at all) for expert work.

> 'I have been involved in so many workplace activities where I have put forward ideas or initiatives but they almost never make the final cut. It's frustrating and feels like consumer workers' ideas are not valued equal to others.' Wanda Bennetts, consumer worker

## 4: Examples of peer work in states and territories

An additional problem for lived experience workers is the part-time nature of most of the positions offered. There are usually many reasons put forward for this, one most often being that people with mental health issues cannot manage full-time work. This is reflective of some of the discriminatory decisions that are sometimes made by employers. For example, a service that has received enough funding for three full time equivalent lived experience positions advertised for six part time positions because they believed that a person with a mental illness would not cope with full time work, or that it's better to give more people jobs. This does not happen when advertising other professions. So if there are three full time equivalent nursing vacancies on an inpatient unit, that is what is advertised with a note that part time work or job sharing would be considered.

These actions, while often attempting to come from a place of good intentions, can have the opposite effect on workers, creating more demanding jobs (the work can't be completed in the hours allocated), difficulties in connecting with other workers because they all work different days and the lack of time for professional development. In many instances, due to the typically low rates of pay, workers will hold more than one part time role in order to make ends meet, which can be more challenging than being employed in one full time role.

> 'Since entering the consumer workforce, I have had to juggle several part-time jobs in order to keep my head above water. I am living on the poverty line with a committed heart and an empty pocket.' DM, consumer worker

Whilst rapid expansion has bought opportunity, the development of structures and supports has not happened at the same pace as workforce growth.

With a small workforce dispersed right across Victoria, the implementation of statewide initiatives is challenging. For example, regional training is often unavailable, with a need for already stretched workers in regional and rural areas to travel to participate in training. Even communication can be a challenge, with no one central point of contact such as a professional association to broadcast information and to facilitate the connection of workers.

Despite these challenges (and the many more that individuals face across the state), there is a strong sense of achievement in the positive growth in the development of the lived experience workforce in Victoria. The majority of the workforce continue to work in these difficult circumstances because they know, on a very personal level, how important the work is.

## Conclusion

The priority focus for lived experience workforce development in Victoria over 2018 and 2019 will be to continue to strengthen the identities of both the consumer and carer lived experience workforces and to promote the unique value that these roles have in supporting people who access public mental health services in Victoria. People from both workforces are participating in co-design processes to further define the values and principles that underpin consumer perspective and family/carer perspective work. This work will form the foundations from which other resources and promotional materials can be developed.

The longer term vision for the lived experience workforce includes the evolution of a sustainable 'home' or 'homes' for the workforce, much like the professional associations and bodies that other disciplines have access to. Parity of access to supports that other professions benefit from is aspirational, but fair, as is parity of wages, and access to conditions such as full-time positions for those that want them. Parity has been highlighted as a key issue for lived experience workers, with the peak bodies for consumers (Victorian Mental Illness Awareness Council) and carers (Tandem) having a key role in advocacy, together with the relevant unions.

It will be important to monitor positions over time to measure growth of the workforce and advancement of lived experience workers into leadership positions. It will also be important to understand the migration of lived experience workers from mental health community support service organisations as the National Disability Insurance Scheme is rolled out.

In concluding this chapter, the authors would like to recognise the past and present leadership of people with lived experience that have lobbied for lived experience to be acknowledged and developed as a legitimate knowledge base and included as a discipline within the mental health service system. Acknowledgement should also be given to the lived experience workers who bring so much of themselves to work, and who make a real difference in the lives of the people they work alongside, despite the professional and personal

## 4: Examples of peer work in states and territories

cost that comes with being the 'face' of lived experience within their workplace.

## References

Australian Healthcare Associates. (2013). Evaluation of the community mental health intentional peer support training and consumer operated services: Final report. Melbourne: AHA. Retrieved from www.ahaconsulting.com.au/wp-content/uploads/2015/07/ips_cos_final_report_june2013.pdf

Department of Health and Human Services Victoria. (2015). Victoria's 10-year mental health plan. Melbourne: DHHS. Retrieved from https://www2.health.vic.gov.au/about/publications/policiesandguidelines/victorias-10-year-mental-health-plan

Department of Health and Human Services Victoria. (2016). Victoria's 10-year mental health plan: Mental health workforce strategy. Melbourne: DHHS. https://www2.health.vic.gov.au/about/publications/policiesandguidelines/mental-health-workforce-strategy

Epstein, M., & Wadsworth, Y. (1994). Understanding & involvement (U & I)—Consumer evaluation of acute psychiatric hospital practice: A project's beginnings. Melbourne: Victorian Mental Illness Awareness Council.

Gallagher, C. & Halpin, M. (2014). The lived experience workforce in South Australian public mental health services. Adelaide: Central Adelaide Local Health Network. Retrieved from http://mhcsa.org.au/wp-content/uploads/2016/09/The-Lived-Experience-Workforce-in-SA-Public-Mental-Health-Services.pdf

Kling, L., Dawes, F., & Nestor, P. (2008). Peer specialists and carer consultants working in acute mental health units: An initial evaluation of consumers, carers and staff perspectives. *International Journal of Psychosocial Rehabilitation, 12*(2), 81–89.

Lawn, S., Smith, A., & Hunter, K. (2009). Mental health peer support for hospital avoidance and early discharge: An Australian example of consumer driven and operated service. *Journal of Mental Health, 17*(5), 498–508.

McLean, J., Biggs, H., Whitehead, I., Pratt, R., & Maxwell, M. (2009). Evaluation of the delivering for mental health peer support worker pilot scheme. Scottish Government Social Research. Retrieved from www.gov.scot/Publications/2009/11/13112054/0

Roper, C., Grey, F., & Cadogan, E. (2018). Co-production: Putting principles into practice in mental health contexts. Retrieved from http://www.synergyresearch.edu.au/wp-content/uploads/2017/05/Coproduction-Putting-Principles-into-practice-in-mental-health-contexts.pdf

© State of Victoria (Department of Health and Human Services) 2018

This work, Honouring, developing and growing Victoria's lived experience workforce, is licence under Creative Commons Attribution 4.0 licence [link to http://creativecommons.org/licences/by/4.0/]. You are free to re-use the work under that licence, on the condition that you credit the State of Victoria (Department of Health and Human Services) as author, indicate if changes were made and comply with the other licence terms. The licence does not apply to any branding, including government logos.

Copyright queries may be directed to livedexperienceworkforce@dhhs.vic.gov.au

# Section 5

# Values and experiences in implementing peer work

# Why peer workers do their work

*Darren Jiggins*

*Darren Jiggins has been working as peer worker in the Richmond Fellowship Tasmania for fifteen years has been a joyful and fulfilling experience. Writing about working as a peer worker will hopefully help convince organisations to get on board to employ peer workers. Future recovery services that embrace the peer workforce will be a great leap forward for people seeking help with mental distress.*

Being a peer worker is so much more than a job for me, it is my raison d'être, my reason for living. I wish a peer worker could have been there for my eight-year-old self. I wish at that time of my life that I knew that other people lived like me, with obsessive-compulsive disorder. I wish someone could have told me that 'you are not alone, and you are not going to be taken away for being different'. I hid my obsessive-compulsive disorder for fifteen years very well, too well, suffering in silence while living in a normal loving family, acting my way through life trying to be 'normal' in desperation not to be found out as being different. Later this would come at a cost, with almost fatal consequences. Fear of being found out for being mentally ill, living in a world that stigmatised those who were different, prevented me asking for the one thing I needed most—help.

At the age of twenty-three I met my first peer worker who was just like me. She was the coordinator of the Perth obsessive-compulsive disorder self-help group, and meeting her was a life-changing moment. For the first time I met someone who would open up and share her lived experience of thinking wacky thoughts like me, who talked openly about her torturous mental and physical rituals like me, yet was happy in life, very much unlike me at the time. Later I too came to accept my obsessive-compulsive disorder as part of my life as she did, and thanks to her kindness and the personal connection she made with me, I was inspired to later become a peer worker. I too went on to dedicate myself to turn up each week for eight years in my first peer worker role in co-facilitating the obsessive-compulsive disorder group and supporting her, as an unpaid peer worker, until it wound up in 2001. This group of like-minded people saved my life, and the lives of so many others, and gave me hope and purpose.

The second form of peer support work that I want to share with you is my fifteen fabulous years of working at the Richmond Fellowship of Tasmania. When I first started working as a support worker at the Richmond Fellowship of Tasmania in 2001, I remember telling a friend from Western Australia, who was working very hard on getting her social work degree, that I had got the job as a support worker, as there was no such role defined as a peer worker back then. She replied 'How the hell did you pull that off?' in her lovely way. What she didn't know was that I had in my youth been a resident at the Richmond Fellowship in Fremantle residential support community in 1993 for six months. When I moved to Tasmania in 2001 I felt that I was ready to 'give back' in this support worker role; today we call this role a peer worker. Starting work was my coming out experience in 2001 as a person living with obsessive-compulsive disorder. I decided that I was ready to be open to everyone about my lived experience of mental illness outside of the obsessive-compulsive disorder group, especially with my peers at work.

From my previous volunteering in the obsessive-compulsive disorder group I knew that I could try to be a peer worker as I felt, and still feel, that people with mental illness were my people, and I could connect with them and hopefully do some good at work. This was not just another job for me. I wanted to succeed so badly that nothing would stop me. Writing about this work as a peer worker reminds me of the television series *The West Wing*, where one character who is an alcoholic tells his co-worker who has just been diagnosed as having post-traumatic stress disorder a tale:

> 'This guy's walking down a street, when he falls in a hole. The walls are so steep. He can't get out. A doctor passes by, and the guy shouts up "Hey you! Can you help me out?" The doctor writes him a prescription, throws it down the hole and moves on ... Then a priest comes along and the guy shouts up "Father, I'm down in this hole, can you help me out?" The priest writes out a prayer, throws it down in the hole and moves on ... Then a friend walks by "Hey Joe, it's me, can you help me out?" And the friend jumps in the hole! Our guy says "Are you stupid? Now we're both down here!" and the friend says, "Yeah, but I've been down here before, and I know the way out." '(Sorkin & Wells, 2000)

There is great value in peer workers jumping back down in the hole to stand beside our peers in despair to inspire hope in others for a better future. My approach to peer work is that if I found my way out of that feeling, of being stuck in a hopeless hole, others can as well. This is why I began my journey in the role of peer worker, to help others see that living with a mental illness is possible and that we can contribute much to the world. For myself I was glad, as part of my recovery journey, to have worked as an electrician for eight years after leaving hospital. I don't think that I was ready to fill the role of peer worker during that time. Call it destiny, or luck, or just committing to what I loved best, I honestly feel that working with my peers is what was meant for me. Most people want to leave the labels of mental illness and the stigma of having a mental illness behind and move on with living life with mental illness as a personal matter that no-one other than their support people need to know about. And that is fine, as stigma and discrimination are crippling in our society. This calling to be a peer worker is not for everyone. This is why when organisations find peer workers with the 'right fit' for the job role we need support from the organisation, other staff and other peer workers to successfully implement this change.

When I explain what I do for a living, and what I have done, people usually remind me that I could be earning twice as much money working as an electrician, rather than doing peer work, and they are right. But money is secondary to me now compared to the joy that I get from people who share their fears and secrets with me as I listen to them and watch people move on in life after crisis. To be able to give back to people like me, as my peers did for me in the obsessive-compulsive disorder group, is a very good reason for me to live and thrive. Work is almost an odd word when describing peer support work at the Richmond Fellowship of Tasmania. At the Fellowship , we build communities where staff get to welcome broken people enter the community after a crisis in their lives and all residents leave, to varying extents, that much stronger and ready to live life again.

### What do peer workers do

Firstly, I would like to explain my experiences of being volunteer peer worker in the obsessive-compulsive disorder self-help group in Perth, Western Australia. The first person I ever met who had obsessive-compulsive disorder like me was in 1994 when I was in hospital. In a visionary act of kindness and understanding of what people needed most, one nurse invited an ex-patient to meet me with the aim of me joining a non-clinical obsessive-compulsive disorder self-help group as he had as a patient. This nurse, in taking a bold step to help me connect with my peers, changed my life, and most likely saved it. So, a few days after I encountered this remarkable idea of being able to meet someone like me, in walked a person a year or two younger than me, but many steps in front of me in his recovery journey. He sat with me and I spoke through tears and he listened to me as I, for the first time, was telling another soul like me what I had been very successfully keeping secret. My secret that I kept from family, friends, workmates until I was found out at the age of twenty-three was that I was mad, I'd wanted to die a decade previously and I thought that I was like no other person in the world. Yet here was a person who listened, and shared that he too was like me living with this disorder I had never heard of until the nurses told me that I had obsessive-compulsive disorder.

When this kind ex-patient with obsessive-compulsive disorder came to the hospital, he reached out and connected with me and encouraged me to come to his group's next meeting. He was successful where the nursing staff had not been, as he was my peer and I felt our obsessive-compulsive disorder connected us. Two weeks later I went to my first meeting of the Perth obsessive-compulsive disorder self-help group, maybe the greatest step of my recovery journey. When the group started, we all took turns listening to how each other's week had been and then it was my turn to talk. And I did what I would do for weeks to come, I cried all the pent-up tears of fear and anxiety of the past fifteen years in this one room. Eventually I shared my secret shame of a life of rituals, obsessions and compulsions as I said that no-one could understand surely, what is in my mind, as I am the only person who is so terribly weird and bad. And, as I would see time and time again in the years to come, people just nodded as they connected exactly with their lived experience of obsessive-compulsive disorder. They just 'got me' at the deepest level. This feeling of being bad as the basis for obsessive-compulsive disorder is told in a very good book about obsessive-compulsive disorder called *Because we are bad*, by Lily Bailey (2016). She portrays the depth of the experience of obsessive-compulsive disorder from a genius perspective.

In our obsessive-compulsive disorder self-help group, we could discuss much pain and suffering and yet make fun at ourselves and have a great time as well.

We as a group understood that obsessive-compulsive disorder and mental illness need only be a single part of your life. Many of us came to accept that obsessive-compulsive disorder was for life, but all other facets of life, including love, health, family, hobbies and spirituality, were all part of what we strove to regain focus on. Life for me took off six months later when I fell in love, found work and even found meaning in social justice campaigning in Perth. My obsessive-compulsive disorder has always stayed the same but my peers encouraged me to build up all other areas of my life. Within a year I had gone from a chronic alcoholic, pot-addicted, totally isolated person with no friends or family in Perth, to having a loving life with a partner and friends. With peers that loved me and falling in love with my wife-to-be, all aspects of my life recovered rapidly except for my obsessive-compulsive disorder. I came to understand that the disorder is just a part of who I am.

I realised over time attending the group that I was actually quite good at listening to people and encouraging them when I could. Many hundreds of the people that I met in the following years live like I do and have also realised, like I did, that they are not alone. Family members were welcomed as well and respectfully contributed stories about their week and realised they too are in the room with other families struggling to understand this obsessive-compulsive disorder experience. Our group included carers, family members and friends who came for many reasons. This connection with people like me is one of the greatest experiences and gave me hope at a time of absolute crisis. I was able to go on and flourish in life when that had seemed impossible while I was in hospital for all those months.

My second role as a peer worker started when I got a support worker job at the Richmond Fellowship of Tasmania working in a residential support service for people with mental illness just like the Richmond Fellowship Fremantle program that I lived in back in 2001. In Hobart in 2001, peer workers like myself did this role in practice but not yet in title—we were called support workers. Unlike volunteering outside the 'mental health sector' in the obsessive-compulsive disorder group, working in the Richmond Fellowship of Tasmania is much more complex. Working beside residents in our program, within the mental health system, means that we also have to support residents to negotiate the overwhelming number of supports and services available. Whether they be related to family, clinical services, medical services, allied

## 5: Values and experiences in implementing peer work

health or housing, the list of supports for residents within the medical model is complex for any staff member to navigate and understand. This is a very special service in a residential setting for peer workers to work beside residents to help them find the systemic help they need, that is, services within our current medical model.

This places myself as a peer worker beautifully in that social position between 'us', the consumers, and 'them', the staff in the current medical model. In this job I feel that I have challenged the standard model of mental healthcare that consists of the 'well' staff, who are encouraged not to share their life struggles, and 'sick' patients who must be cured. One reason I love this job is bridging that divide, by simply saying to residents 'yes, me too' when they arrive in our program and struggle with living at the Richmond Fellowship of Tasmania. As a peer worker I share that I too have lived in a Richmond Fellowship in Fremantle in my youth. I love this moment. This is a moment of, for some residents, a connection with a staff member who has had a lived experience of being a resident. For some new residents, hearing this is not believing—it is just not believable. According to the medical model they have experienced, staff are 'well' and patients are 'sick'. They experience cognitive dissonance as confusion sets in as they try to comprehend the possibility that a staff member who has had a lived experience of mental illness like themselves can work and thrive. I believe that this experience is at the heart of changing and challenging the medical model to become the recovery framework we all strive for.

This is why I love my role as a peer worker, as we are equipped with the knowledge and experience that can change the way residents see themselves as people on a journey through life with its ups and downs, like many other people. Peer workers have the ability to share just enough of their lived experience to connect with others, to openly and unashamedly admit to having lived in their shoes, with a simple story to connect with another person's suffering. In my work at the Richmond Fellowship of Tasmania I always try to be for others as down-to-earth, kind, compassionate and authentic a peer worker as the coordinator of the obsessive-compulsive disorder support group was for me in the 1990s. She was also a great listener. A leader by example—living life to her fullest with a mental illness. A strong citizen who could make her own decisions about her life with a mental illness, to take life's risks, to fall in love, to choose treatments that work for her, to be empowered and rediscover hope for a fulfilled life. This is the standard of peer worker that I aspire to be.

## How do peer workers do their work?

From a human resources management perspective, I believe that I have a unique set of knowledge, skills and abilities as a peer worker learnt through the experience of living with mental illness. Experiential learning is a vastly underestimated form of knowledge in the medical model, but highly valued in the recovery framework that we are all striving towards. This lifetime of knowledge and experience is invaluable to connect with others living with a mental illness. This is one of the most important messages that I would like to impart. A peer worker who has used services and has gone through a recovery journey will make a strong team member. As a staff member the peer worker enters the workforce with extra knowledge from the perspective that a lived experience provides of the mental health system, stigma, discrimination, despair and isolation—all are used as tools to connect with consumers. I found when I began working at the Richmond Fellowship of Tasmania that I knew what my team leader call 'the Richmond Fellowship way' before I even started my first day at work.

## Knowledge of peer workers

Peer workers bring a vast array of knowledge of the experience of being mentally ill and struggling through the system itself. The experiential learning that peer workers have of living through the struggles common to those people we now seek to support as peer workers is something that should never be underestimated. I believe that knowing the feelings of shame, fear, isolation, despair and hopelessness makes the job of connecting with others that much easier. I can say truthfully 'yes I know what that feels like' and share brief examples of my experience. I very much accept that most people who work in the mental health system also have had experiences of mental distress and mental illness. The medical model stifles these professionals and requires them to keep these experiences secret. We as peer workers encourage staff to embrace the recovery framework and share experiences with consumers. Some mental illnesses are totally foreign experiences to me as well and I struggle to understand what it must be like to hear voices or live with the fear of delusions.

However, there is much common knowledge that we all share of the fear of coming out as a person with a mental illness, the feelings of being hospitalised and the fear of being stigmatised by society. Some experiences are so difficult to understand and explain to others as lived experience that finding peer workers who are able to truly understand is invaluable. Obsessive-compulsive disorder is a classic example for me. For eight years volunteering and participating in the obsessive-compulsive disorder group I listened to similar experiences over and over again. Hundreds of new people over the years would tell their experience of obsessive-compulsive disorder with tears and plenty of frustration, believing that none of us would understand. Yet my experience in the self-help group was one of watching the people come to understand that even the group coordinators had an intimate knowledge of this common experience.

**Skills of peer workers**

Our work is very much about making connections with consumers. I believe that this is key to the much-needed reform needed in the mental health system. Peer workers who use skilfully selected parts of their lived experience to connect with consumers are changing the medical model to a recovery framework of service delivery. Recently I was seconded for six months to the chief executive officer role in an organisation called Flourish, the voice of Tasmanian mental health consumers. I would visit the hospital wards to let patients know what we did. In one hospital there was a particular staff member who understood the value of my lived experience. This non-clinical staff member ran the art group for decades and always welcomed me into her art space. Every time I came to talk with patients she would always say, after me doing a bit of an introduction of myself, with perfect timing, 'Tell Sally your story. Darren'. She had seen a peer worker's skill firsthand as the conversations had quickly changed when patients in the past had come to realise that I was one of their peers. Having peer workers in the team gives all staff the ability to utilise the skills of peer workers to make rapid connections with consumers to provide support. Fifteen years ago, in my job interview, the chief executive officer of the Richmond Fellowship of Tasmania at that time later told me that she was mainly focused in the interview process on how interviewees related to, and managed to connect with, the consumer on the interview panel. I congratulate her on the visionary use of a peer worker on the interview panel to see if interviewees had the skills to connect with this consumer. For me I felt like I had a peer, one of us, on the panel and the chief executive officer told me later that we connected very easily. That is why she employed me.

**Abilities of peer workers**

A peer worker's strength lies in the stated solidarity of a shared lived experience. Many times, while listening to others tell their stories of struggle with daily life, and the limitations of a person's obsessive-compulsive disorder experience, I witnessed amazing solidarity. I vividly remember one woman's lament that because of her obsessive-compulsive disorder the family could never go on holidays for fear of contamination in the shower. The group of a dozen or so participants and their carers or friends all sat silent while she sobbed. After thirty seconds a group member had an idea and said 'How about you buy a few pairs of thongs [rubber sandals or flip-flops for non-Australian readers] and throw them out each time you have a shower?' he asked the group member. The three family members later returned and told us of the wonderful holiday that they all had, due to a non-clinical, practical solution found by a peer in the obsessive-compulsive disorder group. Where clinical and non-clinical staff, in my experience, would have looked to cure her, a peer thought of a simple practical solution. The ability to put yourself in another person's experience and try to imagine a solution is a much valued ability of a peer worker. It is common for peer workers to come up with practical solutions to what seem like the most impossible situations.

I too had a major issue. Since I was seven or eight years old I had an obsession that sweating was bad, more than bad—a disgusting intrusion on others' lives. It was only when I was twenty-three and I mentioned this crippling social disability that a peer suggested a solution. He said '"Hey mate, why don't you just wear a bandana? Then you won't have to worry about the sweat.' Where a psychiatrist would have opted for pills or suggested a sedative medication, where a priest would have prayed for me, a peer of mine who knew what it was like to be stuck in the pit of despair had the ability to look outside the square and offer me a practical solution. To this day I always have a Cancer Council bandana in my left back pocket. And when panic sets in, out comes the bandana and I immediately settle and breathe my way through each moment of horror.

**What were the challenges in being a peer worker?**

On reflection I believe that the obsessive-compulsive disorder self-help group was very fortunate to have such an inspiring leader. The group was also lucky that I stepped up to assist as a co-coordinator when our coordinator could not attend on rare occasions. The challenge that the self-help group model faces is a lack of governance structures that lead to good succession planning and support structures. When I left the group, there was a void that the group members failed to fill to support the coordinator, and once the coordinator also moved on the group ended. Running a volunteer self-help group can be very difficult for the leaders, as it is challenging work for unsupported, unsupervised and untrained volunteers. Many of you would be concerned about how safe it was to be involved with a group that ran without clinical supports, but I never felt that. In eight years we never had a suicide in our group.

In reflecting on fifteen years of paid peer work at the Richmond Fellowship of Tasmania I have come to understand my work in three stages. The first five years work at the Richmond Fellowship of Tasmania, employed as a peer worker under a support worker title, was my dream job. This was a time when the Richmond Fellowship of Tasmania was a small organisation and I was lucky to be working with three forward-thinking people who had no problem with my sharing my lived experience. In the second five years, some community organisations in Tasmania began employing peer workers, giving employees job descriptions as 'peer workers'. I began to bring this information about the benefits of peer workers to my team, and voiced my thoughts on engaging the first wave of peer workers in the Richmond Fellowship of Tasmania like other organisations were doing. For me this began a period of frustration and a decline in my working relationships with those in my team as I was not supported in my views.

This period of a quick expansion of peer workers in Tasmania was well researched later in a peer worker's honours thesis, 'Living a liminal fife: Peer workers' experiences of dual role negotiation in mental health service delivery within Tasmania' by Leticia Saunders (2013). Her understanding of the issues that were raised in her qualitative research were developed by talking to peer workers who had been involved in the rollout of full-time peer worker roles. Saunders came to understand the liminality of the role, meaning 'betwixt and between', as peer workers negotiate a role that exists between the social categories of consumer and professional within a marginalised social space (Saunders, 2013, p. 11). Saunders found through her research that the implementation of peer workers in the workforce had much support from the peer workers she interviewed. The success of the engagement of peer workers by the non-government sector was undermined, however, by the 'absence of any clear guidelines and specific structures for the role of peer worker [that] led to an inevitable lack of policy translation' (p. 42). I lived this existence of working in this isolated liminal space, while not feeling quite like a 'real' consumer and also being side-lined from the team as someone, from other staff's perspective, who thought that peer workers were better than the other staff.

I am pleased to say that now in this third stage of implementation of peer workers in the Richmond Fellowship of Tasmania, times have changed again. And recently I have been encouraged by the National Disability Insurance Scheme legitimising the rollout of the peer workforce. This has recently led my chief executive officer at the Richmond Fellowship of Tasmania to employ a peer worker to engage consumers in focus groups to provide authentic feedback from consumers to the organisation. Also, I was motivated by recently being approached to assist in the development of guidelines and a strategic implementation of peer workers to be formalised in the Richmond Fellowship of Tasmania job roles. We now have a better understanding of why the implementation of peer workers in the non-government sector and mental health services failed, a failure described by Saunders (2013, p. 42) as 'lack of policy translation'. We will take these lessons forward to a new era of engaging peer workers.

5: Values and experiences in implementing peer work

**In conclusion**

For fifteen years I have had the ability to honestly make connections with the fears and feelings of being a resident at the Richmond Fellowship of Tasmania as a peer worker. That is what drives my work ethic—to help others find solutions to their issues as I have done over the years. I sometimes regale my peers with stories of frustration at having lived in a share house where people drank straight from the milk carton or a hundred other common issues. I am, however, even more fortunate than many other peer workers as I have lots of time to spend with residents at the Richmond Fellowship of Tasmania to solidify and form strong connections. As a peer worker I have found that it can take residents a long time to truly understand that even today I am still unwell. People living with obsessive-compulsive disorder can hide their symptoms, rituals and anxiety very well. We all put on a show that all is fine in life. Fortunately, over time, residents do get to see and know that while I always suffer from the disorder, I live a full life and maybe this inspires them to believe that they too can live contributing lives.

**References**

Bailey, L. (2016). *Because we are bad*. Crows Nest, NSW: Allen & Unwin.

Saunders, L. (2013). Living a liminal life: Peer support workers' experiences of dual role negotiation in mental health service delivery within Tasmania. Honours thesis, University of Tasmania.

Sorkin, A., & Wells, J. (2000). Episode 2.10—Noel (Television series episode). In T. Schlamme (Director), *The West Wing*. Warner Brothers Television and NBC. Transcript by Giorgio, BumbleLion, Joshsgirl, Irene and LocalGomer8, retrieved from http://www.westwingtranscripts.com/search.php?flag=getTranscript&id=32

# Peer work and climate change

*Tim Heffernan*

*Tim Heffernan is a consumer peer worker. He is a life member of the NSW Public Mental Health Consumer Workers' Committee and currently works as mental health peer coordinator for the South Eastern NSW Primary Health Network. He was motivated to write because we need to record the work that we do.*

When thinking about peer work, I like to use the analogy of climate change. We know that we need to change the way we live on planet Earth, and the way we fuel our modern lifestyles, yet we remain dependent on oil, gas and coal while alternatives such as solar, wind, hydro and thermal remain under-developed and under-funded. We know the Earth is in crisis, yet our policies and systems are dominated by climate change deniers and those with vested interests in keeping things the same.

In a similar way we have a biomedical mental health system that is not working, and the futures of hundreds of thousands of people are at risk as a result. We know that things must change, yet change is slow to come. We know that we must move to a recovery-oriented, trauma-informed psychosocial mental health system so that people do not continue to be harmed, yet traditional approaches, evidence bases and workforces still attract funding and resources to prop up a system floundering in inappropriate places like hospitals and prisons.

If we think of workforce as the fuel that feeds the mental health system, then the peer workforce is a lot like alternative fuel sources such as solar and wind power. Peer workers are the renewable resource of the mental health system. The traditional workforces are the fossil fuels that sustain the biomedical model. Things are obviously worsening in this system, but as with climate change, there are significant vested interests whose survival depends on maintaining the status quo, regardless of the damage done.

Many oil companies know that their traditional way of doing business is no longer sustainable, so they are diversifying and innovating—investing research and infrastructure dollars into sustainable energy. Mental health systems must do the same, and so as we move into an era of responsible, renewable energy consumption, we must also move into the era of the 'expert by experience' working to assist others to become experts themselves—the era of the peer worker.

## The NSW public mental health consumer workforce

*The Consumer Consultants Project*

The first National Mental Health Plan and Strategy (Australian Health Ministers, 1992) was critical to the development of consumer rights, participation and workforce. The New South Wales (NSW) public mental health peer workforce evolved directly from a meeting held in late 1992 at Rozelle Hospital, then a 270-bed psychiatric hospital. In the room were the hospital's general manager and 'a number of Sydney Consumers and some people who had provided much support for consumers' (as worded in the submission for the 1998 TheMHS Awards by consumer consultants at Rozelle Hospital). The resulting Consumer Consultants Project was a defining moment for the peer workforce across Australia.

Helen Blum wrote of the motivation for the project, 'The group thought that consumers, because of their experience coping with mental Illness, had certain expertise in the mental health field. They were ideal to advocate for patients, because they have a consumer's experience of the mental health system, and could understand and empathise with problems patients were facing.'

Helen was one of two consumers employed by the hospital for fourteen hours a week to create a training package and to orientate staff and consumers at the hospital. Over the next twelve months, working with the original consumer group and the general manager for guidance, they trained a further six consumers as consumer consultants to work on the wards. Helen became the coordinator of consumer consultants, remaining on fourteen hours per week. The consumer consultants were employed to work three hours per week.

As coordinator, Helen encouraged a 'therapeutic attitude' borrowed from psychologist Carl Rogers, 'to listen empathetically to the patients and allow them to resolve their own problems'. She wrote of the different work in the 'acute' and 'rehabilitation' wards. While advocating for consumers in both, consumer consultants tended to 'to share their experiences in the hope that they will help patients' on the acute wards, while on the rehabilitation wards there was a focus on 'recreational activity'.

The consultants also delivered education of consumers about their rights under the Mental Health Act, promotion of self-advocacy, supporting consumers before and during doctors' reviews and at tribunal hearings and supporting ex-patients in the community.

This first formal peer work was 'consumer designed and ... effectively consumer controlled'. As Helen wrote in the submission, 'Although we are paid by the Hospital and work in close partnership with hospital staff, the jobs and training were designed by consumers and the Consumer Coordinator makes most of the day to day decisions.'

These peer workers gave hope and the path to recovery to the consumers at Rozelle Hospital, and they also clearly began to disrupt and change mental health services. In 1998, the coordinator of consumer consultants was invited by the hospital's general manager to join the hospital management committee. And peer workers were moving into the community. In 1995 Peter Schaecken was employed as coordinator of consumer initiatives to run a peer counselling and advocacy service in the community. This became a full-time role in May 1996 overseeing community participation in the community (Escott et al., n.d.).

**Peer work in public mental health**

*The Illawarra Shoalhaven reflecting national trends*

By the time I came into my position as a consumer rehabilitation assistant in 2009 the lived experience workforce was already well established in the Illawarra Shoalhaven region. The workforce grew out of volunteer representation on various mental health service committees, beginning with the Community Consultative Committee in 1987. An increased impetus for consumer representation coincided with the implementation of the 1992 National Mental Health Strategy and first National Plan and the associated Mental Health Statement of Rights and Responsibilities (Mental Health Consumer Outcomes Taskforce, 1991). The strategy and plan prioritised the improvement of the rights of consumers and carers, and this saw the

## 5: Values and experiences in implementing peer work

establishment of peak bodies—consumer advisory groups—at national, state and territory levels to represent the interests of mental healthcare consumers and carers. In 1996 the National Standards for Mental Health Services (Commonwealth Department of Health and Family Services, 1996), which included relevant service delivery standards for ensuring protection of consumer rights, were established.

The evaluation of the National Mental Health Strategy released in December 1997 (National Mental Health Strategy Evaluation Steering Committee, 1997) gives a good picture of the embryonic growth of consumer and care participation.

> In 1994, two years into the Strategy, only 33% of public sector local mental health service organisations had established a specific, formal mental health consumer and carer group to advise on service planning and delivery (see Figure 2). By 1996, this figure had increased to 49%. However, one third of all organisations remained without any formal process for consumers and carers to contribute to service development.

It also flags some ongoing resistance:

> In general, all groups were positive about the new roles for consumers and carers in local service planning, with some important differences. Staff employed in hospitals were more cautious about the value of consumer and carer involvement than community-based staff.

And the evaluation identified an emerging workforce:

> Differences between the four sites reviewed suggest that the transition has been more far reaching where management unambiguously demonstrated its commitment to consumer and carer involvement, for example, by investing funds in consumer advocates or providing assistance to local groups with establishment costs. The notion that we 'pay for what we care about' has much merit in this context (pp. 11–12).

The first step towards a paid consumer workforce were these consumer advocates.

Finally, the evaluation called for the establishment of 'guidelines and assistance to local agencies, public and private, [which] need to be established to accelerate the empowerment of consumers and carers' at the local level (p. 26). These guidelines pre-empted the action to establish a peer workforce framework and guidelines in both the fourth and fifth National Mental Health

Plans. There has now been a twenty-one-year wait for such guidelines and so disempowerment continues.

So, in this context, paid consumer and carer representation began in the Illawarra Shoalhaven region in 1998, and in 1999 the consumer workforce was first established, with the employment of two consumer initiatives coordinators. They were employed two days a week in both Wollongong and Nowra. The Consumer and Carer Consultative Committee began in 2000.

Around the same time the Illawarra Mental Health Service participated in the Mental Health Integration Project, a national demonstration project sponsored and funded through the Australian Government's Department of Health and Ageing as part of the Second National Mental Health Plan. This funding enabled the Illawarra Area Health Service (AHS) to develop a number of innovative programs including the establishment of consumer rehabilitation assistants in Wollongong, Nowra and Ulladulla. The aim of the consumer rehabilitation assistants in the project was to improve access and integration for consumers to a broader range of mental health services. The project concluded in 2004, but the positions were retained following a positive evaluation: 'Components of the [Mental Health Integration Project] undoubtedly provided a broader range of services and some increased access. [Consumer rehabilitation assistant]s are feasible and appear to be making a significant contribution to integration' (Eager, Owen, & Burgess, 2004, p. 45).

The Mental Health Integration Project 'demonstrated that there is an ongoing need for planning and incentives to achieve better integration between the public mental health sector, the private mental health sector, general practice, community health and the NGO sector. The [Project] has also demonstrated that consumers and carers are critical stakeholders who have a central role in any integration agenda.' Importantly it demonstrated the evidence for the peer workforce as an effective agent for integration.

Following a review of consumer and carer programs in 2001, the Illawarra AHS appointed Fay Jackson as full-time director of consumer and carer affairs, a lived experience position, and expanded the workforce with the appointment of a number of part-time consumer and carer advocates to specialised positions such as adult, youth, culturally and linguistically diverse and Aboriginal. Things were moving forward.

## 5: Values and experiences in implementing peer work

Also, in 2001, a partnership between the University of Wollongong, Illawarra Institute for Mental Health and the Illawarra AHS established an innovative example of co-designed research, the Consumer Evaluation of Mental Health Service Framework. The project aims were to improve mental health services by empowering consumers through 'credible' research and to demonstrate the as yet untapped resource of consumers as mental health researchers and the implication of this resource to health service evaluation.

At the beginning of the project fourteen consumer research assistants (seven men and seven women) were employed as casual research assistants by the University of Wollongong. Consumer researchers were recruited via the consumer initiative coordinators of the Illawarra AHS who were the associate investigators of the project and awarded fellowships with the University of Wollongong (Viney et al., 2004, p. 20).

The Consumer Evaluation of Mental Health Service project was critical to the development of the Mental Health Consumer Perceptions and Experiences of Services (MH-CoPES) Framework (NSW Department of Health, 2006, p. 41).

Consumer worker involvement in research partnerships with the University of Wollongong has continued on such projects as the Collaborative Recovery Model and the School of Nursing's Recovery Camp project. Consumer workers provide education to the University of Wollongong nursing and psychology students on an ongoing basis.

### What is in a name?

South Eastern Sydney and Illawarra AHS was formed in 2005 from the amalgamation of the Illawarra AHS and South Eastern Sydney AHS. The pioneering consumer initiatives coordinators became consumer advocates in 2006 and a carer advocate was appointed in the Shoalhaven area. A South Eastern Sydney and Illawarra AHS consumer participation coordinator was appointed in 2008.

In 2011, with the establishment of the Illawarra Shoalhaven Local Health District (LHD), all consumer worker roles, including advocates, began to use the generic title of consumer worker. In 2015 with the rollout of the Certificate IV in Mental Health Peer Work, we chose to be known as consumer peer workers.

A part-time Illawarra Shoalhaven LHD consumer participation coordinator was appointed in 2015.

Consumer peer workers continue to provide peer and advocacy support across all mental health units in the Illawarra area and in community rehabilitation teams in Wollongong and Nowra. All peer workers work as part of multi-disciplinary teams and some work across teams. Recently the workforce has been considering the creation of a peer work hub that could seek to service more equally the needs of consumers of mental health services. Currently community mental health lacks peer worker support.

In 2017, a successful Partnerships in Recovery grant application saw the creation of the Illawarra Shoalhaven Professional Peer Worker Network. The network brings together peer workers from across the region to engage in networking, education and professional development activities led by peer workers. The network aims to provide a more navigable experience for mental health consumers. and hopes to be sustained with the support of the mental health peer coordinators from the South Eastern NSW Primary Health Network. In 2018, similar networks have been established in the South Coast and Southern Tablelands regions of NSW.

## You don't go to the doctor

Peer work made sense to me and it clearly provided a valid alternative to traditional clinical interventions in public mental health. My own experiences of mental health services were that they took away my power, my autonomy and my sense of self and connectedness. They replaced these things with a dependence on others, a diminution of ambitions and world view and an identity constructed by those others. I feel it has been a mistake in our development as a workforce to position ourselves as complementary to the dominant clinical workforces. We need to start saying that we can do much of the work carried out by clinicians, which is stale and diminishing in effectiveness. This is especially the case in the community where traditional management and involuntary community treatment can be replaced by the development of connections, communities and pathways to recovery.

## 5: Values and experiences in implementing peer work

In 2010, a year after I began as a peer worker, I presented a paper at the Mental Health Services (TheMHS) conference in Sydney titled, 'Early intervention recovery in acute mental health units and beyond'. The paper was about peer work and the possibilities for this profession. It was inspired by a consumer helping me round up people for a recovery discussion group. He was very convincing and spoke clearly about the ancient evidence base of peer work: 'Come on everybody, you need to come to this group! My grandmother in Italy used to say to me when I was a little boy: "When you are sick you don't go to see the doctor to get better, you go to see someone who has recovered from the sickness".'

The paper explored how peer workers provide 'helpful relationships' supporting individuals in their own ways of dealing with problems and struggles and how essential peer workers are in any transition or transfer of care. I argued that consumer peer support workers, running recovery groups in acute units, are ideally placed to spark the recovery journey. When those peer support workers also work in community teams and in community rehabilitation they can move with the uncertain traveller through the early stages of the journey, into the transition from hospital to home, to establishing links with community supports and agencies. The peer support worker then remains available to help refuel, redirect and travel with the consumer when the consumer chooses not to travel alone.

The paper proposed that important questions about consumer peer support need to be answered through appropriate funding, planning, implementation and research:

1. What does a career as a peer worker look like? What are the career pathways?
2. How do peer workers educate the clinical workforce? In the workplace, in universities.
3. Should peer workers move into other roles? What about designated lived experience 'clinicians'—nurses, psychologists, psychiatrists? Should we have scholarships for people with lived experience to move into and transform these workforces?
4. Should people with lived experience who are working outside health be part of this recovery story? Should we identify and recruit those who work

in the professions, the trades and the services to act as peer mentors, vocational and life coaches?
5. How do we learn from peers and peer worker elders? How do we maintain their wisdom, their understanding of the past and vision for the future?
6. Should peer workers always replace unfilled positions in mental health services? What are the essential competencies for these positions?
7. Should peer workers in public mental health be free to work across all services to walk with consumers as they move from hospital to home to community?
8. Should hospital to home peer support be available to all consumers?
9. Can peer workers just do things with their peers? Things like writing, art, music, exercise, cooking …
10. How can peer workers be proactive advocates, rather than reactive advocates? How can we empower consumers to influence the treating team's decision before they are made? How can we shift the power imbalance?
11. Should peer workers become shared decision makers? How might peer workers be involved in guardianship arrangements?
12. How many peer workers? How many in government and community-managed organisations?

## NSW Mental Health Consumer Workers Forum

*A framework for the public mental health consumer workforce*

Many of these questions were already being answered by one of the most influential peer worker groups in Australia. A rapid growth of consumer workers in the public mental health system in the 1990s meant that consumer workers were employed in an ad hoc manner, with nothing by way of consistent guidelines, orientation, adequate training or clarification of their job descriptions, roles and responsibilities and award rates (Sandy Watson, quoted in McDonald, 2010). In response to these concerns and to provide a place for consumer workers to network and obtain peer support and development, Sandy Watson, one of the original six consumer consultants in public mental health, was instrumental in organising the first New South Wales Consumer Workers Forum, held at Rozelle Hospital in 1998 (McDonald, 2010). The Consumer Workers' Forum organising committee would continue to organise the annual forum until 2012 when it became the New South Wales Mental Health Consumer Workers' Committee.

Unfunded for its first five years, the forum organising committee was granted $20,000 per annum from 2004 to 2008 to run the annual forum and also for the new NSW Consumer Workers' Forum Project, which was tasked with examining the consumer workforce in NSW Area Mental Health Services and made recommendations around standardised work practices.

By the end of the funding in June 2008 the Consumer Workers' Forum produced *The NSW Consumer Workers' Forum Project: Report to the Mental Health and Drug and Alcohol Office*, which was presented initially at the 2008 Forum in March, and then later in the year to the Mental Health Program Council (NSW Consumer Workers' Forum Organising Committee, cited in McDonald, 2010). This marked the end of what was to become known as Stage 1 of the Consumer Workers' Forum Project. The project had examined the job descriptions, functions, work conditions, training, supervision and work orientation, policies and protocols and codes of conduct for public mental health consumer workers.

Originally, it was intended that Stage 2 of the project would incorporate input from the Mental Health Program Council and the report, once formally approved, would serve as guidelines for mental health services. However, at the end of 2008, the report remained in draft form and the guidelines were not made policy.

Significantly, in 2008, the Consumer Workers' Forum identified that it was now a 'de facto peak body' and it sought extra funding for the development of peak body functions. A decade later there is still no peer workforce peak body.

Following a funding request from the Consumer Workers' Forum in February 2008, the Mental Health and Drug and Alcohol Office agreed to funding of $58,000 per annum for three years 'to further examine and support the role of Area Health Service Mental Health Consumer Workers'. This became Stage 2 of the Consumer Workers' Forum project.

Key strategic deliverables of Stage 2 included 'to provide support to assist the Consumer Workers Forum to make recommendations regarding the standardisation of good practice in consumer workers roles across Area Health

Services', and 'to finalise, disseminate and work with Area Heath Services and MHDAO to implement the NSW Consumer Workers Project report.'

Among other general deliverables the Mental Health and Drug and Alcohol Office agreed to 'feedback to the Forum the response by the Mental Health Program Council of the draft report on the standardisation of Consumer Worker's distribution, role definitions and skill development across NSW'.

## The NSW Consumer Advisory Group, the Consumer Workers' Forum and the Framework

A collaboration between the Consumer Workers' Forum and the NSW Consumer Advisory Group began in 2009. The NSW Consumer Advisory Group was contracted to provide secretarial support to the Consumer Workers' Forum, coordination of and secretarial support to the annual Consumer Workers' Forum and to undertake the work of the NSW Mental Health Consumer Workers Project. The project was to complete the framework for the Mental Health Consumer Workforce, have it endorsed by Program Council and then develop and initiate a framework implementation plan.

Building on the substantial work of the Consumer Workers' Forum in Stage 1 of the project, the NSW Consumer Advisory Group and the Consumer Workers' Forum were able to move confidently into Stage 2 of the Consumer Workers' Forum Project. In the first year the project officer conducted a review of Stage 1 of the project, surveyed the sector on the purpose of the mental health consumer workforce in NSW and completed a literature review (NSW Consumer Advisory Group, 2010, p. 18).

By June 2010, consultations focusing on the roles, functions, responsibilities and titles for the consumer workforce were held with more than 50% of the consumer workers employed by AHSs, as well as AHS staff and executives in eight AHSs.

The final consultation paper draft framework for the NSW Health Consumer Workforce was published in November 2011. The draft framework included detailed recommendations regarding:
- the range of roles for consumer workers within the public mental health sector

## 5: Values and experiences in implementing peer work

- where each of these roles should be positioned within public mental health organisations
- the minimum number of each position
- the content of position descriptions
- the award under which consumer workers should be paid
- line management arrangements for consumer worker positions
- the structure and minimum requirements for the supervision of consumer workers
- professional development and best practice training including a list of core knowledge and skills that need to be included in induction and orientation training for consumer workers.
- a code of professional standards regarding the NSW mental health consumer workforce
- a workplace adjustment implementation plan.

### The NSW Mental Health Consumer Workers Committee

In 2012 the Consumer Workers Forum organising committee changed its name to the NSW Mental Health Consumer Workers. The Consumer Workers' Committee and the NSW Consumer Advisory Group incorporated the feedback from the consultation paper and by 2013 had settled on a draft framework that was submitted to the Mental Health Program Council. The framework was endorsed by the Clinical Advisory Council meeting on 25 October and was endorsed 'in principle' by the Mental Health Program Council on 5 December 2013. It seemed that the framework was a reality.

In early 2014 a working party of the NSW Ministry of Health was established to complete work on the framework, but it did not become operational. A Ministry policy officer began a rewrite. The Consumer Workers' Committee requested that they could complete the fine detail by working directly with the Mental Health and Drug and Alcohol Office. The framework stopped. No process could be negotiated with the Ministry to complete this work. At this time, the Consumer Workers' Committee voiced concern about its influence in decision making and about the relationship between itself and the Ministry of Health.

The release of the NSW Mental Health Commission's 'Living Well' strategic plan in 2014 gave hope that the framework would become a reality when it made as an action of the plan that 'NSW Health will implement the Framework for the NSW Public Mental Health Consumer Workforce' (pp. 99–100).

However, by late 2014 the Ministry had ceased all work on the framework and commissioned a consumer participation consultation which identified that the emergence of local health districts in 2012 had impeded the final adoption of the framework: 'Many of the stakeholders consulted highlighted the ongoing pressing need for guidance in regard to developing the consumer workforce, particularly in light of changing healthcare structures and roles over recent years which have seen the establishment of Local Health Districts in 2011 with greater autonomy than their predecessors, Area Health Services. These changes took place while the draft Framework was under development' (p. 22).

As an initial response to the Living Well plan, the Ministry established 116 scholarships over three years to support peer workers to obtain Certificate IV qualifications. It promised a mental health workforce plan that would include the peer workforce by 2016, and a statewide consumer workforce coordination service based in the non-governmental sector with a brief to provide coordination, advice and advocacy in the development of the consumer workforce across both Local Health Districts and non-government organisations (NSW Health, 2014).

### Living Well—the strategic plan for mental health in NSW

Like the National Mental Health Commission's 2013 Report Card, the NSW Mental Health Commission's Living Well plan (2014) mapped out a strong future for the peer workforce. Now the Ministry of Health's strategic plan for 2014–2024, Living Well is the catalyst for workforce reform in NSW public mental health. From its inception the NSW Mental Health Commission included a strong peer worker presence in the Deputy Commissioner Fay Jackson and in the inclusion of peer workers on the Community Advisory Council.

## 5: Values and experiences in implementing peer work

Actions from Living Well included:

- The development of a NSW Mental Health Workforce Plan, including the peer workforce
- The implementation of the framework for the NSW public mental health workforce
- Peer worker roles in the Department of Family and Community Services
- Benchmarks for peer workers in public and community-managed organisations and in housing, disability and justice (NSW Mental Health Commission, 2014, pp. 99–100).

In May 2016, the Ministry appointed a statewide peer workforce coordinator and in 2017, following advocacy from the NSW Consumer Workers' Committee, a 'senior project officer—peer workforce' position was established. The project officer provides secretarial support to the NSW Consumer Workers' Committee while also supporting the peer workforce coordinator with all aspects of project management associated with the design, development and implementation of the Framework (NSW Health, n.d.).

The peer workforce coordinator's role is to 'support, enhance, expand and define the NSW peer workforce', including the public and community managed sectors. The coordinator is responsible for the final development and implementation of the framework for the NSW public peer workforce, the development of benchmarks for the peer workforce in Local Health Districts and all Ministry-funded programs in community-managed organisations.

Twenty-five years after the visionary beginnings at Rozelle Hospital the public mental health consumer peer workforce continues to build and to provide hope for consumers and to bring cultural change to public mental health services. The NSW Public Mental Health Consumer Committee has provided support and leadership, a framework of sorts, for the workforce for most of these twenty-five years.

### References

Australian Health Ministers. (1992). *The national mental health strategy.* Canberra : Australian Health Ministers' Conference.

Australian Health Ministers' Advisory Council. (1992). *National mental health plan 1993–1998.* Canberra: Australian Health Ministers' Advisory Council.

Commonwealth Department of Health and Family Services. (1996). *National standards for mental health services.* Canberra: Commonwealth Department of Health and Family Services.

Consumer Workers' Forum Project. (2010). Literature review on the mental health consumer workforce. Sydney: NSW Consumer Advisory Group—Mental Health Inc. Retrieved from http://old.being.org.au/files/our_work/cwf_literature_review_final.pdf

Eagar, K., Owen, A. & Burgess, P. (2004). National Mental Health Integration Program (MHIP): National evaluation synthesis. Wollongong: Centre for Health Service Development, University of Wollongong.

Escott, P., Moore, S., Dauncey, S., Blanchard, L., Hobbs, S., & Schaecken, P. (n.d.). What are consumer workers and what do we do? Retrieved from https://www.slhd.nsw.gov.au/MentalHealth/pdf/What_are_Consumer_Worker

McDonald, J. (2010). Consumer Workers' Forum Project: Literature review on the mental health consumer workforce. Sydney: NSW Consumer Advisory Group, Mental Health Inc. Retrieved from http://being.org.au/wp-content/uploads/2015/06/cwf_literature_review_final.pdf

Mental Health Consumer Outcomes Task Force. (1991). *Mental health statement of rights and responsibilities.* Canberra: Australian Government.

National Mental Health Strategy Evaluation Steering Committee. (1997). *Evaluation of the national mental health strategy: final report.* Canberra: Mental Health Branch, Commonwealth Department of Health and Family Services. Retrieved from http://www.health.gov.au/internet/main/publishing.nsf/Content/mental-pubs-e-strateval

NSW Consumer Advisory Group. (2010). *NSW Consumer Advisory Group 2009–2010 annual report.* Retrieved from http://being.org.au/whatwedo/publications/annual-reports/

NSW Department of Health (2006). *A statewide approach to measuring and responding to consumer perceptions and experiences of adult mental health services: A report on stage one of the development of the MH-CoPES framework and questionnaires.* North Sydney: NSW Department of Health.

NSW Health. (n.d.). Statewide peer workforce coordinator (fact sheet). SHPN (MHB) 170134. Sydney: NSW Health. Retrieved from http://www.health.nsw.gov.au/mentalhealth/reform/Factsheets/mh-statewide-peer.PDF

NSW Health. (2014). Investing in workforce (fact sheet). SHPN (SRC) 140511. Sydney: NSW Health. Retrieved from http://www.health.nsw.gov.au/mentalhealth/reform/Publications/investing-in-workforce.pdf

NSW Mental Health Commission. (2014). *Living well: A strategic plan for mental health in NSW 2014–2024.* Sydney: NSW Mental Health Commission. Retrieved from https://nswmentalhealthcommission.com.au/sites/default/files/141002%20Living%20Well%20-%20A%20Strategic%20Plan%20(1).pdf

Viney, L. L., Oades, L. G., Strang, J., Eman, Y., Lambert, W. G., Malins, G., ... Tooth, B. A. (2004). A framework for consumers evaluating mental health services. University of Wollongong, Illawarra Institute for Mental Health.

# The world according to me: A Western Australian peer work journey, some history, reflections and thoughts

Lyn Mahboub

*I am many things, such as parent, daughter, teacher, student, glue- and glitter-lover and person with a lived experience on a recovery journey of over forty years (so far), as well as a person inhabiting roles from within the peer workforce spectrum. I am responding to the invitation to contribute to the literature on peer workforce development and given that so little is documented on work undertaken by the peer workforce I am delighted to do so. Specifically, I am focusing on a spattering of significant historical developments here in Western Australia that I have come to intersect with and know about.*

I feel privileged to contribute to the growing literature on peer work. In so doing, I would also like to tip my hat to some of the key influencing projects and initiatives which have shaped my learning and motivated me to work in the peer space. Therefore, this chapter will highlight some of these enterprises which I believe have significantly contributed to peer workforce development in Western Australia. Some of them I have been involved with personally, or people passed them down to me via stories and situational anecdotes. I acknowledge that because much of our history is oral, with very little emerging in print formally, my account and recollections will likely be incomplete, and will likely differ from the accounts of others. Below, I will discuss the contributions to the peer workforce of the Consumer Consultant Trial, the HealthRight Project and the Hearing Voices Network, and will culminate with a summary of a project I am currently heading up at Curtin University, the Valuing Lived Experience Project. First, as is our custom in the consumer movement, I would like to acknowledge the contributions of our elders and colleagues—past, present and emerging. Their efforts inspire me to stay connected to, and involved in, the Australian 'consumer movement'.

Everything that exists is the result of what has come before. I am who I am because of the teachings of others who have reached out from the past. I feel blessed to follow in the tracks of advocates and activists from around the world, dating as far back as the seventeenth century (for example, the 1620 'Petition of the poor distracted people in the house of Bedlam', Buhagiar, 2013) and probably even earlier. It is on the shoulders of these often-unacknowledged giants that I stand. As I reflect on my journey through the consumer movement, I am instantly reminded of my peers who have taught me so much through their writings, personal stories, teaching and generous sharing of their wisdom. But I am especially motivated by the thousands of hours they have given to the mission of mental health reform. I have built solid and lasting relationships with some, intermittent but deeply meaningful acquaintance with others, and eagerly await the knowledge and learning still coming from those I have yet to meet.

My entry into the peer workforce is relatively recent (2003), but I luxuriated in many stories passed down to me as part of my induction into the peer movement. There were tales from the east of the visionary Deakin workshops (1999), the amazing Understanding and Involvement Project (1991–2001), the work of the Victorian Mental Illness Awareness Council (VMIAC), the Consumer Advisory Network, the Pitane Recovery Centre and the Australian Mental Health Network, to name but a few. This work drew strength from the heady days of the 1970s civil rights movement and came to fruition in the 1990s, when the launch of the National Mental Health Strategy, and the first National Mental Health Plan, signalled for the first time in policy the importance of consumer (and carer) involvement. Such initiatives inspired us in the west and initiatives like the Health Consumers' Council Mental Health Advocacy Project (1995–2003) were born. Spanning seven years, it was hugely effective in building the capacity of people with lived experience to act as peer (consumer) representatives across a range of domains, including mental health and consumer advocacy.

In 2004, the Consumer Consultant Trial commenced. Borrowing from the massive learnings from the Mental Health Consumer Advocacy Project, this project was another brick in the foundation of the peer workforce in Western Australia. It added 'consumer consultant' to the existing, somewhat accepted, role of 'consumer representative'. Seconded to a mental health service, the project had two roles. One role was to facilitate the establishment of focus groups, which advocated for the patients of the Southern Mental Health Area Service (which was made up of five mental health services) and made

## 5: Values and experiences in implementing peer work

recommendations for change from a consumer perspective (Ambrosius et al., 2005). The second role was to design and recommend a model for consumer participation for the state. Though this model created was considered, it was not taken up. Instead, another model called Statewide Advocacy, Education, Training and Information Service was initially endorsed in 2005, but ultimately not funded. Instead, the Mental Health Division provided recurrent funding to the North Metropolitan Area Mental Health Service as the lead agency for the Statewide Consumer Participation Program.

An additional, memorable enterprise that also significantly paved the way for mental health peer work in Western Australia was the HealthRight Project and its offspring the Peer Advocacy and Support Service. To my knowledge, in addition to the Hearing Voices Network, HealthRight was among the first in Western Australia to employ peers (Kemp, Bates, & Mohan, 2008, p. 26). The project, which was responding to the ground-breaking *Duty to care* report (Coghlan et al., 2001), sought to attend to the huge physical health disparity of those with mental health issues. HealthRight did not utilise peer work in the same sense that we know it today. The mental health peer workers delivered a 'lifestyle intervention' (Kemp et al., 2014, p. 217) helping mental health consumers to set and reach physical health goals and to access medical and other appointments and physical health information (HealthRight Project Overview, 2009). As a member of the HealthRight reference group, I witnessed at first hand how this project's success broke the ground for peers to be considered employable in mental health. Champions of the project, Margaret Cook, Ginger Gordy, Pauline Miles, Anne Bates, Vivien Kemp, Dr Mohan Isaac and others were our trailblazers in this ground-breaking work. HealthRight's success inspired a number of agencies to employ peer workers, and so our journey began.

Many other initiatives past and present have contributed to the development of the peer workforce landscape in Western Australia, including the Association of MH Consumers WA Inc. (2001–2004), the West Australian Mental Illness Awareness Council Inc., now called Consumers of Mental Health WA (CoMHWA), Recovery Rocks Community Inc., the Body Esteem peer-facilitated self-help groups, Mental Health Matters2, the WA Peer Support Network (hosted by CoMHWA) and Cyrenian House's Alcohol and Other Drugs Peer Support Plus Program (to name a few). Incorporated in 2005 and rebranded in 2010, CoMHWA was funded in 2011 and is the peak consumer body in Western Australia. A number of us were early founding members, led by Debbie Waddingham, creator and instigator, who commenced the foundational work in 2004. Recovery Rocks Community Inc. is a small, unfunded Perth-based peer-led and -run mental health recovery community founded in 2012 by Amanda Waegeli. Mental Health Matters2 is a Western Australian community action and advocacy group led by peers (families and individuals).

The continuous proliferation of such initiatives demonstrates the growing competence, experience and sophistication of peer power in Western Australia. Clearly, the breadth of the peer workforce has no end in sight with new roles emerging regularly (see Figure 1).

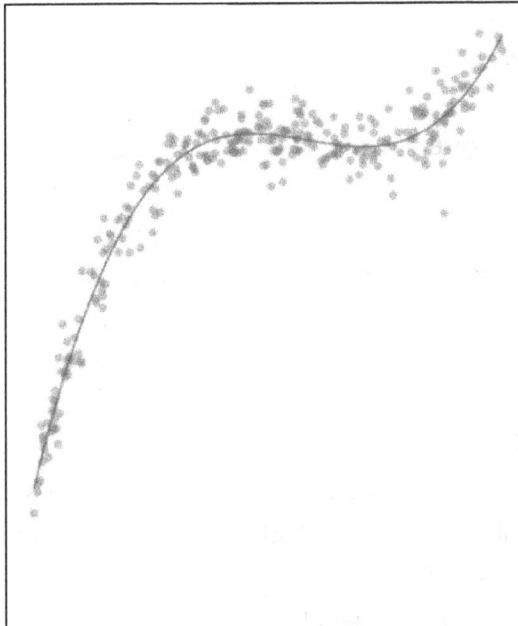

| Peer workforce roles |
|---|
| Consumer representative, consumer consultant, consumer advocate and/or activist, consumer adviser, consumer assessor, consumer liaison officer, consumer policy officer, consumer reviewer |
| Hearing voices group peer facilitator, hearing voices network director or coordinator |
| Peer worker, peer support worker, peer trainer, peer/consumer/lived experience researcher, peer specialist, peer/lived experience supervisor, peer respite worker, peer mentor, peer advocate, lived experience practitioner |
| Carer peer, family member peer/advocate |
| Consumer/lived experience academic, recovery adviser, peer/lived experience educator |

Figure 1: An imagined scatter plot of the growing roles within the Australian peer workforce with a non-exhaustive list of peer workforce role titles

## 5: Values and experiences in implementing peer work

Another influential contributor in shaping the peer landscape is the Hearing Voices Movement. Fundamental to the hearing voices philosophy is the validation of 'expertise by experience'. This acknowledgement of the centrality of lived experience and peer support provides the foundation for its development. It was and, many of us would argue, should be led and developed by peers. This is not to say there should not be others at the table: indeed, having others as a part of the decision making team can often create additional opportunities for hearing voices networks, programs or groups to be co-produced, co-designed and co-facilitated. Historically, this was the model used here, and, importantly, it was grassroots-driven.

In August 2005, fellow Perth consumer, Jen Stacey and I independently went to Richmond Fellowship (nowadays called Richmond Wellbeing) to volunteer to start a Hearing Voices Network. Both of us rose to the charismatic, Scottish war cry challenge of international trainer, speaker, writer and voice hearer Ron Coleman. Those were the days—Jen and I strategised and planned by day (and some nights)! We were surrounded by enthusiastic, courageous professionals who were our allies. (The term 'ally' is often used in the Hearing Voices Movement and here and there in the consumer movement to acknowledge those professionals who stand up and support peers in our endeavours. The Movement is made up of voice hearers, family members (and carers), allies and other members of the community. For example, the co-founders Marius Romme and Sandra Escher were professionals who were key champions working with voice hearer Patsy Hage to enable the voices of experts by experience to be heard.) Significantly, the allies believed in us and the ideas underpinning the hearing voices approach, such as: (1) that voice hearing was not in and of itself a sign of mental illness but a meaningful and meaning-filled experience that could be explored and made sense of; (2) that one did not have to eliminate the voices, but could change the relationship with the voices and gain mastery over the experience; and (3) that voice hearer peers could offer peer support via hearing voices groups.

Our work built on the accomplishments of Michael White in South Australia's Dulwich Centre (Verco & Russell, 2009) and Arana Pearson (working in both New Zealand and some eastern states of Australia) but especially on the massive work undertaken in the United Kingdom and the Netherlands. This prior work inspired Richmond Fellowship champions Rob Rowe and Bill

Bennett (acting chief executive officer) to bring Ron Coleman and Karen Taylor to Western Australia in 2005. (Rob, Bill and I were all taught critical psychology by the late Mark Rapley (1962–2012), a maverick professor and staunch activist for the normalisation of humanness and the de-medicalisation of misery (Rapley, Moncrieff, & Dillon, 2011).) Soon afterwards, new chief executive officer Joe Calleja was equally enthused and ultimately became our single most active ally. Thanks to Joe's vision and willingness to listen and approve proposals from us 'service users', we created one of the first (if not *the* first) initiatives for voice hearers to be employed in Western Australia delivering mental health recovery peer support to voice hearers. Especially helpful were our volunteers on the Hearing Voices Network Development Working Party (a group made up of amazing, passionate people, both service providers and consumers) and the mentoring from Ron Coleman (patron 2006–2015) and Karen Taylor, who inspired us and taught us much over the years.

Of significance, it was the organisation's belief that that 'we peers' brought important knowledge and credibility to the work we were doing: knowledge about the lived experience of mental distress, hearing voices, life recovery, peer support, consumer perspectives and the lived experience of many of the social determinants contributing to loss of wellbeing. Equally, the rest of the team brought to the table important skills and knowledge in program development, grant writing, organisational contexts and much more. The belief in peers was demonstrated with the appointment of Jen as a project officer in 2005, myself as founding director of the Hearing Voices Network Australia in 2006, and all subsequent Hearing Voices Coordinators (Marlene Janssen, Amanda Waegeli and Jacqui Day), as lived experience roles. Today the Richmond Wellbeing, Hearing Voices Network WA employs a peer coordinator and three peer support workers to run hearing voices groups and raise awareness of this important adjunct to mental health recovery.

Looking back, it sure wasn't all smooth sailing. This was new to us all and we were making it up as we went along. We were called 'heretics' and were accused of giving false hope for 'recovery'. But still we forged on, knowing it was a necessary time of change and challenge. In understanding the backlash, worry, and debate about the hearing voices approach, it is important to note that back then, in 2005, in Western Australia, this was New with a capital N, and, like many innovative ideas which challenge the status quo, it raised fears, concerns and questions. We saw this as a positive sign, however, understanding that it is only in the debate and discussion that questions can be raised and fears deeply heard and responded to. We were also mindful that, at that time, 'peer work' in mental health had not been initiated in any formal way in Western Australia and here we were suggesting a model that included having people who might still be actively hearing voices employed as peer workers. We had to remember that while many of those who went before us had been advocating for peer work roles for numerous years, there were some potential funders, and many mental health service providers, who still held much confusion, fear and mistrust in the idea of having the 'mentally ill' provide services. It should be noted that the notion of 'personal recovery' (living a meaningful, contributing life in the presence or absence of 'symptoms'), while possibly known by a few, was little understood at this time. Even today, 'personal recovery' is not well understood by funders, mental health services and others. Primacy is still routinely given to 'clinical recovery' or 'social recovery' (rehabilitation), and the focus on living a meaningful life (personal recovery) is not commonly in the picture. This is largely due to the dominance of the biomedical model. (See more on the difference between 'personal recovery and 'clinical recovery' in Slade, 2009, and for more on 'social recovery' see the chapter in Coleman, 2011, pp. 28–62.)

In 2008, a three-day Recovery from Psychosis Conference (with about eighteen internationally renowned keynote speakers, many of them peers), along with the Annual International Hearing Voices Congress, was held in Perth. This was the first time the Congress was held in the southern hemisphere. This was replicated in 2012 in Melbourne by Voices Vic (Victorian Hearing Voices Network). Thanks to the collective effort of peers and allies, these events put peer work in the hearing voices space and the lived experience of people who hear voices and or have other perceptual experiences on the map.

Across the country there have been scores of people who, like me, have found ourselves in the thick of things (hearing-voices-wise), and contributed to the peer work space in Australia. Some names that come to mind from the early days are Indigo Daya (founding coordinator of Voices Vic), Marlene Janssen (coordinator of the Western Australian Network in 2009–2011), Amanda Waegeli (who formalised the Hearing Voices Network WA and was coordinator from 2012 to 2014), Arana Pearson (owner-director and principal trainer for Keepwell Ltd in Australia and New Zealand), Sue Belmore (former coordinator of Voices Vic, trainer and consultant), Douglas Holmes (chairperson and public officer for Hearing Voices Network NSW), Kellie Stastny (née Comans, Australian voice hearer rep on the international hearing voices board Intervoice), Sarah Reece (foundational involvement in the Hearing Voices Network South Australia) and Bruce Roberts (president of the Melissa Roberts Foundation), as well as scores of others who I didn't meet and those whose names my ageing brain could not retain such as the Albury–Wodonga mob, the Queensland crew, the south Australian contingent and the Top End team.

All of the work in the hearing voices space, I would argue, has contributed to the acceptance of peer support, particularly as Hearing Voices Networks began to multiply. This is not to say hearing voices groups and hearing voices training had not existed previously; certainly the work of Michael White (Dulwich Centre, Adelaide), Arana Pearson (trainer) and others (a hearing voices group in the Dandenongs, outside Melbourne) predated our involvement. The fact that there are now several state-based Hearing Voices Networks (funded and unfunded), such as Voices Vic, Hearing Voices Network New South Wales, Hearing Voices Network WA, Hearing Voices Queensland and the Hearing Voices Network SA as well as a multitude of hearing voices groups dotted across the country from Busselton to Brisbane, which is a true testament to the tenacity of those who made it happen—the many allies and peers. Andrea Minca is the current program manager at Voices Vic working alongside Janet Karagounis and others. Douglas Holmes is chair of Hearing Voices NSW. Jacqui Day is coordinator (since 2014) of Hearing Voices WA, with her team Corina, Soraya and Julie, and Dave Facer is organiser of Hearing Voices Queensland.

Further evidence of the development of the peer workforce can be seen in the increase of the lived experience voice within education and training. This is emblematic within the ideas underpinning recovery colleges (where peers are central), the incorporation of peer trainers into many mental health organisation's training initiatives and also within school and university education. I will now describe one such initiative that is within Western Australia's Curtin University.

## 5: Values and experiences in implementing peer work

The Valuing Lived Experience Project co-created by me and colleague Dr Robyn Martin for the Curtin University School of Occupational Therapy, Social Work and Speech Pathology aims to embed lived experience within course curriculums. (For a more comprehensive overview of the project see Dorozenko et al., 2016.) While starting with Occupational Therapy and Social Work, we are keen to extend to different disciplines and schools within and without Curtin University and are in discussions with Speech Pathology and Exercise Physiology. I am delighted to report that our project is strongly supported and valued right from the top, with the head of School, Professor Angus Buchanan, and other senior leaders such as Dr Donna Chung and Dr Courtenay Harris, as our key champions and funders. Additionally, we have many academics from the School who are joining us and enabling very creative work in their teaching with our lived experience educators such as Sophie Ridley, Kate Dorozenko, Sue Gillieatt, Stuart Youngson, Annalise O'Callaghan, Nigel Gribble, Tina Fernandes, Judi Anderson, Kate Duncanson, Antonia Hendricks, Paula Clough and more.

The mission of the Valuing Lived Experience Project is to privilege the voice of lived experience within teaching and to touch the hearts and minds of professionals and students as to the value of learning from lived experience. We endeavour to do this by

1. building the capacity of people with a lived experience, both individuals and carers and family members who identify as such, to contribute to educating professionals both outside the academy and within the academy (via co-marking, co-curriculum design and co-lecturing and more); largely this aim is achieved by the Lived Experience Educator unit for people with lived experience (peers) and some other activities
2. building the capacity of academics to involve people with a lived experience in their teaching
3. developing resources as teaching aids (filmed footage (simulations) and diverse tutorial activities) drawing on voices of peers
4. researching and promoting the project (writing up and presenting our findings and learnings within the literature, at briefings and at conferences).

While Robyn (academic project support) and I (lived experience academic and project lead) are fixtures in the project, we have the capacity to expand and contract the team. This elasticity affords us the flexibility to recruit peers and academics into different activities as they arise each semester. The project is informed by our positionality, which embraces a number of themes such as: privileging lived experience; enacting reflexivity; prioritising process; being open to feedback and learning; being ethical, equitable, relational and embedded; taking a critical stance (and an attention to power); highlighting the social determinants of wellbeing; and valuing 'personal recovery' (Department of Health and Ageing, 2013). This way of working lends itself to also draw on Slay and Stephens's (2013) co-production principles which are: taking an assets-based approach; building on people's existing capabilities; reciprocity and mutuality; peer support networks; blurring distinctions; and facilitating rather than delivering (p. 3).

The achievements of the project so far have been broad-reaching. For example, we have delivered two workshops (tutorials) to a number of people so as to test the waters (and have more in train), and supported the delivery of a research reading group led and facilitated by our volunteers. We then developed the Lived Experience Educator unit. The unit's learning outcomes were co-designed with an advisory group made up of peers with a background in teaching or curriculum design, academics and a student, and our curriculum was co-developed with a second advisory group made up of the some of the same and some additional peers. The areas covered are: (1) the history of the consumer and family movement and a deeper understanding of the political nature of activism and involvement; (2) an examination of recovery, mental distress and 'madness' from a critically informed perspective; and (3) the application of self-awareness, self-reflection and self-compassion and an introduction to some relevant academic concepts and practices to enable future involvement in teaching within the school. Given the inclusion of critical thinking about power and engagement with the literature on the contestation of language in mental health, many would agree that the content resonates with some of the material within the emerging discipline of mad studies. The term 'mad' uses reclaimed language to politicise the knowledge and power imbalances within mental health and psychiatry and also links people to the consumer (or mad) movement and history of oppression. Mad studies is an emerging, interdisciplinary field, mainly in the social sciences and humanities, that expresses a radical new voice in academe about madness' (Gillis, 2015).

## 5: Values and experiences in implementing peer work

The Lived Experience Educator unit has been delivered twice over two years. It currently is made up of fourteen three-and-a-half-hour workshops run over a semester plus about ten hours of non-contact hours to do the weekly readings, challenge questions, reflective practice and three assessments. It runs at the intensity of a third- or fourth-year unit and is offered to people with a lived experience of mental health recovery (both individuals and carers and family members who identify as such) who have had some experience with study before and who have an interest in educating professionals. We have had sixteen people complete and now have a pool of eighteen people, both graduates and former advisory group members, who are eligible to be involved in the various Valuing Lived Experience academic projects.

Whilst the Lived Experience Educator unit is useful for peer lived experience educators' involvement within academia, there have been a number of recommendations for its application to peer work generally, particularly as we are able to draw on powerful writings such as Brosnan (2012). We have found that by advancing people's knowledge of the difference between two distinct models of participation, the 'consumerist'' and 'democratic' models (Brosnan draws on Peter Beresford's work here in naming these different models), it can be a powerful tool in reducing self-stigma and institutionalised oppression. In addition, we find that by enabling people to access current and contemporary literature about mental health, recovery and critical thinking about notions of illness and distress that indeed 'knowledge is power'. For many people, getting access to the critical literature which signals the lack of evidence for things like the 'chemical imbalance' theory and discovering that the evidence for the construct of 'schizophrenia' is heavily contested is very empowering. At the same time the resulting paradigm shifts in knowledge and identity can be troubling and unsettling, so our attention to self-compassion, journaling and self-care is essential.

So far a number of Lived Experience Educator unit graduates have joined our academics in a range of projects. They have thus far marked over 300 student assessments, co-marked numerous student in vivo presentations, undertaken targeted guest lectures and contributed to curriculum development of a unit (with another in the pipeline). Our lived experience educators are seen as an extremely valuable asset to our School, and the project has been highly praised by both occupational therapy and social work curriculum visiting accreditation boards. Last semester we were able to bring both Lived Experience Educator students and volunteer peer tutors on as university associates, which afforded them library access and swipe card 'keys', which goes some way toward minimising some power inequalities. Even though the project is still in its infancy in many ways, we have new ideas emerging each year (too many to mention here). Additionally we are researching as we go. It is our hope (and plan) to continue to open the doors of the academy to peers with diverse lived experience in the future, and to keep growing from strength to strength.

To conclude, I have shared some snippets of projects and initiatives which have contributed to the peer workforce landscape in Western Australia. There are likely many more stories that could be told here, but due to word constraints I have had to select only a few. Nevertheless, this snapshot demonstrates the power of people with mental health recovery lived experience and their incredible capacity and resilience to forge a place in history. For some the journey was started long ago and for others it is new and exciting. It is true to say there are growing pockets where peer involvement is happening and happening well; however, there are still many places without peers, so we aren't finished yet! It must be acknowledged that the journey to date has not been without pain. Along the way some of us experienced oppression, stigma, ignorance and institutional power at its inanest and bureaucratic as well as, at times, verbal abuse, incivility and the acting-out behaviours of our peers (sometimes called horizontal or lateral violence). However, the Pollyanna part of me believes the tide has turned. Now that compassion and self-compassion have entered the language (and hopefully practice), people are starting to think differently about ways of relating. There is recognition, based on the many voices of lived experience, that the medical model as a first and only line of response is flawed and that things like co-production and co-design can be very useful methodologies for creating new approaches or ways of being and doing mental health. Certainly, I have witnessed change occurring often, and with it new life for peer work continues to germinate and grow. I believe we can go from strength to strength as long as we keep learning from each other and keep relating to each other with compassion. As for me, I have never felt so authentic as when I came out as 'mad' and I am thrilled to be a part of this movement (whatever we call it) with others as we all work toward a more humane, compassionate and accepting society. I deeply thank my fellow peers and, too, my supporting allies, from whom I have had the privilege of learning much. Together we can and do make a difference, I reckon!

## References

Ambrosius, B., Mahboub, L., Powell L., & Sawer, H. (2005). *Consumer consultant trial recommendations report: A review of South Metropolitan Area Mental Health Services—A consumer perspective June 2004 – June 2005.* Health Consumer's Council, Perth, WA.

Brosnan, L. (2012). Power and participation: An examination of the dynamics of mental health service-user involvement in Ireland. *Studies in Social Justice, 6*(1), 45–66.

Buhagiar, J. (2013). *Psychiatric survivors and narratives of activism.* (Professional doctorate thesis). University of East London. Retrieved from http://roar.uel.ac.uk/3479/)

Coghlan, R., Lawrence, D., Holman, C. D. J., & Jablensky, A. V. (2001). *Duty to care: Physical illness in people with mental illness.* Perth, WA: University of Western Australia.

Coleman, R. (2011). *Recovery: An alien concept?* Isle of Lewis, Scotland: P & P Press.

Deakin Human Services Australia. (1999). *Learning together: Education and training partnerships in mental health.* Canberra: Department of Health and Aged Care.

Department of Health and Ageing. (2013). *A national framework for recovery-oriented mental health services: Policy and theory.* Canberra: Australian Government. Retrieved from http://www.health.gov.au/internet/main/publishing.nsf/Content/mental-pubs-n-recovfra

Dorozenko, K., Ridley, S., Martin, R., & Mahboub, L. (2016). A journey of embedding mental health lived experience in social work education. *Social Work Education, 35*(8), 905–917.

Gillis, A. (3 November 2015). The rise of mad studies: A new academic discipline challenges our ideas of what it means to be 'sane'. *University Affairs* (Canada). Retrieved from https://www.universityaffairs.ca/features/feature-article/mad-studies/

HealthRight Project Overview (2009). HealthRight provide community and health services committed to improving the physical health of people with mental illness. Perth, WA: School of Psychiatry and Clinical Neurosciences, University of Western Australia. Retrieved from http://www.psychiatry.uwa.edu.au/research/community-culture/healthright

Kemp, V., Fisher, C., Lawn, S., Battersby, M., & Isaac, M. (2014). Small steps: Barriers and facilitators to physical health self-management by people living with mental illness. *International Journal of Mental Health Promotion, 16*(4), 216–230.

Kemp, V., Bates, A., & Mohan, I. M. (2008). Mental health consumers as peer supporters in Western Australia. *Health Issues, 96,* 23–27.

Rapley, M., Moncrieff, J., & Dillon, J. (Eds.). (2011). *De-medicalizing misery: Psychiatry, psychology and the human condition.* Basingstoke, Hants.: Palgrave Macmillan.

Slade, M. (2009). *Personal recovery and mental illness: A guide for mental health professionals.* Cambridge: Cambridge University Press.

Slay, J., & Stephens, L. (2013). *Co-production in mental health: A literature review.* London: New Economics Foundation. Retrieved from http://b.3cdn.net/nefoundation/ca0975b7cd88125c3e_ywm6bp3l1.pdf

Verco, J., & Russell, S. (2009). Power to our journeys: Re-membering Michael. *Australian and New Zealand Journal of Family Therapy, 30*(2), 81–89.

Wadsworth, Y., & Epstein, M. (2001). *The essential U&I: A one-volume presentation of the findings of a lengthy grounded study of whole systems change towards staff-consumer collaboration for enhancing mental health services.* Melbourne: VicHealth.

# Section 6

# Specialised developments in peer work

# How a collective consumer and carer voice shaped a national qualification for mental health peer work: the Certificate IV in Mental Health Peer Work

*Michael Burge*

*Michael Burge OAM has been advocating for consumers and carers for over twenty-three years. He is a World Federation for Mental Health (WFMH) board member and vice president Oceania Region. He has written this paper to highlight what a ground-breaking advancement the Certificate IV in Mental Health Peer Work will prove to be with regard to increasing the credibility and profile of peer workers across Australia.*

### Introduction

It is predicted that in Australia the peer workforce will be one of the largest 'go to' workforces in mental health, potentially spreading across most of the human service landscape over the next decade. It is anticipated that it will expand even further when the National Disability Insurance Scheme is fully implemented. Peer work is a relatively new approach to service delivery for many organisations here in Australia. Despite its exponential growth in the past decade, it is not possible to say with any real precision how many peer workers are currently employed in Australian mental health services. However, there is evidence that the workforce is growing, with many workforce development initiatives being undertaken across public, private and non-government sectors (Keyes & Burge, 2014).

Many people with a lived experience of mental health issues consistently state 'I don't think I would be here today if I was not able to reach out and speak with a peer worker when I needed to.' It is imperative that we not only promote peer work as a professional role, but look after and preserve the integrity and values of the peer workforce, because in their role they provide support and encouragement to vulnerable peers, inculcating hopefulness, coaching wellness habits, mentoring to ensure suicide prevention and much more.

If given the right training, support and opportunities the peer workers will uniquely provide valuable resource for framing a recovery focus in supports

## 6: Specialised developments in peer work

and services. The Certificate IV in Mental Health Peer Work will provide a valuable tool to enable peer workers to have their competencies recognised and be properly utilised in roles that are consistent with the values, principles and practice of peer work.

Mental health peer workers, irrespective of their position title, are people employed to work specifically from the perspective of personal lived experience of mental health difficulties, who have assimilated their experience of recovery from mental health issues and who have accessed mental health support services. In some places people employed to work specifically from their lived experience of supporting family or friends with mental health issues are seen as carer or family peer support workers.

This chapter will outline the history and development of a nationally consistent qualification in mental health peer work in Australia—the Certificate IV in Mental Health Peer Work.

> 'What I love, is that no one organisation owns this. This is a collaborative qualification that came from shared knowledge and cooperation, we can all be proud of it.' As reflected by a reference group member (Keyes & Burge, 2014)

### History

Consumers and carers have been active in advocating for the creation of a peer workforce for many years. The mental health peer workforce hasn't just emerged overnight. There is a long and valued history of mental health consumers providing informal support to their peers (other consumers). The value of self-help support groups, social and friendship groups, telephone support trees, and consumers connecting with each other individually on an informal basis, whether in hospital or living in the community, has existed for well over fifty years. However, the acknowledgement and recognition of its value and important contribution to holistic mental health service delivery have occurred only relatively recently in Australia.

The first formal dedicated recruitment of people in Australia with personal lived experience in mental health support roles (that specified lived experience as a criterion of appointment) took place back in late 1992 at Rozelle Hospital when Helen Blum was appointed as the first Australian paid peer 'consumer consultant'. She began work in early 1993 and following that, several others were recruited—and thus began the peer workforce in Australia. From 1993 to 1996 in Victoria, moves were afoot to begin employment of people who lived with mental health issues to evaluate the quality of consumer participation in mental health. Their report 'Understanding and Involvement' (Wadsworth & Epstein, 1996) was a landmark in peer literature in Australia. These were not the only peer initiatives that were happening at this time, but they were the ones from which the elements of what we now call peer work were derived. It is important that we acknowledge the history and contribution of the many consumers and carers in Australia (far too many to mention) who advocated for and worked tirelessly over the years towards shaping the peer voice and the peer role in its many guises, thus leading to the development of the national qualification for mental health peer work.

The past two decades have seen the introduction of various types of peer-led programs in mental health service provision across Australia. When peer work initiatives are being proposed it can be confusing for everyone to have a shared understanding of exactly what is being discussed. Peer work is a service delivered by people with a lived experience. Peer work and peer-operated services are planned, operated and managed by people with a personal lived experience of a mental health issue with the appropriate level of training and/or education. Regrettably peer work isn't always done by those with appropriate training and education. For the purposes of this chapter, 'peer work' and 'peer-operated services' refer to services that are planned, operated, managed and delivered by people with a lived experience of mental health issues who have an appropriate level of training, education and/or experience.

Many lived experience leaders across Australia have been involved in the historical development of the Certificate IV in Mental Health Peer Work from the early draft competencies in 2007 through to the rollout of the qualification. It is not feasible to acknowledge all of them individually, but their input has been invaluable. Janet Meagher AM and I are two consumer leaders who deserve special mention as we have been passionately involved since the beginning of this journey. In 2007, as part of the former Australian Mental Health Consumer Network, Janet chaired a committee, supported by me, to work on establishing nationally recognised values, ethics and competencies for peer work. We recognised that we had been waiting a long time for an

6: Specialised developments in peer work

opportunity for peer workers to gain formal recognition of their skills, values and knowledge (Burge, 2016).

Through the intervening years these needs were met by some Australian organisations developing their own peer worker training or utilising packaged peer worker or peer support training from overseas. Much of the training for peer workers occurred in-house or was outsourced to registered training organisations or other providers, for example Janet Meagher and Desley Casey's 'How to be a peer worker' course, run in Toowoomba, Queensland, in 2011.

**A national qualification for peer work**

Over the years it became more difficult to get consumers and carers involved in the development of the Certificate IV in Mental Health Peer Work. People now expected remuneration for their professional expertise, but this was not available. Many within the movement understood why people were reluctant to participate without being appropriately reimbursed for their time and expertise, but the sheer significance of this project made a few feel that consumer and carer participation was imperative. Consequently, Janet, Jenny Burger and I decided to volunteer to participate to develop the curriculum and the units of competency in 2010.

In 2010 the NSW Mental Health Coordinating Council (MHCC), the peak body for community mental health organisations in NSW, lobbied for the development of a Certificate IV in Mental Health Peer Work to the Mental Health Peer Workforce Competency Development Project of the Community Services and Health Industry Skills Council. As a result, the Skills Council consulted nationally and formed a project reference group to develop the units of competence.

This group included Janet, Jenny and me. The Mental Health Coordinating Council funded the project with the aim of understanding the role of this workforce and to support development of the competencies. This project aimed to develop the curriculum for the Certificate IV in Mental Health Peer Work.

In 2010, the National Mental Health Consumer and Carer Forum released a position statement that outlined recommendations for supporting and developing the mental health consumer- and carer-identified workforce as a strategic approach to recovery. They called on Australian governments to urgently address the needs of consumer and carer workers by developing a National Mental Health Consumer and Carer Identified Workforce Development Strategy. There were policy drivers in relation to promoting the mental health peer workforce which included the Fourth National Mental Health Plan, the National Mental Health Commission Report Cards (2012, 2013), and the National Health Workforce Innovation and Reform Strategic Framework (Health Workforce Australia, 2011).

By 2012 a nationally accredited qualification, Certificate IV in Mental Health Peer Work, was completed.

In September 2015, Craze Lateral Solutions were commissioned by the NSW Mental Health Commission to produce *Grow well: A guide for the sound development of mental health peer workforces across NSW*. This recognised the growing role of peer work, its value in mental health service provision and the need for best practice around training and in the development of formal qualifications.

The development process involved a rigorous process with input from technical and advisory groups including peer workers and people with a lived experience.

The six core units that the Certificate IV in Mental Health Peer Work covers are:
- Applying peer work practices in the mental health sector
- Contributing to continuous improvement of mental health services
- Applying lived experience in mental health peer work
- Working effectively in trauma-informed care
- Promoting and facilitating self-advocacy
- Contributing to work health and safety processes.

A further nine elective units were developed.

Additionally, to complement peer workforce development directions, two additional nationally recognised skill sets have been developed for peer leadership and peer management. The peer leadership skill set provides an

## 6: Specialised developments in peer work

early career pathway for peer workers who have completed the Certificate IV; the peer management skill set is intended for line managers of peer workers (both peer and non-peer) (Mental Health Coordinating Council, 2013–2015).

The original version of the Certificate IV in Mental Health Peer Work (CHC492912) was released in 2012 and was superseded by a second version (CHC43515) in 2015. Both require the completion of a total of fifteen units.

Like all nationally recognised training in Australia, the Certificate IV in Mental Health Peer Work will undergo regular review and update.

For a full copy of the latest version of the mental health peer workforce qualification, download it from the National Mental Health Commission website (http://www.mentalhealthcommission.gov.au/peerwork) or the Australian Government's training website (www.training.gov.au at https://training.gov.au/Training/Details/CHC43515).

I believe that it is absolutely crucial that clinicians and other mental health practitioners embrace the amazing opportunities that peer work offers. I also believe that it must be supported by governments that are willing to assist with appropriate training and qualification, and then funded to ensure that peer workers are able to work their magic in the many areas where they can contribute a real value in terms of the mental health sector—particularly the non-government sector, but also in areas like emergency departments of hospitals and as bridges between clinicians and clients (Craze Lateral Solutions, 2015).

If you are a consumer or carer peer worker employed by government, private or community-managed mental health services, you can now convert your knowledge and experience into a nationally recognised qualification.

### The impact of training for the workforce

The positive outcomes the Certificate IV in Mental Health Peer Work fosters and what this will achieve for the peer workforce:
- Consistent delivery—minimising inconsistencies that may arise with different registered training organisations implementing the training
- Validating the lived experience of consumers and carers
- Raising the standard of the peer workforce

- Increasing staff confidence with competency levels of peer workers.
- Reinforcing and raising awareness with service providers that peer workers complement the crucial role of mental health professionals in their teams
- Influencing a culture of hope for recovery
- Resources for life that will be utilised for ongoing mentoring, personal development, supervisors and organisations. that can be utilised to provide structure, scheduled activities that promote socialisation, recovery, self-advocacy, development of natural supports etc.

**Who is this training for?**

This qualification is specific to workers with lived experience of 'mental illness', as either a consumer or carer, currently working in roles supporting other consumers or carers.

The development of the Certificate IV was targeted with the intention of training people who met the following experience criteria:
- lived experience of 'mental illness' as a consumer or carer
- employment in the mental health sector in government, private or community-managed services
- working in a role that supports consumer or carer peers.

The National Carer and Consumer Peer Work Qualification Reference Group recommended that those people who were about to commence work in a peer support position would also be suitable for the qualification and in some cases, to ensure readiness, other courses may be undertaken prior to commencing (Keyes & Burge, 2014).

The experience of training providers since the qualification began to be offered in 2016 is that the above criteria were limiting the growth of the workforce, particularly as people are keen to commence study as a pathway to entering a peer position. Some organisations have also chosen to require peer workers to have already commenced enrolment or completed training to be eligible to apply for advertised peer positions. This has led training providers to revise their approach and seen some engage in work placement and scholarship initiatives (Keyes & Burge, 2014).

## 6: Specialised developments in peer work

**How is training delivered?**

Trainers need to have:
- experience in working as peer workers
- trainer and assessor training (hold current Certificate IV in Training and Evaluation)
- completed the Certificate IV in Mental Health Peer Work

Specific peer work units are to be delivered by people with lived experience as a consumer or carer.

**How to enrol**
- Find a registered training organisation that offers the qualification.
- To find an organisation that offers the qualification in your area, go to www.training.gov.au
- Different RTOs will deliver the training in different ways, so contact them directly for details.

**National Mental Health Commission principles and requirements**

In 2014 the Commission developed a number of principles and requirements to underpin the development of the peer workforce in Australia:

- A peer worker has acknowledged lived experience of mental health issues and recovery.
- Peer workers should be respected and regarded as an essential part of the support team with equal status to their team colleagues. They should not be an add-on or a time or cost saver.
- Peer workers should be remunerated appropriately at a level commensurate with their skills and training— a good and willing volunteer is just that, not a peer worker.
- Peer workers are adequately supported and sustained in the role with quality ongoing training and supervision.
- The peer workforce should be supported by national competencies and standards.
- The peer workforce should have a career trajectory.

## Development of Certificate IV learning resources

In 2013 the National Mental Health Commission funded Community Mental Health Australia to coordinate the production of national development and training materials, resources to assist the uptake of the new Certificate IV in Mental Health Peer Work qualification across the sector. They subcontracted the New South Wales Mental Health Coordinating Council to develop the resources. A small number of pilot projects were undertaken testing the new qualification, and the training resources were developed and tested based on understandings gleaned from this. This project was led by a national network of peer work expertise and a process driven by peer values (Keyes & Burge, 2014).

## A co-design approach

The project was shaped by a collective voice of consumer, carer and service representatives across public, private and community sectors. Three different reference groups contributed to ensure a high-quality and collaborative process (Keyes & Burge, 2014).

The National Management Steering Committee (six members) guided the overall project and endorsed final versions of all resources. The National Technical Reference Group (eight members) contributed subject matter expertise in peer work and in developing accredited training. The National Carer and Consumer Peer Work Qualification Reference Group (twenty-two members) made recommendations on major content areas, key messages, delivery strategy, assessment strategies, duration. They always started with— what does the peer workforce need to know?

- The resources developed included: resource books, training books, PowerPoint slides, training plans, practice logs and handouts around the original core units of:
- Foundations of mental health peer work,
- Working effectively in trauma-informed care
- Supporting wellbeing and physical health
- Promoting and facilitating self-advocacy
- Working with carers.

6: Specialised developments in peer work

These resources are available for download at no cost to registered training organisations via the Mental Health Coordinating Council (www.mhcc.org.au) and the National Mental Health Commission (www.mentalhealthcommission.gov.au).

As mentioned earlier, in 2015 the course underwent a review with changes to the core and elective units. Although the resources on the National Mental Health Commission website have not been updated for the newer (CHC43515) version of the qualification, organisations delivering the course need to update them to meet the requirements of those units. (See http://www.mentalhealthcommission.gov.au/our-work/mental-health-peer-work-development-and-promotion.aspx)

**Consumers and carers train together**

There was agreement that units in each stream were important for both consumers and carers, for example 'Supporting self-directed physical health and wellbeing' and 'Working with carers'. These have been written to apply to both consumer and carer peer work. The 'work effectively' units have assessment tasks that can be answered from either perspective. Training together leads to new ways of thinking and increases the understanding of the other role and finding ways to work collaboratively to support either the consumer or carer journey.

**Project and resources**

We were fortunate to have twenty-five highly expert and absolutely committed people across the country who worked incredibly hard to ensure the resources would propel the peer workforce forward. The group enabled an environment to be created based on the core values that define peer work, a reciprocal exchange based on respect, valuing of lived experience, sharing responsibilities and mutually agreeing. This was distilled into a high-quality resource for the future of peer work (Keyes & Burge, 2014).

## The significance for peer workers

It cannot be over-stated what this means to peer workers, consumers and carers to finally have a nationally consistent qualification and training resources that have been co-designed from the ground up. The following are some sentiments from the National Carer and Consumer Peer Work Qualification Reference Group who researched, wrote, reviewed, shaped and endorsed the training material:

> 'The most exciting and ground-breaking advancement for the Australian peer workforce in decades!'

> 'This is a watershed project and one of the most exciting, ground-breaking advancements for peer work in decades. These resources are world class and will assist in increasing the credibility and profile of peer workers across Australia.' (Michael Burge)

> 'I believe that this is the resource that is going to support the emergent peer workforce [to] take its place as a recognised, valued and integral part of mental health services in Australia.' (Eschleigh Balzamo, Brook RED, 2015)

## Peer worker roles

Peer workers are providing support for people who may be experiencing mental health crises and are walking alongside people who do not wish to, or are unable to, engage with mental health services upon discharge from emergency departments or from hospital. Whilst not completely peer-run, many organisations offer services that are staffed by significant numbers of peer workers, and which provide step-up, step-down services and other alternatives to hospitalisation. They also provide peer support during hospitalisation and upon discharge and transition into community living.

The Certificate IV in Mental Health Peer Work is a national qualification relevant to a wide range of positions or occupational titles with workers who have a lived experience of mental health problems, as either a consumer or a carer, and who work in mental health service roles that support consumer or carer peers (www.training.gov.au) (Keyes & Burge, 2014). Position titles include consumer consultant, consumer representative, peer support worker, peer mentor, youth peer worker, carer consultant, carer representative, Aboriginal peer worker, participation coordinator and family advocate.

## Benefits of the peer workforce

The limited quantitative and qualitative evidence available suggests that the peer workforce can be as effective as the professional mental health workforce in some roles, and may offer benefits to consumers, carers, peer workers and service providers (Health Workforce Australia, 2014a).

As one consumer said to me once, 'it was like having someone who you can talk to who can really show genuine empathy and understanding with what you are going through'. He was hearing voices, on the disability support pension, and he said to me that he felt like he would never own a television, a car or a house. Now he has a colour television and a car, and has been offered a loan for an apartment. He said talking with a peer worker changed his life … he will always be grateful.

## Benefits for individual peer workers

Following a comprehensive review of the research and literature, the National Mental Health Commission identified the following list of benefits for people using mental health services when peer workers are employed:
- more time and engagement with the community
- better engagement with treatment
- greater satisfaction with life
- greater quality of life
- greater hope and increased resilience
- better decision-making
- fewer problems and needs
- a greater sense and longer periods of wellbeing, including less symptom distress
- reduced use of health services, including hospitals (less inpatient use)
- improvements in meaningful activities and practical outcomes, e.g. employment, housing and finances
- increased sense of self-efficacy, self-esteem and self-confidence
- increased quality and number of relationships, self-support, social networks and functioning
- increased ability to cope with stress

- increased ability to communicate with mainstream providers
- stable housing
- increased motivation to implement life changes (National Mental Health Commission, 2015, pp. 62–63).

**Peer work value recognised**

Service managers have indicated that peer workers are a highly valued asset, and some services are seeking to expand the number of peer workers employed. An increasing number of managers are experiencing positive outcomes for people using their services—for carers and families, for services and systems, for other workers, and for peer workers themselves. However, it should be noted that the uptake of peer workers is still slow in many areas (Keyes & Burge, 2014).

> Peers can provide many types of services, but peer work is not so much defined by what is done but by *who* does it and *how* it is done. The '*who*' must be people with lived experience of mental distress or addiction and recovery. The '*how*' is guided by peer values. All peer workforce roles are defined and underpinned by values intrinsic to the mental health consumer rights, self-help and recovery movements spanning mental health and/or addiction (Te Pou, 2017).

Statements of mental health peer work values from around the world traverse similar ground. The values of mutuality and experiential knowledge feature prominently. Values that are frequently identified are reflected in the Scottish Recovery Network; Values Framework for Peer working.

**Workforce challenges and barriers**

We have faced many challenges since the introduction of peer work into Australia. The challenges include, but are not limited to the following:
- lack of consistency across industrial and employment agreements; no legal requirement for peer work to be paid work
- no nationally recognised Australian practice standards for peer work
- no national ethics or values framework for peer work
- inconsistency and some unclear roles and responsibilities of peer work
- no agreed nationally accepted definition of a peer worker
- no agreed entry-level role delineation for peer workers

## 6: Specialised developments in peer work

- lack of organisational readiness and awareness of how peer work can add value to service delivery
- vague and uninformed concerns about the capacity of peer workers to contribute, leading to the role being under-utilised and under-appreciated
- uninformed attitudes and expectations regarding the boundaries of peer work requiring a strong educational response
- lack of peer opportunities to express leadership, to access peer supervision and to embark on a structured career pathway
- isolation and a lack of networking and support opportunities among peer workers, particularly in rural and remote areas.

The Certificate IV in Mental Health Peer Work is an important step towards addressing some of these workplace challenges by at least offering a uniform standard of training and education for peer work. Employers can be confident that qualified peer workers have met competencies in relation to using their lived experience effectively in their work, applying peer work practices, contributing to continuous improvement, workplace health and safety, and promoting and facilitating self-advocacy. Having set training standards may potentially also allow for clearer role descriptions and improved recognition of peer workers' skills by other professionals.

### Organisational readiness

The benefits to mental health services of employing peer workers include that there can be a positive change in organisational culture and an improved focus on recovery (Health Workforce Australia, 2014b). However, for the reasons discussed above, it is important for organisations and services wanting to employ peer workers to ensure that they have the right systems and supports in place to support a peer workforce. Potential employers must take the time to ensure that peer roles are clearly defined, well-supported, provided with appropriate mentoring and supervision, remunerated appropriately, and provided with good networking and development opportunities. Ideally there should be a minimum of two peer workers in any team to avoid professional isolation. The Certificate IV in Mental Health Peer Work offers an exciting opportunity to ensure that peer workers have a relevant, current, nationally recognised qualification to assist them to best perform their unique role.

## Workplace supports and reasonable adjustment

Peer workers should have the same access as other workers to industrial protections and benefits such as employee assistance. Jobs in mental health are stressful, and self-care is an important area of focus for all mental health staff. Organisations using peer workers should operate in accordance with human rights, disability and discrimination legislation, including implications for employment and the provision of *reasonable adjustments* for all staff (Health Workforce Australia, 2014b).

## Mentoring and supervision

Professional supervision and supports are important for all staff. They ensure that a work role is delivered successfully, and they address issues that may arise on the job. As for any position, the requirements of the job need to be mastered, and workers need to manage their time and productivity. Similarly, the peer worker should receive professional supervision that concentrates on job skills, performance and support, and not the person's health status, and which establishes expectations of peer workers that are equivalent to the organisation's expectations of other employees (Health Workforce Australia, 2014b).

## Future of peer work

Facilitating and supporting new ways of working, including the greater use of peer workers, is an important task for leaders in human services. Associated with this is the need to provide others with the knowledge and skills necessary for change, to provide an environment where change happens, and to acknowledge and address the risks of change.

Strong leadership is needed to overcome barriers to the expansion of the peer workforce and to support organisational change. We need to continue to develop leadership capacity at all levels to support and lead the mental health peer workforce innovation and reform. Recognition of, and support for, peer leaders promotes people-centred services and system improvements in mental health and across other human services areas of growth. Peer advice, experience and expertise can contribute to better policies, services and programs with an enhanced recovery orientation as well as improved service outcomes.

## 6: Specialised developments in peer work

Though peer work as a disruptive technology is growing, resistance remains. Some literature mentions that staff and clinicians without a mental illness could feel threatened by the influx of newcomers whose experience with mental health issues is considered an asset (Health Workforce Australia, 2014a). Traditional staff could also worry about being replaced or seen as less effective because of the presence of peer workers. The focus needs to be on complementing rather than taking away from the crucial role of other professionals.

The peer role functions primarily at the individual level. Peer workers do not replace the role of professional services that are crucial for promoting and maintaining positive mental health. Peer work is an additional, unique service that can provide important listening and expert information-sharing services, advocacy, resource identification, linkages and especially providing an avenue for improvement of social skills.

It has been found, for instance, that some people who have been alienated from or who have perceived negative experiences towards their service may re-engage through initial contact with the peer worker. This role primarily provides low-impact advice about living with mental health issues, which can help ease the way for a person to re-engage with services. These days people are demanding more peer initiatives and with very good reasons: relevance, cost effectiveness, identification of gaps in services and better outcomes. Consumers, their families and support people see that much more is possible.

Peer work creates a culture of healing. As people practise new ways of 'being' through even the most difficult times, possibilities for breaking old patterns and creating new opportunities are endless.

### Conclusion

The possibilities for peer work in Australia are endless, but we need more dynamic and visionary organisations backing what we do to achieve what we are capable of. Policies related to recovery focus and frameworks need to be about more than just a change in language or jargon. Their goal should be for a fundamental shift to occur in the way all of us think and in what we do regarding mental health supports and about the genuine potential for recovery for every person who uses our services.

There are many positive outcomes to be achieved through the utilisation of peer workers, having a recovery focus, and enabling self-directed care. But the most important one is that we genuinely believe that recovery is possible for all who use our service.

Hope is an essential element of wellness. If we have no hope, we find many areas of life challenging. Many of us have experienced times when we did not have hope and a special person in our life held that hope for us. When we have hope the sky's the limit. We can see endless possibilities that await us and we know that whatever happens, we will continue to recover.

Peer workers are uniquely placed to help foster the essential elements of hope and connection that so many people living with mental health issues struggle to hold onto. However, it is essential that those working in this rapidly evolving field are provided with appropriate training, education, professional development, mentoring and supervision. Otherwise we are just setting them up to fail, and risk doing harm to those they are trying to support. The Certificate IV in Mental Health Peer Work offers us the opportunity to have a formal, nationally recognised qualification, developed in consultation with consumers and carers, which can meet the training and educational needs of peer workers. It can also help with the recognition of peer work as a discrete profession in its own right.

When you provide hope, you help people to move forward. The grass is greener, the sky is brighter and music sounds better. Who better to provide such hope than someone who has lived experience of recovery—an appropriately qualified mental health peer worker?

## References

Burge, M. (October 2016). Valuing the lived experience. Presentation at Recovered Futures, 12th Biennial Asia Pacific International Mental Health Conference, Brisbane 2016. Abstract retrieved from http://aspacmentalhealth16.com.au/wp-content/uploads/2016/03/ASPAC-Conference-Abstracts-A4-FINAL.pdf

Craze Lateral Solutions. (2015). *Grow well: A guide for the sound development of mental health peer workforces across NSW*. Sydney: Craze Lateral Solutions. Retrieved from http://crazelateralsolutions.com/our-recent-presentations

Health Workforce Australia. (2011). *National health workforce innovation and reform strategic framework for action 2011–2015*. Adelaide, SA: Health Workforce Australia.

## 6: Specialised developments in peer work

Health Workforce Australia. (2014a). Mental health peer workforce literature scan. Adelaide, SA: HWA. Retrieved from https://www.hwa.gov.au/sites/default/files/HWA_Mental%20health%20Peer%20Workforce%20Literature%20scan_LR.pdf

Health Workforce Australia (HWA). (2014b). Mental health peer workforce study. Adelaide, SA: HWA. Retrieved from https://www.hwa.gov.au/sites/default/files/HWA_Mental%20health%20Peer%20Workforce%20Study_LR.pdf

Keyes, C., & Burge, M. (2014). A collective consumer and carer voice shapes national qualification for peer work. In Kellehear, K., Lane, A., Cassaniti, M., et al. (Eds.), *What we share makes us strong: Proceedings of the 24th annual TheMHS Conference, Perth, WA*. Retrieved from http://themhsdev.micko.fatbeehive.com/pages/2014-conference-proceedings.html#contents

Mental Health Coordinating Council. (2013–2015). Mental Health Peer Work Qualification Development Project. Canberra: National Mental Health Commission. Retrieved from http://www.mentalhealthcommission.gov.au/peerwork

National Mental Health Commission. (2014). Thirty 'champions' to be selected to help grow the mental health peer workforce. Retrieved from: http://www.mentalhealthcommission.gov.au/media-centre/news/thirty-%E2%80%98champions%E2%80%99-to-be-selected-to-help-grow-the-mental-health-peer-workforce.aspx

National Mental Health Commission. (2015). *Certificate IV mental health peer work: Foundations of peer work, resource book 1.* Canberra: NMHC. Retrieved from http://www.mentalhealthcommission.gov.au/peerwork

St George, L. C., O'Hagan, M., Bradstreet, S., & Burge, M. (2016). The emerging field of peer support within mental health services. In M. Smith & F. A. Jury (Eds.), *Workforce development theory and practice in the mental health sector* (pp. 222–250). Hershey, PA: IGI Global.

Te Pou, Northern Regional Alliance & Midland Health Share Ltd. (2017). *Service user consumer and peer support workforce: A guide for managers and employers*. Wellington, NZ: New Zealand Ministry of Health. Retrieved from https://www.tepou.co.nz/uploads/files/resource-assets/service-user-consumer-and-peer-support-workforce-a-guide-for-managers-and-employers.pdf

Wadsworth, Y., & Epstein, M. (1996). *Understanding and involvement (U&I): Consumer evaluation of acute psychiatric hospital practice: 'A project unfolds'* (Illustrated ed.). Melbourne: Victorian Mental Illness Awareness Council.

# Brook RED

*Eschleigh Balzamo*

*Eschleigh has worked in lived-experience-run organisations in both Canada and Australia. She has been general manager of Brook RED since 2013 and is continually amazed by the wisdom, creativity and kindness that her co-workers bring to their work each day. She is passionate about seeing the lived experience workforce grow in Australia and is honoured to be a part of this incredible movement of people who are changing systems, challenging stigma and innovating with their hearts and heads.*

> 'Clearly, Brook RED had reached a stage where no longer could the guiding hands and minds of the organisation canvass the views of the entire community and moot the consequences of different approaches to every scenario.'

Brook RED is an entirely lived-experience-run organisation operating in Brisbane, Queensland. All of Brook RED's personnel—including its governance committee, management, and operational employees—bring personal lived experiences of recovering from and overcoming mental health concerns or distress and use these experiences actively, intentionally and explicitly in their roles. This chapter has been written to share the Brook RED story.

As happens over time, and, as people come and go in the life of an organisation, some of the details and specifics about Brook RED's history have become blurry and I acknowledge that my recounting of its history may be in some ways not wholly accurate or complete. Accordingly, being unable to provide a full and detailed accounting of the people that shaped Brook RED, I have elected to provide a generalised history of the organisation and focus on particular aspects of the organisation's development, rather than to mention specific individuals. There were, of course, a great many people without whom Brook RED would not be the organisation it is today. Brook RED is grateful for the contributions of these people and recognises that we stand on their shoulders: their efforts have made possible everything that followed them and everything that will be.

## 6: Specialised developments in peer work

**The early years**

Conceptually and rather informally, Brook RED began in the late 1990s with the intention of being an organisation that provided mutual support. At the time, the founding members of what became the Brook RED community may not have had a clear idea of what lived experience work might look like. What was clear was the intention to be an organisation run by and for the lived experience community, and to draw on the unique insight and knowledge that derives only from lived experience.

Though now infrequently used, Brook RED's formal name is the Brook Recovery, Empowerment and Development Centre Inc. The organisation began its life in a small Queenslander-style house located in Brook Street in the Brisbane suburb of Highgate Hill. There, prior to Brook RED's existence as such, existed a satellite vocational rehabilitation program run by occupational therapists and case managers from the Princess Alexandria Hospital. It was these pioneering clinicians who saw the potential for what could be achieved by a group of people with lived experience and laid the foundations for Brook RED to develop into what it is today. These clinicians took notice of the powerful mutual support that the community of people accessing the vocational rehabilitation services were providing to one another, and resolved to advocate for and support this organically occurring peer support to be recognised and empowered to grow. The clinicians supported the community of peers at Brook Street to establish a steering committee and to identify an existing organisation to auspice the group's activities. They also assisted in preparing the application for the new organisation's first funding. This funding allowed the organisation to hire its first employee and to begin operating two days a week—initially in partnership with the Princess Alexandria Hospital staff and gradually more independently.

In 2002, the Brook RED community resolved to formalise its existence as an incorporated association, and accordingly undertook the steps necessary to achieve full independence and to become an entity in itself. For the first few years of its operations, Brook RED undertook to integrate a more purposeful way of working and began to explore how to deliver its services within an overarching framework of peer support. These early efforts carried with them their own challenges and conflict, leaving the members of the organisation with more questions than answers as to how it could successfully deliver services using a peer work approach.

While on one hand these experiences represented something of a false start, they were also very much the catalyst of a serious questioning and consideration of what exactly it was that the Brook RED community wished to achieve. In 2005, some members of the Brook RED community were introduced to Shery Mead and her 'intentional peer support' (IPS) approach, which provided a perspective from which some of the early challenges could be addressed and questions about peer work practices could begin to be answered. Over the next several years, Brook RED worked closely with Shery to develop its peer support practices and to integrate this into every aspect of its operations, with concordant gains in its understanding of, and approach to, peer work. Additional funding streams were entered into, additional employees were engaged, and Brook RED began to operate five days a week.

In 2009, Brook RED undertook to deliver the Consumer Operated Services program established by the Queensland Department of Communities. This program was considerably more robust in terms of both funding and scope than any of Brook RED's previous operations. It included obligations not only to provide centre-based group and individual peer support services during the regular business day, but also to open and manage a four-bedroom, around-the-clock, peer-run residential service, and to establish an after-hours 'warmline' providing telephone support. These operations were commenced at a second site with services delivered in the suburb of Upper Mount Gravatt.

As is often the case when small organisations undertake rapid expansion, this growth presented the Brook RED community with new and unforeseen challenges. It took a significant time for adjustment: Brook RED struggled to regain its footing. To a considerable extent, the way business had been done prior to the growth of the organisation and expansion could not and did not scale effectively. The grassroots community-governed approach that had worked so well when everybody could gather in the lounge room over tea to make decisions was inadequate to support the provision of critical services in an efficient and effective manner. Disagreements over relatively trivial matters, previously decided by collective—such as what exact shade of red to paint a gate—were crippling the organisation. Clearly, Brook RED had reached

## 6: Specialised developments in peer work

a stage where the guiding hands and minds of the organisation could no longer canvass the views of the entire community and moot the consequences of different approaches to every scenario.

These issues led the Brook RED community to again perform some introspective analysis and consider what the organisation should be, and how it should get there. The community was forced to grapple with the realities of (relative) success in unanticipated ways: many members of the community held the idea that the old way, the entirely collaborative way, of running the organisation should persist within and across a rapidly changing environment, regardless of scale; others recognised that the foundations of how the organisation operated and how peer support services were offered needed to change and adapt to balance the competing interests of all stakeholders, with policies developed and processes needing to be instituted and decision-making delegated to individuals. The latter viewpoint represented what became a watershed for Brook RED: moving from a casual and ad hoc service provider where roles and friendships often crossed over, to an establishment of sorts as a going concern with more clearly defined roles. To further complicate matters, in 2012, in the midst of all this confusion and chaos caused by the growth spurt, Brook RED's long-serving general manager sadly and unexpectedly passed away. The organisation was left in turmoil, with additional uncertainties about its future and the community experiencing profound grief.

After several months of uncertainty during which Brook RED questioned its very ability to go on, I was appointed to the role of general manager. It became immediately apparent to me that a number of significant and serious issues had developed within Brook RED. The more concerning of these included issues of basic competency in the provision of services, compliance issues, fiscal uncertainty and potential insolvency, workplace bullying and harassment, and duty-of-care issues that bordered on negligence. Undoubtedly, my appointment as an outsider also represented a significant change and source of uncertainty and concern for many members of the Brook RED community. This was obviously a difficult time for Brook RED, and the next two years saw significant introspection with efforts directed towards working out how to address our issues and determining how to move forward. A number of significant changes were implemented, dramatically altering the form and substance of the organisation, including the renewal of nearly 80% of the employees, with hiring focusing on role competence in addition to values compatibility and fit. One of the biggest changes made was the decision to move away from the intentional peer support approach after it had served as the underpinning of our work for approximately eight years. These changes were polarising and disruptive for members of the Brook RED community at every level: the management, myself included, were accused of abandoning the community's time-honoured and deeply rooted peer work values in favour of a corporatised approach.

### Recent times

Despite the aforementioned difficulties, there were moments during these times that shone brightly. For example, we successfully introduced the Partners in Recovery program, representing a significant departure from commonly held beliefs about peer work's potential and demonstrating the efficacy and utility of lived experience practice in roles beyond the traditional and typical peer support role. This was only made possible through the sheer will of our employees and their unflagging desire and determination to succeed.

When we moved away from the intentional peer support platform as our approach to peer work, we deliberately did not replace it with any other manualised approach to peer work. Instead, we made a conscious decision to enter a sort of practice freefall and shifted our emphasis towards creating a space in which Brook RED and its community could find our own approach to lived experience practice, and not be dependent on any external framework. We made the decision to trust ourselves and each other and to believe that our collective lived experience would provide sufficient guidance. As a community of people with lived experience, we understood that we could not but create a way of working that was based in and driven from our experiences. This 'trust the process' approach left us with limited structure and required that we learn to have confidence in ourselves and each other—neither an easy nor a comfortable process. It forced a reliance on values, intuition, reflection and a willingness to be courageous and to move into relationships without scaffolding. Because this approach is dynamic and derived from the individuals who shape it, it is open to continual reflection and adjustment as we grow, acquire knowledge, are inspired by others, and change.

6: Specialised developments in peer work

Out of all this, what has emerged for us is a shared set of stable values: the watchwords that guide us are connection, self-determination, possibility, bravery, hope, integrity, authenticity and relationships. We ask ourselves in all of our work if we are advancing these values; if the answer is anything other than yes we stop and work our way back home to them. Our values have provided effective and appropriate guidance and serve as the stalwart foundations of our practice.

In 2014, with a renewed confidence in our work and our ability, Brook RED expanded to a third permanent site, opening a centre in the suburb of Beenleigh. This perhaps best exemplified Brook RED's moving beyond its internal focus and into the next stage of its story. Currently, Brook RED employs over forty people. All employment positions with Brook RED are lived-experience-identified, meaning that all members of our team (including administration and management), identify as having a lived experience and a willingness to actively incorporate this characteristic into their roles. As our programs have expanded and we have attracted additional funding sources and consequent responsibilities, the work of our team has expanded to include group and individual support, linking and connecting roles, National Disability Insurance Scheme (NDIS) supports, and suicide prevention services. Brook RED is primarily funded by the Queensland Department of Health, the Australian Government Department of Health, Brisbane South Public Health Network and individuals choosing to work with us to provide them with supports funded by the NDIS.

**Policy development**

Historically, administration has not been a strong point for Brook RED. We made a decision to be audited against the National Standards for Mental Health Services in 2016; this necessitated attention to be paid to policy documents and their attendant consequences. While the desirability of developing policies for best practice had been previously identified a number of times, other squeakier wheels demanded precedence time and time again. While we are the largest completely lived-experience-run organisation in Australia, we have always maintained a relatively compact organisational structure with a heavy focus on providing frontline services. We did not allocate the necessary personnel, let alone the required time, to focus meaningfully on purely administrative tasks. Eventually, drawing on the lessons from our past, we realised that continued growth in the coming years was likely (and desirable) and that committing the resources necessary to develop the proper administrative structures would be highly conducive to smooth operational scaling. We made what was for us a difficult decision and hired a policy and human resources officer. This decision was difficult because it saw priority placed on a back-office function rather than direct services even though we understood that improving frontline service provision remained our paramount interest.

Designing our policies has carried its own challenges, particularly where there is tension or discord between legislative requirements and our firm determination to stay true to our values and lead with lived experience. To address these tensions, we employ a highly consultative approach and revisit our policies as needed until we are comfortable that they support, rather than detract from, our organisational goals and values. While we may never be quite sure we have struck the optimal balance, or whether such a thing is even possible, acknowledging the existence of tensions is itself beneficial to us through its demand for constant reflective practice. As well, the process of reducing abstract ideas to writing has unexpectedly assisted us in assessing and affirming our organisational position for a number of issues. We are particularly satisfied with our research participation policy underscoring our commitment to working with lived experience academics and researchers, and our credentialing policy, which outlines our commitment to supporting our team members in acquiring formal qualifications that might assist them in their lives beyond Brook RED.

## Supervision

We have always approached day-to-day supervision from a structural perspective, intentionally designing our teams to ensure responsiveness to any required support, guidance, coaching or mentorship. While Brook RED provides regular in-house monthly supervision for staff members, issues are immediately addressed wherever possible as they arise: we believe that this practice best promotes resilience and wellbeing. As well, every employee is offered external supervision with a supervisor of their choice for up to fourteen sessions each year. We believe that the supervision relationship is

## 6: Specialised developments in peer work

between the supervisor and supervisee and accordingly is non-reportable. Many members of our staff accessing supervision engage with psychologists, social workers or life coaches; feedback from our team has led to the inclusion of allied practices including speech therapy and exercise physiology in this program, where team members have identified that these supports would assist them in their roles. While we have noticed that there is a dearth of high-quality lived experience practitioners offering supervision, feedback received indicates a strong preference by our employees to engage with such practitioners. The primary purpose of supporting and encouraging our employees to engage in external supervision is to support their wellbeing; an important additional purpose is ensuring that our employees continue to have experiences of seeking support and accessing services themselves, in order to provide perspective into their practice.

**Training and development**

At the time of writing, Brook RED continues to experience considerable and fast-paced growth. The issue of how to effectively recruit, train and maintain a high quality of practice within our workforce is the topic foremost in our minds. Our team has worked tirelessly over the past several years to build a culture based on our values and to ensure that the work we do is outstanding and showcases the valuable contribution of lived experience practice. We challenge ourselves as to whether our norms are scalable. Will we lose the qualities that make us unique, responsive and effective as we grow? While so far we have been able to rely on day-to-day relationships and intimate teams as a means for training and mentoring new employees, we are concerned that significant growth will necessitate the formalisation of processes. Overly prescriptive approaches would risk compromising our culture, creating the risk of rigidity where procedures rather than relationships form the basis of our work. On the other hand, we want to share our work with more people, and sustainability seems best served by growth and diversification.

With an increasing diversity of services delivered, such as suicide prevention in acute settings, we have found the need to engage training for our teams which goes beyond training specifically created or identified as being for peer workers. Our decision as an organisation to be run by and for people with a lived experience was in part born from a belief that mainstream and clinical systems were at times ineffective and occasionally counterproductive and self-serving. Consequently, it has been somewhat confronting to explore and consider the value and benefits of training based in tools and approaches otherwise traditionally in the domain of mainstream and clinical workers. Currently we accept a wide range of tools and approaches, with the overarching condition that they can be used in a manner consistent with our values. For example, our suicide prevention team recently trained in Griffith University's Screening Tool for Assessing Risk of Suicide (STARS); we have decided to implement this assessment as a part of our standard practice. We have commenced a qualitative research project to explore what impacts the tool (which has its foundation in clinical practice and was developed for use by clinicians) has on our practice (or, for that matter, what impact we have on the tool). We will be looking at the outcome of this research to guide us as to whether and how we do or do not integrate other such tools into our work in future.

We have identified the nationally accredited Certificate IV in Mental Health Peer Work as baseline training for all of our employees, and we have made a commitment to supporting all of our staff to achieve this qualification within a year of their commencing employment with us. While the Certificate IV in itself does not replace the need to internally train and mentor our team, it provides a basic common foundation and is usable as a catalyst for thought and discussion about approaches to lived experience practice. To encourage the learning process itself to be structured around peer interactions, small learning circles of four to six people meet regularly to collaboratively work through the learning materials and assessments. This process has also resulted in groups of employees teaching and learning from one another, and provides an opportunity to achieve a desired fidelity and quality of learning experiences. Feedback indicates that this approach offers an opportunity for reflection and promotes shared understanding, which in turn supports consistency in day-to-day practice and also in team relationships.

**Human resources challenges and adaptation**

Brook RED's growth was and is accompanied by a need for staff who not only have skills-based competencies in areas such as service coordination, management and business administration, but who also have the ability to work from their lived experiences. Finding suitable candidates—who are willing and able to actively apply their lived experience to tasks which are historically not associated with lived experience practice, while also demonstrating compatibility with the values of the organisation—can be difficult. Even purely administrative functions are informed by our lived experience and this makes a substantial difference to Brook RED, underpinning and informing all other functions.

Holistically, employing a lived experience workforce demands essentially similar approaches to employing any other workforce: we are people just like anybody else. What is clear is that our lived experience values require and enable us to be thoughtful about the relationships entered into as an organisation; organisation–employee relationships are particularly important. Brook RED takes the view that its employees are, in addition to being part of its team and community, individuals with discrete abilities and goals and not merely generic workers fulfilling a function. Brook RED acknowledges that what is best for the organisation and community is for its employees to care where the organisation will be in the future, whether remaining employed with Brook RED or not. In turn, Brook RED needs to care about where its employees will be in in the future, whether or not their life journeys remain intertwined with ours. We consider that asking employees to bring their lived experience with them is to ask them to share their whole self, and not park part of their personality at the door.

This chosen approach to the employment relationship is not about how an organisation should treat a lived experience workforce, but rather it is about how an organisation should treat any workforce in a decently caring manner. Over time a number of our informal or discretionary practices have made their way into policy. Some of the things we do to foster wellbeing for our team include: offering an additional week of paid annual leave beyond the statutorily required minimum, up to two weeks discretionary paid leave to support people to be able to properly attend to life transitions and crises, the option of taking additional leave of up to eight weeks a year, external supervision, flexible working hours wherever possible, piloting of self-managing teams in some of our projects, a 'wobbly fund' to support employees in exigent circumstances, and making a significant and continued investment in everyone's professional development. Employee retention has been quite high in recent years.

**We are proud of**

It was not so many years ago that we were nearly buckled by our own growth and it has really been in the past couple of years that we have again been able to look at ourselves as an organisation and at the work we do with a sense of pride and achievement. Echoing our individual experiences, our organisational journey has been very much one of recovery. For a period of time, we had lost our path, our purpose, our sense of self, and to a large extent our hope. To be frank, we did not know if we would make it; some days we are still awed to be here. We have had to work hard, to face some uncomfortable realities, and to make some difficult decisions. But in the end, looking at ourselves today, we are proud of what we have become.

Perhaps we are most proud that we do what we do with integrity. The funding and policy environment recently has been rife with invitations for mission drift. Many times, we have made decisions to take a harder approach in order to stay true to our values. While at times an easier path was obvious and made us question our commitments and whether we were making things more challenging than needed, the outcomes have been worth the effort. Overall, we are satisfied that working from our lived experience base makes a real impact and change in our communities.

We consider that as a lived-experience-run organisation, it is our responsibility to push at the boundaries of what lived experience practice is considered capable of; we believe that it is incumbent upon us to do so. We have made deliberate decisions to expand our work into what may be seen as less traditional avenues for a peer workforce. This is in no small part because of our beliefs in the benefits of approaching interactions from our lived experience and the quality of our work has seen funders choose our lived experience approach over others when commissioning. For example, our Partners in Recovery team is a fully lived experience team delivering services for individuals requiring multifaceted support coordination. Our team has been able to deliver the program to a high standard, meeting and exceeding the same key performance indicators as any other team while additionally applying the added value of lived experience practice to their roles. As far as we are aware, it is the only openly identified lived experience Partners in Recovery team in Australia.

In 2017 we began delivering a pilot suicide prevention program in an emergency department of a local hospital and, as part of this, contributing to the evidence base for the role of lived experience practice in suicide prevention through an affiliated research project.

We are pleased with our approach to delivering services in the new NDIS environment, meeting the requirements of the scheme with work that is true to us, is based in lived experience, and refuses to compromise on quality of service or on employee wellbeing. In particular, we are very proud to be delivering a wide range of NDIS supports in addition to the peer support specific line item included in the scheme, and to be approaching what could easily be a transactional model of service in a holistic and relationally based manner.

At the time of writing, we are planning Dialogue 2018, the third Lived Experience Workforce Conference. We began hosting the conference in 2015, in part to raise the profile and credibility of peer work in Queensland and Australia, and also to bring together the collected wisdom of peer workers around the country so that we might all learn from and inspire each other in a collaborative setting. We are grateful to the Queensland Mental Health Commission, Mind Australia, Flourish Australia and Queensland Public Health Networks for their support for the Dialogue 2018 conference.

**Our next steps**

The next few years for Brook RED will almost certainly involve further expansion and diversification. Our approach to growth and change is marked by adaptation and agility, allowing advantage to be taken of emerging opportunities where an appropriate and correct fit is found. It is fair to say that while strategically minded, we are also an intuitive organisation and we rely very much on 'feel' to guide our decision making. We hope to expand our centre-based services, to continue delivering supports to individuals with NDIS packages, and to continue pushing into previously unexplored territory. We have decided that it is vital to retain our ability to have close relationships with everybody we work with: this is expected to naturally bound our growth to what is sustainable within our value system. I am sure there will be a number of challenges facing us in our efforts, the biggest of which might be workforce development. We are looking forward to developing ideas around restructuring and shifting to more autonomous 'business' units because we want local community-based responsiveness, instead of centrally controlled authority; this will require some divestment of responsibility and oversight.

One of our main priorities in the next year is to clearly document our work and our unique approach so that we can share what we have learned and also to support our own fidelity of practice. We have recently begun to focus on providing external training and supervision to support the development and capacity building of other lived experience organisations and teams. A further priority is to partner more closely with lived experience academics and researchers to contribute to the evidence base and understanding of lived experience work.

While doing all of this we would also like to take some time to slow down, breathe and be present with our community.

# Youth peer work: building a strong and supported youth peer workforce

*Nicholas Fava, Bridget O'Bree, Rose Randall, Hamilton Kennedy, Jesse Olsen, Emily Matenson, Sarah Fitzpatrick, Magenta Simmons*

*Nicholas Fava is a policy research assistant and youth participation project officer at Orygen, the National Centre of Excellence in Youth Mental Health. He has focused on supporting partnerships between researchers and young people to improve research outcomes, and has provided support to research in youth participation and youth peer work.*

## Background

Despite more than three-quarters of the onset of mental health issues occurring before the age of twenty-five, young people are unlikely to seek help from mental health professionals (Australian Bureau of Statistics, 2010; Rickwood, Deane, & Wilson, 2007). As young people are more likely to seek support from their peers, the inclusion of youth peer workers in a mental health service may reduce barriers to care (Rickwood et al., 2007).

It is worth noting that there are multiple titles, roles and definitions in peer work. This framework defines peer support as the reciprocal task of mutually sharing support between people who have a shared lived experience. Mental health peer work refers to people with a lived experience of mental health issues who are able and willing to use their lived experience to support others with mental health issues (Chinman et al., 2014). Youth peer workers are involved in activities such as advocacy, connecting people to resources, relationship building, group facilitation, goal setting and building self-esteem, providing spaces to share common experiences and serving as role models in recovery (Jacobson, Trojanowski, & Dewa, 2012). However, a lack of role clarity still exists in the peer work field (Moll et al., 2009). Although youth peer workers are becoming crucial to youth mental health services, there is very little research that focuses on peer workers in youth mental health services. The continued growth of youth peer work programs requires a detailed process for clarification and effective implementation.

## Youth mental health

Young people have unique needs that should be catered for by specialist youth mental health services, focusing on early intervention and recovery. The youth mental health field often engages in collaborative and exploratory processes. Compared to adult services, youth mental health services are designed to be a 'one-stop shop', and do not require young people to have a diagnosis or to be experiencing clinically diagnosed mental health issues. Youth peer workers are more likely to work with people experiencing distress, and less likely than adult peer workers to be working with people who have a mental health diagnosis or a history with the mental health system. Differences between the youth mental health system and the broader mental health system require that youth peer workers have distinct role clarification, processes, values and training, even more so than peer workers working with adults.

## Policy context

The National Mental Health Commission and the Australian Government have expressed support for the peer workforce. This is evidenced by a recommendation in the Commission's national review that advocates for improved supply, productivity and access to mental health nurses and the mental health peer workforce (National Mental Health Commission, 2014). The Fifth National Mental Health and Suicide Prevention Plan dictates that the government will develop guidelines for the peer workforce, and describes peer work as a role that is important to recovery-oriented approaches (Commonwealth of Australia, 2017).

## Youth peer work research

A recent review of youth peer work initiatives in the United States highlighted both the rapid growth of such initiatives and the lack of research in the area (Gopalan et al., 2017). However, one Australian study has evaluated a youth peer work program designed to promote shared decision making at an enhanced primary care (headspace) service in New South Wales (for results, see Simmons et al., 2017a; for an overview of the intervention and implementation, see Simmons et al., 2017b). The Choice Project employed eight youth peer workers to welcome new clients in the waiting room of headspace Gosford. They helped clients to complete the required administrative tasks and promoted and facilitated a shared decision making approach for their initial assessment with the clinician. Using historical comparison data, the evaluation showed that the combined peer work and shared decision making intervention resulted in clients of the service feeling more involved in the assessment with their clinician (Simmons et al., 2017a). This feeling of involvement, along with feeling less confused about what to do, was associated with higher client satisfaction.

Qualitative focus group data from the Choice Project (manuscript in preparation) tracked the experiences of the youth peer workers over time (when they started their roles, then three months and six months later). These data highlighted three main themes over time: a trajectory from fear to hope, as the youth peer workers developed skills and experienced an improvement of personal factors over time; an improved understanding of the purpose and benefits of their role for clients, the mental health service, and their own recovery journey; and an evolving understanding of shared experiences being a primary asset. A separate study used qualitative research interviews to document the expectations, motivations and experiences of twelve youth peer workers from Orygen Youth Health and headspace centres (Allsop, 2017). These data showed that youth peer workers experience many of the same challenges faced by peer workers from adult mental health services, including multiple benefits of engaging in peer work, role confusion, complexities in maintaining appropriate boundaries, and a need for specialised supervision and training. However, the study also highlighted the unique aspects of youth peer work, including the fact that youth peer workers are at a critical developmental stage in terms of career trajectories, a greater emphasis on support from their fellow youth peer workers, and the nature of the activities undertaken in the youth peer work relationship (e.g. less focus on sharing experiences and more focus on enjoyable activities).

### How youth peer work differs from peer work

Youth peer work differs from other peer work in various ways. The following list is adapted from the youth peer work toolkit (Orygen, 2017).

- Having significant gaps between the ages of two people can create unintended power imbalances, which is a dynamic that peer work attempts to avoid.
- Young people know what it's like to be a young person now. What it's like to be a young person changes over time (e.g. across generations).
- Young people are in a rapidly changing developmental stage where they are forming independence and autonomy. They may feel more comfortable talking with someone who isn't of a similar age to those who have authority over them in other settings (e.g. parents, teachers).
- Young people are more likely to have complex ties to family, peers and educational institutions. Other young people can empathise with the relationships experienced in these contexts.
- Sometimes the experience of mental health issues can be different for young people compared with older adults (e.g. irritability in the context of a depressive episode). If an older peer worker experienced mental health issues later in life, then the ways in which these issues manifest themselves may be different from the way they would during adolescence.
- Young people are relatively new to their early experiences of mental health issues and seeking and receiving help from services. This means that they are more likely to have been treated in the same types of services.
- Youth-specific services often have a strong focus on early intervention, which can involve a distinct philosophy about recovery and care. This includes a strong focus on youth participation and the important role that young people play in creating youth-friendly services.
- Youth peer work can be performed in specialised, youth-friendly settings, such as community youth mental health centres, online forums and chatrooms, schools, universities, youth mental health inpatient units and discharge support.
- The goals are different in youth peer work, as they may focus on vocational goals or exploring relationships that are unique to a younger age group.

## Peer work roles

Multiple peer work roles exist within the youth peer work field. Some peer workers will engage in many types of peer work within their role.

6: Specialised developments in peer work

- One-to-one peer workers work directly with service users. They can be employed as specialised peer workers, for example providing vocational support or support for people who use alcohol and other drugs.
- Peer educators share their lived experience with groups of people to deliver psychoeducation or workshops. They may also engage with the media to share their stories and advocate for people with mental health issues.
- Group facilitators work with a group to coordinate longer term recovery programs.
- Case managers may liaise with community organisations, make referrals, prepare individual recovery plans, and focus on social or recreational wellbeing.
- Consumer advocates may be involved in strategic planning, legal advocacy, working with the Mental Health Review Board, or assisting with delivering and addressing complaints.
- Consumer researchers share their lived experience to design, guide, lead or improve research projects.
- Consumer consultants design, support or implement strategic projects.

**Critical components of peer work**

*Shared experiences*
- Peer workers have a lived experience relating to mental health and a willingness to share those experiences to support others.
- Peer workers help each other to move towards what people want, rather than away from what people don't want.

A central task of intentional peer support is to focus on moving towards something, and what we need to do to get there, as opposed to focusing on developing strategies or solutions to problems (Mead, 2014).

*Willingness to work with, and be open to, other worldviews and frameworks*

As peer workers work with people seeking help and within multidisciplinary teams, it is essential that they are open to other people's opinions.

*A stage of recovery*

Peer workers shouldn't be expected to experience no level of mental health issues, but they should be at a stage of recovery that allows them to feel comfortable with sharing experiences and providing hope to the people that they are working with. Some peer workers report that they feel limited by low expectations. Like all staff members, peer workers can be relied upon equally and work within organisational requirements. It is important for organisations to support the wellbeing and mental health of all staff members.

*Emotional intelligence*

Peer workers must understand empathy and emotions independently and interpersonally.

*Hope*

Hope is one known benefit of peer work, as peer workers provide service users with hope for recovery or a better future (Repper & Carter, 2011).

*Goal-setting*

Peer work relationships involve setting and adhering to achievable goals, as directed by the person seeking support.

*Strong interpersonal communication*

Discussion and communication are required in all peer work roles.

*Culturally competent*

All staff should be culturally competent, but peer workers may need to be especially proficient in this area, given the need for strong communication, empathy and relationship building.

*Reflection*

Reflection is critical to improve and examine the peer work relationship.

## 6: Specialised developments in peer work

### Critical components of youth peer work

Although the above list of critical components applies to youth peer workers, additional components apply in the youth mental health setting.

### Age

Peer workers should be similar in age, but 'ageing out' of the role (i.e. becoming older than your peers) can be responded to in a flexible way. One example is that the commencement of contract cut-off is two to three years older than the upper age limit of the service users, with an upfront understanding that they will need to transition from the role at a certain age. (The peer work working group acknowledged that this idea needs further consultation from older youth peer workers, who may have different views on transitioning from the role.) Roles developed specifically for young people are appropriate when the role requires them to be young, when the opportunity promotes equality, and when it is undertaken in good faith.

### Diverse experiences

A range of ages, experiences and diversity should be seen in the peer workforce. There may be large differences between the experiences of a sixteen-year-old and a twenty-five-year-old, who may require different approaches from different peer workers.

### Understanding and being comfortable working with young people

Youth peer workers should be able to build rapport and develop an understanding of the people they are working with, as well as the factors which impact on their wellbeing and a broad range of issues relating to young people.

### Capacity to advocate for young people

Youth peer workers play an important role in advocating for the needs and rights of the young people at their service. It is important that peer workers are supported to develop their advocacy skills, and that organisations see their advocacy as integral to their role.

## Recommendations for including a youth peer workforce

*Design*

Plan and define the role. Peer workers should work in a clearly defined role with a clear job description. Design the program with peer workers. Experienced peer workers should be consulted during the design stage of a peer work program.

*Implementation*

Hire a diverse peer workforce. Youth peer workforces should aim to represent their uniquely diverse population, as well as including culturally and linguistically diverse and sex- and gender-diverse peer workers, because a diverse workforce will better ensure that young people can work with peer workers who share similar experiences to them. Their lived experiences should represent the lived experiences of people in the service's community, such as specific ethnic or immigrant communities or people who have experiences with inpatient settings.

Employ by values, rather than experience. The youth peer workforce should be recruited on the basis of flexible key selection criteria that reflect the demographic features of the service users. Many youth peer workers have a tertiary education, but a tertiary education may not be essential to the role and may not reflect the experience of some young people seeking help.

Youth peer workers should be paid appropriately at the correct award rate, and be provided a task load appropriate for the hours worked. A peer workforce pay rate was negotiated in the Health and Community Services Union Public Mental Health Enterprise Bargaining Agreement (Health and Community Services Union, 2016).

Adopt an organisation-wide approach. It is vital to train all staff on the role and benefits of peer work, as well as having leadership express the value of peer work to set the tone.

Be transparent. Be clear and discuss at the outset what happens when peer workers 'age out' (i.e. become older than the people accessing the service).

## 6: Specialised developments in peer work

*Maintenance*

Recognise the skill set of youth peer workers and respect different approaches. Youth peer workers aren't hired to be therapists or clinicians. They provide a unique skill set to mental health teams. Organisations should recognise that peer workers are team members who can contribute to informing both clinical and strategic decisions.

Provide professional development. There should be a focus on training and supervision, particularly that delivered through experienced peer workers. Training should be provided before the commencement of peer work with young people. Organisations such as Psychiatric Disability Services of Victoria (VICSERV), Wellways and Intentional Peer Support provide training for peer workers. A Certificate IV in Mental Health Peer Work is available as a nationally recognised qualification. Storytelling workshops also provide useful skills that assist youth peer workers to share their lived experience.

Consider how the workforce can grow. As employment for youth peer workers is still at an early stage, some peer workers experience job insecurity. Youth peer workers may reach a point where they are older than the peers they seek to engage with. Youth peer workers should be supported to understand the career pathways available to them, both within and outside peer work. Unclear career progression may result in high turnover for service providers, and a lack of continuity of care for young people.

**Peer work in action**

A group of peer workers developed descriptions of their own experiences in their role, or included examples of people that they have worked with. Names and any other identifying details have been changed.

*Peer work at headspace: Emily Matenson*

I am a youth peer worker employed at headspace Sunshine. headspace Sunshine provides support for young people aged twelve to twenty-five, across a range of areas including general health, mental health and wellbeing, alcohol and other drugs, education, employment and other services. My role is relatively new, and includes community awareness, peer education, in-centre engagement and peer support. Peer support is a developing service at headspace Sunshine, and is still in its early stages. It is intended to be short-term support delivered alongside therapy or other engagement with headspace. It aims to connect young people with peers who might have shared experiences and relate on a non-clinical level.

My role involves working with young people who might be struggling to engage with the service, are in need of additional support, or who require non-clinical support. Most of them are managing challenges, and many feel as if no-one fully understands what they're going through or can relate to their situation. Peer support may involve sharing experiences and modelling recovery with young people to help break down stigma about mental health and help seeking. It might also include skills-based training, and focus on building capacity and confidence in a practical way, such as transport training or conversation practice. It may simply be a warm introduction and orientation to the service so that it seems less daunting. It might involve assistance with study or homework, or simply the chance to connect with another young person when feeling a bit isolated.

For example, I recently saw a young person, Sam, who was struggling with social anxiety and wanted to build social and conversation skills. Sam and I met for several sessions, each focusing on a different aspect of conversational skill building, e.g. beginning conversations, ending conversations and body language. I shared several experiences of also feeling anxious or shy, and we spent time talking and building rapport. Over time, we were able to practise some of these skills outside the centre, e.g. making small talk with staff at the supermarket. Peer support gave Sam an opportunity to build skills in a safe and supportive environment, complementary to Sam's ongoing therapy.

Peer work is different from other roles because it is built on a foundation of mutuality, and requires both parties to be prepared to show vulnerability. It doesn't have the same capacity to provide formal support, risk management, and/or intervention that clinical roles do, but provides support in a different way. Peer support involves a great deal of empathy and the capacity to be vulnerable and genuine. It also requires a strong awareness of boundaries, and capacity to work closely with other sources of support. Sometimes the role can be a bit unclear or blurry, and that can make it challenging for both the young person and the peer worker, but that ambiguity is also a strength in that it allows the role to be tailored and flexible enough to meet the young person's needs.

Providing peer support can be incredibly rewarding, as it allows me to work in a way that validates my experience and aligns with my values. However, it can also be difficult, as it requires a great deal of self-awareness and self-monitoring. Revisiting parts of my life that have been challenging is not always easy, making self-care an important part of peer work practice, in addition to adequate and regular support. I think that most people can benefit from peer support in some form as it helps to break down stigma, and demystifies the process of help seeking, which can be daunting if it is not something you've done before. Peer support is a valuable tool in a therapeutic toolbox, as it can help young people to feel more connected and understood at a time when feelings of isolation and disconnection are common. Given that peer support is still relatively new in this setting, the more we practise and learn about it, the more beneficial it can be.

*Youth peer work in an inpatient unit: Hamilton Kennedy*

John is a young man who required support in the intensive care unit for some time, and he is comfortable with me sharing aspects of his story. I met him during a group activity. He came to me asking lots of questions about why he was here and what was happening to him, as he was very unsure. I told him that I really didn't know either. I informed him about my role as a peer support worker and spoke to him about my lived experience of mental illness. He was immediately comforted in hearing about my story as he was under the assumption that he was the only person who had experienced such a thing. Further, he was comforted to be informed of the inevitability of recovery, however difficult it might be.

We maintained a close relationship on the ward until his discharge. I asked whether he would like some support in his transition to home. John was ambivalent about receiving future support so I said that I would call him in a week to see whether he did.

When I called him, he was pleased to hear me and we arranged to meet later that day. John, being the inquisitive young man he is, was keen to know more about my experience of recovery. I told him that my mental health issues had allowed me to understand myself better. John immediately resonated with this. He spoke about how his voice hearing and intense emotions, which were initially distressing, were a useful insight into his own psychology and spirituality.

John asked about what informed my role as a peer support worker, so I spoke to him about the concept of intentional peer support. Our relationships conveniently followed the path set out by intentional peer support. I spoke about how we had formed a good connection during his inpatient stay, and we then shared our experiences and what had led us to being together at this place in time. I then spoke about mutuality. John immediately understood what this term meant as he had felt a genuine sense of mutual respect and connection between us. He did not have many people in his life who he could share his experiences with, and having me support him as he returned home proved to be a vital source of support.

We set mutual goals together, such as encouraging one another to attend social engagements, speak more with our families and continue to attend appointments to support our mental health. I genuinely feel that John was a good influence on my life, and that I was a good influence on John's. Today, I can see that he is more comfortable in accepting and utilising his own lived experience. Because of this, I believe that he is better able to pursue his own interests and have a more fulfilling life.

*Youth vocational peer work at headspace: Rose Randall*

Dan came to a headspace centre as he had heard from an external clinician that there was a new individual placement support vocational program attached to the headspace site and he would be able to access vocational support. The vocational worker met with Dan and after an initial assessment introduced the idea of meeting with a peer worker as an additional support in his search for work. Dan was interested in this as an option, as chatting to someone of a similar age who had had similar experiences appealed to him, and increasing social confidence and sense of comfort with age mates were an identified goal of Dan's. Dan had always previously been accompanied by a parent in these scenarios, and was uneasy when he didn't have someone to guide his behaviour when dropping off résumés or calling folks on the phone. Dan also experienced difficulties in reading and responding to social cues.

## 6: Specialised developments in peer work

Dan and I met fortnightly, alongside his vocational support, for walks in a local park and home visits (Dan had recently got a puppy so this was especially fun for me). In our conversations with one another, we chatted about our interests and the values that drove these things. One particularly poignant reflection I recall from our conversations was a shared experience of being less in touch with a sense of self and a loss of confidence after periods of being particularly unwell. Dan and I both had found ourselves prone to relying on support and encouragement from loved ones, which we agreed left us less empowered as individuals.

Dan expressed a desire to be more independent now that he was managing his health; I shared what that process had looked like for me when recently coming out of a period of ill health. We explored options for developing a network of friends and made a plan for asserting independence in decision making when carers were present. After our conversations, I also committed to being more assertive in situations I felt nervous about at work. I would sometimes sit in with Dan on his sessions with the vocational worker and the family to ensure that his voice was not lost.

Transport support was provided to Dan so that he was able to start résumé dropping without his vocational worker or carer. In accompanying Dan in doing this, I was able to listen actively to what his experiences were like without a figure of authority present. I was also able to validate that his feelings of anxiety and feeling awkward were not, as he believed, related to the fact that he had experienced mental health issues, but totally normal parts of the job searching process. I shared my similar experiences of cold calling and feeling inadequate, but was able to embody that pushing through that feeling has positive outcomes. Functional recovery happens, even when you don't fully believe it will; reflecting on how I had come through this process with Dan retrospectively has been very affirming. After three outings by ourselves, Dan was feeling exceptionally confident in meeting prospective employers, introducing himself appropriately (including reading facial cues and reflecting) and following up with a phone call.

After I had been working with Dan for around six months, he was successful in securing a role close to home that allowed him to apply transitional skills from previous study, and the role was aligned with his long-term goals. Dan and I are continuing to encourage one another to regain confidence in old interests. For Dan, these are things such as getting out in nature, team sports and drama, and for myself, creative hobbies and socialising. I feel the peer relationship with Dan has strengthened my own sense of holistic health and feel he has grown in a similar way.

*Peer work for all ages: Jesse Olson*

As a peer worker with Neami National, I first began working part-time to co-facilitate a self-development program with another peer worker. This program is a six-session program that explores building strengths, identifying values, goal setting, and exploring alternate pathways to achieving personal goals. It also incorporates strategies on how to increase positivity and optimism through mindfulness, gratitude and exploring support networks. Between the fortnightly sessions, there is also an added component of fortnightly coaching sessions with people using the service.

At the beginning of 2017, I attained a second peer work position, which increased my hours to full-time employment. Although my role remained the same, I also began to maintain a caseload and conduct outreach appointments.

I have a caseload of five people of various ages who I provide fortnightly support to. While they all have experienced different events in their life, with some having experienced trauma and others with a lifelong history of anxiety, depression and/or schizophrenia, most exhibit the same challenges: loss of identity, confusion and feeling lost in life, as though nothing they do fills them with a sense of purpose or meaning.

I find that my approach with people of all ages or backgrounds is largely the same across the board: I state I have a personal experience of depression and anxiety, and will support people through tools such as motivational interviewing and intentional peer support. I assist people using the service to identify their strengths and values, and help them to put these into action through techniques such as goal setting.

I will incorporate my own recovery story if I feel it will benefit people, or if it relates to what the person is currently experiencing. I will also use it to share or identify a learning curve.

6: Specialised developments in peer work

In many instances, I have found that mentioning a personal experience and identifying as someone who is still in recovery has sparked interest in people using the service. Some have been curious and asked me about my experience, others have felt comforted knowing that 'someone gets it'.

## References

Allsop, K. (2017). Exploring the motivations, expectations and experiences of peer workers, family peer workers and peer educators in youth mental health services. Graduate Diploma in Psychology (Advanced) Thesis. Melbourne School of Psychological Sciences, Faculty of Medicine, Dentistry and Health Sciences, University of Melbourne.

Australian Bureau of Statistics. (2010). Mental health of young people 2007 (Catalogue no. 4840.0.55.001). Retrieved from www.abs.gov.au

Chinman, M., George, P., Dougherty, R. H., Daniels, A. S., Ghose, S. S., Swift, A., & Delphin-Rittmon, M. E. (2014). Peer support services for individuals with serious mental illnesses: Assessing the evidence. *Psychiatric Services, 65*(4), 429–441.

Commonwealth of Australia. (2017). The Fifth National Mental Health and Suicide Prevention Plan. Retrieved from http://www.coaghealthcouncil.gov.au/Publications/Reports

Gopalan, G., Lee, S. J., Harris, R., Acri, M. C., & Munson, M. R. (2017). Utilization of peers in services for youth with emotional and behavioural challenges: A scoping review. *Journal of Adolescence, 55*, 88–115.

Health and Community Services Union. (2016). 2016–2020 HACSU public mental health EBA key outcomes: An agreement that benefits us all. Retrieved from: https://hacsu.asn.au/file/17657/8564

Jacobson, N., Trojanowski, L., & Dewa, C. S. (2012). What do peer support workers do? A job description. *BMC Health Services Research, 12*(1), 205.

McGorry, P. D. (2007). The specialist youth mental health model: Strengthening the weakest link in the public mental health system. *Medical Journal of Australia, 187*(7), S53.

Mead, S. (2014). Intentional peer support: an alternative approach. Available from www.intentionalpeersupport.org

Moll, S., Holmes, J., Geronimo, J., & Sherman, D. (2009). Work transitions for peer support providers in traditional mental health programs: Unique challenges and opportunities. *Work, 33*(4), 449-458.

National Mental Health Commission. (2014). *Contributing lives, thriving communities: Report of the national review of mental health programmes and services.* Sydney: NMHC.

Orygen National Centre of Excellence in Youth Mental Health. (2017). Youth peer work toolkit. Retrieved from https://www.orygen.org.au/About/Youth-Engagement/Resources

Repper, J., & Carter, T. (2011). A review of the literature on peer support in mental health services. *Journal of Mental Health, 20*(4), 392–411.

Rickwood, D. J., Deane, F. P., & Wilson, C. J. (2007). When and how do young people seek professional help for mental health problems? *Medical Journal of Australia, 187*(7), S35.

Simmons, M. B., Batchelor, S., Dimopoulos-Bick, T., & Howe, D. (2017a). The Choice Project: Peer workers promoting shared decision making at a youth mental health service. *Psychiatric Services, 68*(8), 764–770.

Simmons, M. B., Coates, D., Batchelor, S., Dimopoulos-Bick, T., & Howe, D. (2017b). The CHOICE Pilot Project: Challenges of implementing a combined peer work and shared decision making program in an early intervention service. *Early Intervention in Psychiatry*. Online 12 December. doi: 10.1111/eip.12527. Abstract available at https://onlinelibrary.wiley.com/doi/abs/10.1111/eip.12527

# Intentional peer support: some notes from a roller-coaster ride in Victoria

Flick Grey

*Flick Grey works as an intentional peer support (IPS) facilitator, IPS operations coordinator in Australia, IPS project worker at the Self Help Addiction Resource Centre (SHARC) and peer support manager at PartnerSPEAK. She also works freelance as a supervisor, trainer, consultant and open dialogue practitioner. She not-so-secretly identifies as a professional over-sharer, unicorn and human who listens deeply to trees, rivers and child parts.*

> IPS is a way of putting into words what it is that peer support workers are doing when we walk alongside people. It offers us a clear framework for staying human together in the face of complexity, and attendant uncertainties.

This chapter began its life as a description of the implementation of intentional peer support (IPS) in the context of the Victorian Department of Health and Human Services' post-discharge project, the Expanding Post-Discharge Support Initiative. Sounds exciting, huh? Despite all these titles and acronyms, this project really has been exciting (not to mention, at times, challenging, confusing, frightening, traumatising, heart-breaking, breathtaking, joyful and wondrous, and that's just some of my emotions!). But my heart couldn't finish *that* chapter—this project has been too complex and too personal and involves too many different voices. I could do justice to neither the project nor myself (nor, for that matter, IPS) by approaching this writing with any pretence of 'objectivity'.

So, I've opted to tell some stories instead, hoping these might do at least some preliminary justice to the immense expansion of IPS here in Victoria, centred around the Victorian Department of Health and Human Services' post-discharge project. My hope is that this article might stimulate some reflections, inviting us to go deeper into some of the inherent uncertainties of being human together in a complex world.

Flick Grey

## What is intentional peer support?

Intentional peer support (IPS) is a framework for thinking about what humans in distress need from other humans, and how we might navigate hard times together, in ways that build towards the lives and worlds that we most value. Or that's how I see it. One of the blessings of being an IPS facilitator is that every time we facilitate a training session, we discover more layers of what IPS is, or could be, through hearing how other humans make sense of it all—a call and response, call and response. With every IPS training session, my own sense-making is broadened, deepened—and sometimes defensively entrenched, but I am getting ahead of myself!

IPS has roots in many traditions. Shery Mead, its founder, was deeply influenced by her engagement with the international consumer/survivor/ex-patient movement. The politics, history and diversity of our collective movement are honoured more in IPS than in any other peer support training I have experienced. Shery was inspired by non-violent communication, and brought in elements of that tradition. She was also trained as a social worker, and there are many threads of social work practice that inform IPS. Shery's also a jazz musician, and to my ears, this is one of the best metaphors for IPS—it's a way of 'making music' together:

> Much like improvisation in music, IPS is a process of experimentation and co-creation, and assumes we play off each other to create ever more interesting and complex ways of understanding (Mead, 2018).

Shery's various experiences led her to co-creating a peer-run crisis respite service, Stepping Stones, in 1993 in the United States. In this crisis-oriented environment, Shery observed that while peer workers were often able to relate to each other as equals much of the time, when things became difficult, peer workers would sometimes (unintentionally) fall back into ways of relating that got in the way of a peer relationship. For example, one person might assume they know better, another might let fear get in the way of having an honest conversation, another might take power because they have a privileged position (so they *can* take power), regardless of the consequences. IPS offers a framework for 'staying peer' when the going gets tough. Mead and Filson describe it like this:

## 6: Specialised developments in peer work

> Intentional Peer Support is a process of relationship that seeks to explore the events in our lives and the stories we create out of them. Through dialogue, new meaning evolves as we compare and contrast how we have come to know what we know. Our shared stories create communities of intentional healing and hope. IPS challenges the notion that people need to leave their communities for specialised treatment. When people share their stories without others imposing meanings on them, this creates social change (Mead & Filson, 2016, p. 109).

IPS frames peer support work within a social change agenda, offering us relational tools to expand the possibilities of sense-making.

### IPS in the Victorian context

I personally first came across IPS in 2009. I was on sickness benefits at the time, taking a break from the pressures of studying at university, and radically uncertain about what I was doing with my life or my time (or indeed whether I even wanted to be alive). I had been offered my first mental illness diagnosis in 2005, and (through my nerdy, voracious research) had come across the work of Merinda Epstein, whose sense-making made sense of my life in a way that mental 'illness' frameworks never had. After I had fan-girled Merinda at a conference, we had become friends and one day she rang me up out of the blue to ask me what I was doing next week. 'Why?' I asked. She told me about some training course the next week, that someone had dropped out at the last minute and asked me if I was interested in coming along. 'What is it?' I asked. 'Just come!' she replied. On the strength of Merinda's personal recommendation, I ended up spending a week in a training room at Mind, in Rosanna, Melbourne, with Shery Mead (founder of IPS), Chris Hansen (director of IPS) and many peer workers. I believe this was the first (or possibly the second) IPS five-day core training course in Victoria. Not long after, I began working alongside Merinda Epstein at Our Consumer Place and as part of my role there was able to attend further IPS training courses—train-the-trainer and advanced training—in Queensland (both in 2012, with Shery Mead and Chris Hansen). These courses were all (I understand now) only possible because of the significant commitment in Queensland to peer-operated services (see later in this chapter).

I confess, I was a convert to IPS from the first day—and I will return to this concept of 'the convert'. I still have all my notes from that very first course, including:

- [Reflecting on the moment I was first diagnosed] That social worker 'translated' my experiences [from my words into medical language] and I'm still un-translating!
- [Finding the word 'shame' to be revelatory] It's darkness and secrecy that cause damage—peer support addresses *shame*.
- [Reflecting on the relationship I had with my partner at the time] Rescuers don't get their needs met, often don't like conflict, want everything to be nice, seen as capable. [Little did I know then that this was to become one of *my* default patterns as a lead IPS trainer, but that comes later in this story.]
- [Reflecting on how shrunken my life had become] When you feel safe, you take risks (when you don't feel safe, you don't take risks).
- [After watching a role play between Shery and Chris] Rather than reacting defensively, Shery was patient, connecting and opening up to hear Chris's experiences, before presenting her own experiences, not defensively, but owning them, without that being predicated on invalidating their experiences.
- [In the module on self-harm and suicidality] Self-harm is a language, a way of communicating 'the unsayable' […] I *learn* to speak suicide—it's how I am taken seriously.
- [On the relationship between consumer workers and service providers] Shery observed that the dialogue with service providers (with perceived power) is the most important conversation for us to have. It's *so* important for us to be able to hear their world view.

These kinds of learnings were *huge* for me. There's one particular exercise in the training where we write our story in medical language, and then try to write it in non-medical language. I was shocked when I realised I had no 'second story', all I had was the story (about my life, and my suffering) that had been told to me by the mental health system. And sitting in that room, with all those incredible people, I realised that I wanted to find words for my second story, *my* story. Years later, I would facilitate IPS training in the United States, in a peer-run respite house called Second Story, knowing in my bones the power of finding second (and third and more) stories, through the kinds of conversations we can have together, as peers.

## IPS in the post-discharge environment

Fast-forward seven years, and I can't possibly do justice to the full complexity of IPS in the post-discharge environment, as my voice is just one among many. I will, however, own that, as lead IPS trainer on this project (alongside Tyneal Hodges, from Queensland), I have had—and continue to have—my own

## 6: Specialised developments in peer work

profound IPS journey, and I hope that my sharing a few threads of this might illustrate some of the bigger picture.

In 2015, the Victorian government funded the Expanding Post-Discharge Support Initiative, in which mental health services employed peer support workers to support people leaving psychiatric hospitals, in part to reduce the twenty-eight-day readmission rates. I confess this sounded like a potentially messy project to my ears—suddenly dramatically increasing a devalued and under-theorised workforce, spreading them sparsely across the state and across the diversity of health services. And (since health is devolved) each health service could create their own version of what they thought peer work should be. Peer workers were being popped into the pointiest end of the mental health system (acute hospitals) and then expected to somehow impact the performance targets (readmission rates) of a complex system. What could possibly go wrong, right? (I hope you can hear the sarcasm!) An initial pilot was conducted and concerns about the many foreseeable risks—of peer workers being clinicalised or harmed in some way—brought many Victorian consumer workers to tears. What was to be done? IPS was offered as one possibility, offering at least some theoretical coherence to the emerging discipline of peer work.

There was a small problem, amid all these much larger problems. I was, at the time, the only IPS facilitator in Victoria, and I was about to move to London to pursue my studies in Open Dialogue. By a complete fluke of circumstances, we had just organised an IPS core training course in Melbourne. For years I had been collecting the names of people interested in IPS and putting them on a spreadsheet on my computer, hoping that my limited administrative skills would not harm anyone terribly.

Steven Morgan, the operations manager of IPS, was coming to Australia to facilitate a train-the-trainer course, originally planned to be held in Queensland but moved at the last minute to Melbourne. So, some folks were able to attend a core training course and then a train-the-trainer course *the very next month* (usually, people need to practise for at least year between these two courses—in my case, it was three years). In order to increase capacity quickly, we set about an 'apprenticeship' model, involving three apprentice IPS facilitators—Nathan Grixti, SJ Haywood and Sherie Stiefler—who began co-facilitating IPS training courses within a few months of themselves attending core training. In theory, I was supposed to teach these new apprentices all that I knew as an IPS facilitator. (I wish I could say now that that I didn't actually come in with that mindset.)

IPS was contracted to offer multiple IPS core training courses, managers' training, advanced training, train-the-trainer courses, group co-reflections (the IPS version of supervision), and later, single-day topic courses. More than 220 people have been trained so far, through this project, across the vast majority of mental health services across the state of Victoria. That's 220 different ways of understanding IPS! This includes consumer and carer peer support workers, consumer and carer consultants, advisers and academics, as well as those who work alongside us (as managers or colleagues). There were also many folks trained who came from other contexts (e.g. see below the discussion of the alcohol and other drugs and family violence sectors), including independent peers. Of all those folks, I was the one who had to repeat the class over and over, being brought back from London to relearn and relearn. I say this jokingly, but each time anyone participates in this training, there are new opportunities to learn together, and to challenge our ideas around hierarchy, power, certainty, problem-solving, relationship dances, what is valued in human life, and how we make sense of our experiences, each other and the world. For me, the most powerful lessons have revolved around what it means to be a 'trainer' or 'facilitator'—a 'lead trainer', no less—while exploring *peer* work. How do we bring our own certainties, our own power, our own histories of big feelings (OK, let's be honest, our current big feelings) into the room without diminishing others? How do we receive both support and learning, when we are positioned hierarchically as needing neither support nor further learning? In this context—possibly the most 'big kid' role of my professional life—I learned to cherish the small child parts of myself, and have come away wanting to play in the sandpit of life with all the oddballs, misfits and free spirits ... and the 'emos' and the know-it-alls and the bullies and the prefects and the preppy kids, because at the end of the day, these complexities are within our communities, and within ourselves.

I can't speak to the many varied experiences in this project—the project workers engaged in various acts of creation, networking and defending our discipline from 'peer drift'; the peer support workers sharing music, cups of tea and profound conversations over Uno, crying, laughing, getting frustrated and dancing (yes, there is dancing in some services!); the trainers laughing about how we often teach the very things that we struggle with ourselves (and flinching when participants point this out unkindly on anonymous feedback forms); the carer workers grappling with their sense of professional belonging; the clinicians speaking more humanly about their own feelings and uncertainties, building teams who can hear big feelings and respond to uncertainties with connection and being-with-ness, while defending peer workers to their colleagues who have yet not understood what peer work is or could be; the consumers coming out as carers; the carers grappling with their own clinical training or inner turmoil; the clinicians juggling multiple hats internally; the government workers who have come into training to help answer questions about this whole complex behemoth; the services staff who have humbly admitted they have learned things that they didn't previously know; the supervisors hearing stories of incredible bravery and creativity, shame-filled uncertainties and retraumatisation; the peer workers holding the services accountable; the peer workers holding the trainers; the peer workers holding each other … so many stories that perhaps require music, poetry, academic journal articles, or back-alley cigarettes, tears and laughter (and more workshops with pipe-cleaners, play dough and pieces of material)—more stories than there are stars in the skies!

## IPS in the alcohol and other drugs sector

Meanwhile, some folks working in a peer-run alcohol and other drugs (AOD) service in Melbourne, the Self-Help Addiction Resource Centre (SHARC; www.sharc.org.au), were actively developing training, resources and frameworks for the growing AOD peer workforce. In their research into internationally respected models of peer support, SHARC came across IPS and contacted IPS Central (in the United States) to explore their options for accessing training, unaware of other developments happening simultaneously in Melbourne. It was sheer luck—combined with good timing and goodwill— that SHARC staff were able to attend IPS training, alongside the post-discharge workers. Over the next two years, SHARC were able to send a handful of AOD peer workers to fill spare places in the post-discharge training courses.

There was great affinity between IPS and the work SHARC were already doing, and the two streams met to form one strong river. Two people from SHARC were trained to be IPS trainers (Heather Pickard, the chief executive officer of SHARC, and Crystal Clancy, the coordinator of Peer Projects). Several co-reflections funded through the post-discharge project were held at SHARC with post-discharge peer support workers travelling from nearby services to attend, generating a strong sense of mutual enrichment. Philanthropic funding was secured for a twelve-month project to create an additional appendix for the IPS core materials, specifically for the AOD peer workforce. This work has been closely negotiated with IPS Central. As part of this project, I have been employed one day a week as a project worker at SHARC. For me personally, this was life-changing—Heather had noticed that I was 'out in the cold', struggling as a freelancer to find a sense of professional belonging, and she offered me somewhere to come in from the cold, while also building something that would work for all involved.

At the time of writing, we have held one IPS training in-house at SHARC, using the regular core materials (i.e. with a focus on mental health peer work). We found that most participants were able to connect easily. One SHARC employee described the IPS training as the most profound learning environment she'd ever experienced. But we are aware that some participants can find it disconnecting to have content that focuses on a different sector, and that this can lead to an overall sense that the materials aren't relevant to their experiences and work environment. As part of this adaptation project, we conducted an online survey and a face-to-face consultation, seeking to better understand the experiences of people trained in IPS who have an AOD background. From these feedback mechanisms, we have adapted some IPS materials—keeping as close as possible to the original structures—adding material that will hopefully be relevant specifically to the AOD workforce.

One of the most profound learnings for me from the AOD context is the ways in which the identities of 'consumer', 'carer' and 'clinician' are held less tightly than in the mental health sector. *Lived experience of being impacted by alcohol and other drugs forms the basis of the whole service* and yet many people working at SHARC wear multiple hats, and these experiences are all valued. For example, SHARC has a family drug telephone helpline for affected family members, and many staff have other professional training, as well as personal experiences with alcohol and other drugs. To my mind, this privileging of lived experience has a paradoxical effect of simultaneously decentring it, freeing everyone to inhabit their own complex, multilayered identities. As Heather frequently says, 'at the end of the day, we are all just people'. Holding this both/and stance (we are both 'just people' *and* valuing specific expertise) is one of the greatest gifts SHARC has offered me.

## IPS in the family and sexual violence sectors

In another quirk of timing, in 2016, Natalie Walker, the founder and chief executive officer of PartnerSPEAK, approached IPS Central, also with the intention of exploring IPS training possibilities, but this time in a family violence context. PartnerSPEAK, according to its website (www.partnerspeak.org.au), 'provides advocacy and support for the non-offending partner and family of a perpetrator of child sexual abuse and child exploitation material'.

As an affected partner herself, Natalie founded PartnerSPEAK first in the early 2000s, and then again in 2013, initially as an online discussion forum. Over the years, PartnerSPEAK has partnered with other organisations (family violence services, national media, politicians, police, women's organisations, sexual assault services) and volunteers (basically anyone who comes anywhere near Natalie's orbit!), and the organisation has grown exponentially. PartnerSPEAK has received significant national media coverage (e.g. on Radio National in 2013, ABC News in 2017 and SBS Insight in 2018), and secured Victorian government funding from 2017 to employ four part-time and several casual staff members, including myself as peer support manager. Two PartnerSPEAK people, Natalie Walker and Nijole Lucinskaite, attended IPS core training in December 2016 (prior to PartnerSPEAK receiving any funding), again piggybacking off the post-discharge-funded courses. Subsequently, Natalie has attended train-the-trainer, Nijole has attended advanced IPS training, and two other PartnerSPEAK staff have attended core training.

PartnerSPEAK is a completely peer-run organisation and 'will never employ clinicians on my watch', as Natalie says. PartnerSPEAK partners with other organisations, so that we each do what we do best, and encourage and support other organisations to do (well) what they do best. PartnerSPEAK's board, staff and volunteers have worked towards embedding IPS principles in every level of PartnerSPEAK's strategic planning and everyday operations. Currently, PartnerSPEAK offers peer support online, by telephone, face-to-face, in peer support groups and through opportunities for people to become actively engaged in PartnerSPEAK's work (to end child exploitation). For me, it has been a delight to be involved in an organisation that is predicated on asking not 'what is wrong with you?' but 'what's happened to you?'. We also see partners and family members of perpetrators of child sexual abuse and child exploitation materials as worthy of support, *and* as strong, capable world-changers.

**IPS in Australia, outside Victoria**

IPS was originally brought to Australia, in large part, to support the growth of peer-operated services in Queensland, in the mid- to late 2000s. Gaynor Ellis, who at the time worked in the Department of Health in Queensland, was a key advocate for significant investment in both peer-operated services and IPS specifically. This resulted in Shery Mead and Chris Hansen repeatedly being brought to Australia to offer first core training, and later advanced and train-the-trainer courses, consultancy work and training for managers and colleagues, to ensure that IPS practice was supported by the environments in which peers were working. Each of the peer-operated services (Social Ventures Australia, 2017) has a different relationship with IPS, and with clinical and community mental health services, all of which have evolved over time.

IPS has influenced a number of different contexts in and around Australia, and it's not possible to fully document these influences, but a few of them include:

- **The IPSOD project in Wide Bay**: An initiative of Central Queensland, Wide Bay and Sunshine Coast Primary Health Networks in partnership with the Wide Bay Mental Health Alcohol and Other Drugs Service, Flourish Australia and Central Queensland University. Twenty-two participants completed the Foundation Training by Open Dialogue UK in October 2017. Participants represented a mix of lived experience and clinical mental health professionals and academics. Approximately half the participants identified as lived experience practitioners, including peer support workers currently working for Flourish Australia's peer-operated service, Wide Bay Mental Health Alcohol and Other Drugs Service, Community Solutions and Red Cross (personal communication, Cherie McGregor).

## 6: Specialised developments in peer work

- **CentreCare, Cairns:** Gaynor Ellis and then later Gill Townsend (both non-peer workers with strong commitments to IPS) have had leadership roles at Centacare, a service that employs as coaches both people with lived experience and people with other training. Many CentreCare staff have been exposed to IPS training, although this is not the only approach used. Staff with lived experience are integrated with other staff (including being paid the same wage), and all coaches are encouraged to draw on their own lived experience of moving through difficult experiences.
- **Wellways, Australia:** Wellways are a national, community-managed mental health organisation who have invested significantly in IPS, including training several peer staff members as IPS trainers, and delivering training at a number of locations nationally.
- **Certificate IV in Peer Work:** There are also a number of people who have been influenced by IPS who offer training that is infused with IPS (e.g. some versions of the Certificate IV in Peer Work).
- **Intentional Peer Support Aotearoa New Zealand:** IPS has had a strong take-up in New Zealand, including several peer-run services. They have their own website (www.intentionalpeersupport.nz). (And they may be offended at being considered part of Australia, although they may consider themselves part of the same tribe, who knows?)

### Is IPS a cult?

People sometimes speak as if there is a 'pure' IPS and then there's IPS adapted to contexts in which 'pure IPS' is not possible. This isn't how I understand IPS—to my mind, IPS is a way of putting into words what it is that peer workers are doing when we walk alongside people. It offers us a clear framework for staying human together in the face of complexity, and attendant uncertainties. But IPS is by no means the only way or the right way. Many folks who come to training, to my eyes, are already responding to people in the ways in which IPS encourages us to—valuing relationships, recognising that we don't have the answers for other people, but that we can show up with our humanity, and try to figure out a way forward that works for everyone involved. And many folks (myself included) can 'intentionally peer support' people in ways that are only superficially drawing on the tasks and principles of IPS, but miss the deeper, human, interconnected wisdom.

IPS is sometimes described as 'cult-like', which I imagine has something to do with the fervour and passion of those who find it useful in their practice and in their lives. IPS has offered me—personally—the most profound set of practices and philosophies, and so has a kind of spiritual dimension. But, bear in mind, I've committed to becoming not just a trainer, but a train-the-trainer trainer and a national coordinator—I (personally) have chosen IPS very specifically as the practice I choose to explore more deeply. Over the years, I have witnessed many transformative experiences during the training, and so I honour the impulse to use grand language.

But I also know in my bones what it feels like to not belong, to feel excluded from 'tribes' (including tribes that I had thought were my 'home'), and so I am intuitively troubled by any whiff of exclusiveness, of any message that 'you are either with us or against us'. I have seen many peer workers in the post-discharge project come to IPS training from services in which ardent converts to IPS are in positions of power, and how this can get in the way of connection, trust and a sense that it's OK to have one's own (different) perspective. For my part, I have no doubt contributed to these dynamics at times—it's hard to hold something passionately and lightly at the same time.

A participant in training taught me the importance of framing IPS as 'another option'. This particular participant irritated me intensely for much of the training week—they seemed to have come into the training defensive, convinced that they had nothing new to learn about peer work after many years of practising. Or perhaps it would be more useful to own that *I* came into the training feeling defensive, convinced I had nothing to learn about IPS after many years of practising! We bumped up against each other for the first day and a half, and there was often more heat than light generated. I confided to a co-facilitator that I was confronted by this person's simmering anger (repeatedly aggressive disagreement, crossed arms, glowering looks, agitated leg jiggling), and I requested my co-facilitator support me to *disconnect* and stop feeling like I needed to 'work harder' to connect this person with IPS. Instead, I focused on connecting with the whole group, rather than spending energy on what seemed like a pointed and pointless battle. Over the years, I'm learning (slowly) to appreciate the frame IPS offers for the training itself—first we build connection, and from there we increasingly entrust the group to hold the process. By the final day, this participant no longer irritated me, in fact, I was in awe of their capacity to hold their own truth while softening their resistance to other possibilities. I was also in awe of the skilfulness of the group, who listened deeply, learned together, and held each other accountable—putting into practice what we were learning together right there, in the room.

I will add, as a final thought on cultishness, that there are definitely elements to hold lightly and with good humour—for example, the tendency to put Shery Mead on a pedestal, asking 'what would Shery do?' as a proxy for 'what do I think would be the "right" (IPS) way?' Honestly, I think Shery would turn over in her kayak with laughter at this (understandable, human) absurdity! IPS offers space for us each to show up in our own truth, to be ourselves in our full complexity and colourfulness. Some of us will swear like troopers, some of us will make deadpan jokes, some of us will be meditative and calm, some of us will be irritated by swearing or by jokes or by meditative calmness ... the point isn't to 'do it right' but to self-reflect, be *intentional*, and to increase our repertoire of options in relating to other people, in distress, in extreme states, and in our inherent diversity.

Finally, there are also words that get used by people trained in IPS that can sound like some kind of orthodoxy, shibboleth or sociolect, so I leave you with—IPS lingo!

| We made a really good connection | That's just my world view | Where's the mutuality? |
|---|---|---|
| What might be some other possibilities? | I'm curious to understand ... | Co-reflection (which can seem to mean any act of thinking/talking/breathing) |
| I wonder ... | The untold story | It's not about the nail! |

## References

Mead, S. (2014). Intentional peer support: An alternative approach. Retrieved from www.intentionalpeersupport.org

Mead, S. (2018). What is IPS? Retrieved from http://www.intentionalpeersupport.org/what-is-ips/

Mead, S., & Filson, B. (2016). Becoming part of each other's narratives: Intentional peer support. In J. Russo & A. Sweeney (Eds.), *Searching for a rose garden: Challenging psychiatry, fostering mad studies* (pp. 109–117). Wyastone Leys, Monmouth: PCCS Books.

Social Ventures Australia. (2017). The value of a peer operated service. Retrieved from https://www.socialventures.com.au/sva-quarterly/the-value-of-a-peer-operated-service/

## PartnerSPEAK in the media

ABC News. (2017). Ex-wife of paedophile reveals anguish of finding child exploitation images, slow police response. Retrieved from http://www.abc.net.au/news/2017-10-26/desley-lodwick-discovered-child-porn-on-her-husbands-computer/9086238

Radio National. (2013). Partnerspeak.org: Support for families whose members have accessed child pornography. Retrieved from http://www.abc.net.au/radionational/programs/breakfast/partnerspeakorg/4636402

SBS Insight. (2018). His other life. Retrieved from https://www.sbs.com.au/news/insight/tvepisode/his-other-life)

# Peer supervision: stumbling blocks and ways forward

Aimee Sinclair

*Aimee identifies as a mad sociologist. Alternative frameworks of understanding her distress and alternative responses to her distress have saved her life on many occasions. As a result, she is passionate about ensuring that peer work continues to provide and advocate for alternatives to biomedical approaches.*

> Peer supervision may act as a 'third space', facilitating the development of self-identity, confidence, and collective resources for peer workers to unsettle oppressive practices and sustain our own unique principles and practices.

Despite a long history of informal peer support and peer-run services, peer work as an occupation within mental health systems is a recent phenomenon. Thanks to the long and continuing advocacy work of communities with lived experience, peer work is rapidly being incorporated into Western mental health systems and public policy (Bennetts et al., 2013; Bates, Kemp, & Issac, 2008). Unfortunately, the structures, support mechanisms and cultural change needed to sustain peer work and ensure its integrity have lagged, causing a range of issues for peer workers as we try to navigate confusing and often hostile work environments. Alongside these issues, there are growing concerns around the co-option of peer work as we become included in mental health systems that have traditionally excluded us.

In this chapter I explore the meaning and role of peer supervision, as one of the various solutions recommended to overcome these issues, particularly in regards to peer support work (as opposed to other peer or consumer roles). I focus on my home state of Western Australia, but draw on literature from across Australia and also internationally. My thinking is underpinned by an understanding of peer support best described by Mead, Hilton and Curtis (2001, p. 135):

> a system of giving and receiving help founded on the key principles of respect, shared responsibility and mutual agreement of what is helpful. Peer support is not based on psychiatric models and diagnostic criteria ... [it is] a deep, holistic

understanding based on mutual experience where people are able to 'be' with each other without the constraints of traditional (expert/patient) relationships.

I locate peer support within its historical context as emerging from the survivor movement, demanding radical alternatives to biomedical approaches and coercive practices dominant within Western mental health systems (Chamberlain, 1978; Epstein, 2013). I write unapologetically from a 'mad' standpoint, as someone who reclaims the term 'mad' to reflect and challenge the ways in which madness (including my own) is socially constructed, and to emphasise resistance to psychiatric discourses. I acknowledge, however, that my approach is just one of the many approaches to madness, and by extension, peer support work and peer supervision. I share my thoughts here as a way to offer up one way of thinking about peer supervision, rather than defining my way as 'the right way'.

I argue that supervision for peer support workers has the potential to play an integral role in not only sustaining the peer support workforce, but also in ensuring that peer support retains its original mandate of resisting, and/or providing alternatives to, biomedical approaches and coercive mental health practices. I begin by contextualising peer supervision within the Western Australian context, outlining approaches to supervision for other health workers and some of the issues with replicating these existing models. I explore emerging concerns about the formalisation and co-option of peer support and peer supervision, and suggest there are alternatives for peer support workers beyond inclusion (through co-option), or exclusion (due to resistance). I argue that peer supervision may facilitate these alternatives, but this is dependent on developing our own forms of supervision separate from clinical models.

## Contextualising peer supervision

In Western Australia, peer support has been taken up more slowly by the formal mental health sector than in other states (Bates et al., 2008; Elias & Upton-Davis, 2015). Yet, as in other Australian contexts, the nature of funding models means that when an organisation or hospital has received the go-ahead for a peer support program, this program is often rolled out hastily. Vandewalle et al. (2016, p. 235) note that the move to embed peer roles within these contexts is 'complicated because it requires a radical change of culture and practice'. In many parts of the mental health system, despite the hard work of activists, there remains unwillingness, or a lack of capacity due to time and funding constraints, to consider this radical change of culture and practice. There often exists an underlying assumption that peer workers can, and should, simply be assimilated into pre-existing systems and 'professional' ways of working. Despite what seems like an abundance of policy pieces and grey literature highlighting the 'beneficence' of organisations who employ peer workers, challenges experienced by peer workers in these contexts have been well documented (Vandewalle et al., 2016). Western Australia is similar to most states in this regard, with peer workers reporting a range of issues including lack of role clarity, discrimination, bullying and unreasonable workloads (Kemp & Henderson, 2012).

Peer supervision, as differentiated from managerial supervision, has been recommended as one of many solutions to overcoming these issues (Being, 2017; Kemp & Henderson, 2012; Health Workforce Australia, 2014; Vandewalle et al., 2016). However, in Western Australia, as in most of Australia, peer supervision for peer workers remains under-developed and under-resourced (Kemp & Henderson, 2012; Elias & Upton-Davis, 2015; Bennetts et al., 2013). Further, there exist varying understandings of what supervision for peer support workers means and what purpose it should serve. Approaches to supervision are inconsistent, supervision needs are poorly understood and peer supervision is often confused with line management (Bennetts et al., 2013; Vandewalle et al., 2016).

In many contexts, peer supervision is modelled on pre-existing models of clinical supervision. While models of clinical supervision vary depending on the specific profession, the overall aims of clinical supervision are predominantly linked to accountability, client safety and improvement in clinical practice (Taylor & Harrison, 2010). The Australian Association of Social Workers (AASW), which arguably has one of the more holistic approaches to supervision, defines supervision as a 'forum for reflection and learning ... an interactive dialogue ... a process of review, reflection, critique and replenishment for professional practitioners' (Davys & Beddoe, 2010, in AASW, 2014, p. 2). There is an assumption within clinical models that a clinician with more knowledge and experience than those being supervised will conduct clinical supervision, and this may be a line manager (AASW, 2014; Bateman,

Henderson, & Hill, 2012). With such limited data on supervision for peer workers in Australia, it cannot be said with any sense of authority, but my suspicions from discussion with colleagues is that workplaces expect supervision for peer workers to follow such a format. The Mental Health Coordinating Council, for example, which represents community health organisations in NSW, suggests that despite the 'call for peer supervision which emphasizes independence from professional services … there is no reason to suggest that people with lived experience working in mental health services should not utilize this mode of delivery in exactly the same format' (Bateman et al., 2012).

Alternatively, 'peer supervision' within the context of nursing, psychology and social work tends to refer to 'a collaborative learning and supervisory forum … established by two or more professional colleagues (social work or multi-disciplinary) of *equal standing*' (AASW, 2014, p. 6). Moving away from hierarchical and authoritative modes of supervision, this model functions as a space for mutual support and education more than accountability (Nickson, Gair, & Miles, 2016). Like clinical supervision, peer supervision can be delivered in both one-to-one and group settings. It has been suggested that utilisation of such a model can lead to improved professional and organisational learning, and reduced feelings of isolation, and that it provides professional nourishment and support (Bailey et al., 2014; Hawken & Worrall, 2002). This model of 'peer–peer' supervision is utilised by peer workers in Western Australia through the WA Peer Supporters Network.

However, when the mental health sector talks about peer supervision for peer workers, it does not tend to mean 'peer–peer' supervision. Rather, there is an expectation that the peer supervisor will have more experience or training than those being supervised. This thinking would seem to align more with the definition of clinical supervision. In what could be argued is an overvaluing of educational qualifications over lived experience qualifications, this often results in peer workers 'being supervised by established professionals, most typically nursing, occupational therapy or social work' (Elias & Upton-Davis, 2015, p. 305). The desire for peer supervision to be developed and delivered by individuals with more experience also comes from peer workers, but this desire recognises that this should be experienced members of the consumer workforce, *not* other workers (Bennetts et al., 2013, p. 319).

6: Specialised developments in peer work

Just as clinical supervision for other health workers provides opportunities for increased quality, skills and accountability, these are equally important in peer work. However, peer support workers also have a unique set of values and practices, and face unique challenges within the mental health space that are not addressed by pre-existing models. It is these differences that I turn to next, arguing that while we may draw on certain attributes of these existing models, the supervision needs of peer support workers are unique and therefore we cannot simply replicate models of clinical supervision.

**Why peer supervision needs to be different**

Unlike other health workers, peer workers are working within a system and alongside practices that we have traditionally been excluded from or actively oppressed within. Whilst recognising that 'madness lands and is graphed on bodies' in uneven ways (Voronka, 2016a, p. 197), and therefore each of us will have varying experiences, I argue there are some collective 'stumbling blocks' unique to peer work. These unique challenges make traditional models of supervision unsuitable.

Firstly, individuals with lived experience have previously experienced epistemic marginalisation and often continue to do so (Thatchuck, 2011). That is, our ways of knowing and being are often unrecognised or undermined. Society has traditionally considered these ways of knowing to hold no authority or credibility. This has resulted, amongst other things, in organisational policies and codes of practice being developed for us, without our being consulted or involved in the process. Non-peers are still often responsible for developing our job descriptions (Rebeiro Gruhl, LaCarte, & Calixte, 2016). This means that often our collective values and ethics do not align with these organisational policies and practices. As an example, peer work is unique in that self-disclosure is relevant and valued. However, self-disclosure, as articulated by Elias and Upton-Davis (2015, p. 308), is a 'challenge within the prevailing medical model in psychiatric hospitals' and therefore peer staff are often told by non-peer supervisors that they cannot disclose because to do so would be 'violating boundaries' and against organisational practice (Stratford et al., 2017). Thus, a clinical understanding of supervision as a process that ensures organisational policies, standards and procedures are adhered to (Davys & Beddoe, 2010, p. 21), without critically co-reflecting on these policies, is problematic for peer supervision. Any resistance to oppressive or coercive policies or codes of practice is potentially silenced within traditional models of supervision. By doing so, the space to explore alternatives is closed down. In regards to disclosure, for example, peer workers report not 'knowing how to disclose, how much to disclose and when it is appropriate to disclose'. These are major stumbling blocks (Kemp & Henderson, 2012, p. 339; Moran et al., 2013). Peer supervision needs to provide a space for this to be explored collectively.

Secondly, while clinical models often see no issue with a facilitator of peer supervision also providing line management to a worker, this causes potential issues for peer workers. Unfortunately, the vast majority of peer workers report to non-peer line managers. Peer workers often report that non-peer managers 'do not clearly understand the peer support worker role' (Kemp & Henderson, 2012, p. 339), and do not always recognise (or at worse, sometimes even reproduce) the sanist microaggressions that peers face. By sanist microaggressions, I mean practices that take the form of 'multiple small insults and indignities' that subjugate people who have received diagnoses of 'mental illness' or treatment (Kalinowski & Risser, 2005, p. 1; Poole et al., 2012; Chamberlain, 1978; Sinclair, 2018). Examples of sanist microaggressions that peers experience from non-peer managers include low expectations and judgements in regard to capacity to cope with the demands of the job (Kemp & Henderson, 2012). If we resist these microaggressions and/or organisational practices that we perceive as coercive and damaging to others, we risk being labelled, excluded and even dismissed.

Even if a non-peer manager may theoretically understand the existence of this oppression, I argue this is different from *knowing* what it feels like in one's body, in a way that often only peers can relate to. Deegan (1996, p. 91) perhaps best describes this as a difference between 'knowing' something, and actually seeing 'the form or essence of that which is'. Bennetts et al. (2013) articulate how many non-peer team members assume they are working as equals when peer workers feel otherwise. Further, our experiences of oppression are often embedded in a way that makes it difficult to share with others who do not share the same experiences. For these reasons, a model of supervision that conflates peer supervision with line management, or views a non-peer as appropriate for facilitating peer supervision, at best does not fit with the needs of peer workers, and at worst causes damage to peer workers and peer support practices.

Further, as a marginalised group, peer workers are also exposed to what Brosnan (2012) refers to as invisible power imbalances. Invisible power is the 'shaping of the psychological and ideological boundaries of participation' (Gaventa, 2006, p. 29 as cited in Brosnan, 2012, p. 57). In other words, the ways in which we understand our experiences and the world around us are shaped by deeply ingrained schemas that replicate dominant modes of thinking, feeling and understanding (Crossley & Crossley, 2001). A peer worker uniquely uses 'their own lived experience of recovery, deliberately, intentionally, as a core aspect of their practice' (Watson, 2013, p. 10). Yet in doing so, we must recognise how our understanding of these experiences has often been shaped by dominant models of thinking about madness that potentially re-enforce our oppression. In Australia, the dominant discourse remains that of biomedical understandings of distress that situate the 'deficit' within the individual. This discourse limits the way we may understand ourselves and our practices as peer workers. The deep reflexive work needed to understand and unpack this internalised oppression requires a style of supervisory practice that is often not seen in traditional models. It also requires a supervisor who has lived experience, an understanding about how power and oppression can become embodied, and a commitment to unpack these understandings. Otherwise, as peers we run the risk of making sense of our experiences through the dominant frameworks of society that oppress us in the first place.

Lastly, whilst I have used it thus far due to its common usage in policy and practice, the term 'peer supervision' itself sits uncomfortably for me. A supervisory relationship suggests the presence of an 'expert', which does not align with the peer principles of mutuality and reciprocity. As Mead (2014) articulates, supervision for some of us has meant oversight of our performance by someone with more experience or power. This often leads to us feeling judged, overly evaluated or misunderstood. A traditional learning environment of expert and student does not support peer values and is potentially not a productive place for learning. I propose that Mead's (2014) terminology, and associated practice, of 'co-reflection' fits better with peer values and aligns with reworking or resisting, rather than reiterating, clinical styles of supervision.

I have argued here that peer workers have supervisory needs that cannot be met by traditional modes of clinical supervision. Peer support needs to define its own style of supervision that upholds and reinforces its unique values and practices, rather than that of traditional mental health systems that are often experienced as coercive and damaging. I now move to explore what such a space may look like; however, it is worthwhile to first note concerns about the co-option of peer work and the part that peer supervision may play in facilitating or resisting such co-option.

**Concerns for peer supervision**

Alongside recommendations to formalise peer supervision as a solution to peer workforce challenges, there are emerging concerns from within the consumer movement as to whether this is the right move. These concerns, I believe, relate to two main issues, both of which suggest peer work is at risk of being detached from its 'founding values in a civil rights and social justice framework' (Stratford et al., 2017, p. 1).

The first of these concerns is in regard to the impact that formalisation of peer supervision may have on the ability of individuals with limited financial means to work as peer workers. For the last three years in Western Australia, the Mental Health Commission has funded scholarships for students to study the Certificate IV in Mental Health Peer Work and to access external peer supervision as part of their studies. This qualification is quickly becoming a minimum standard qualification for peer work in Western Australia. Yet without these scholarships, many students report they would not be able to study (Consumers of Mental Health Western Australia, 2017). Further, if peer supervision becomes mandatory for practice, but is not funded by one's employer or by a scholarship program, only peer workers who have the financial means will be able to practise. As a result, formalisation puts peer work at risk of becoming inaccessible to those with limited financial means. Formalisation also leads to models and certifications being 'registered, marked' and monetised by those who may not have the same core values (Epstein, 2013, p. 16). This can already be seen within Australia with community mental health organisations trademarking 'models' of recovery. In the United States, Davidow (2017) has critiqued Mental Health America for their costly national peer specialist certification. These moves have the

## 6: Specialised developments in peer work

potential to steer us away from the origins of peer support as accessible to and practised by those of us with the most minimal access to society's resources.

These apprehensions relate to broader, and in my experience warranted, concerns that peer values and practices are being 'co-opted' through inclusion within mental health systems to achieve the same coercive and controlling aims that peer work traditionally challenged (Voronka, 2017; Stratford et al., 2017; Rose, 2014; Healy, 2018; Penney, 2018). Detached from our radical foundations that require the challenging of 'mental illness' assumptions and coercive practices, peer workers risk becoming another cog in a mental health system that often does more harm than good (Voronka, 2017; Mead, Hilton, & Curtis, 2001). For example, peer workers are generally understood within the mental health system as 'providing a wellness model that focuses on strengths and recovery: the positive aspects of people and their ability to function effectively and supportively' (Repper & Carter, 2011, p. 394). This understanding suggests that a peer worker's role is to use their lived experience to 'role model' appropriate ways of managing madness. Yet this framing of peer work has been criticised for failing to disrupt individual deficit understandings of distress, and the expectation that peer workers should orientate individuals towards self-governance and compliance (Voronka, 2017; Harper, &Speed, 2012; McWade, 2016; Scott & Doughty, 2012; Scott, 2011). While I strongly uphold these concerns in regards to co-option, I also question whether this framework of thinking may lead us to forget alternative possibilities. While incredibly useful for highlighting issues that as peer workers we must be mindful of, they potentially negate the ability of peer workers (and other health providers) to resist co-option. There is a tendency to think that when we come up against oppressive institutions and practices, we only have two options. Either we adapt to clinical ways of working (becoming 'paraprofessionals') to stay included within the system, or we resist these practices, which leads to our exclusion. However, this misrecognises the changes that peer workers *are* able to make within the mental health system, and the advocacy work we undertake to align institutional priorities with consumer aims (however problematic this may sometimes be).

Drawing on ideas such as those expressed by McWade (2015) and Grey (2016), I suggest it may be more useful to explore the complexities in which peer work and peer supervision exist. By working from a place of curiosity about alternative possibilities, we can start to examine what these may look like and how they may be facilitated. I am particularly inspired by Flick Grey's (2016, p. 250) invitation for us to explore '[how] we can live with others domesticating?' (Domesticating can be understood as a process through which professionals within the mental health system making themselves feel more comfortable by dominating, co-opting or excluding us). What are the possibilities beyond inclusion or exclusion? What contexts and resources might enable peer workers to challenge oppressive ways of working while remaining within the system?

Brosnan (2012) suggests 'third spaces' (spaces created by people for themselves, as opposed to spaces they are invited into by authorities) may provide potential for mental health (ref)users to explore such alternatives. Peer supervision may act as a 'third space', facilitating the development of self-identity, confidence and collective resources for peer workers to unsettle oppressive practices and sustain our own unique principles and practices. It is this idea, of peer supervision as a space to facilitate alternatives beyond inclusion and exclusion, to which I now turn.

### Peer supervision as facilitating resistance

Peer supervision, like most forms of supervision, has been upheld as useful because it helps to prevent burnout in peer workers, maintains wellbeing and aids workers in reflecting on and improving our practice. These are all important objectives for supervision, particularly given the negative impacts and barriers that peer workers currently face within the sector. However, as can be seen through concerns about co-option, peer supervision needs to go further than this. Peer supervision cannot be seen as a bandaid solution to these issues; we cannot simply work out better ways of coping with oppressive work conditions or practices. Rather, as Pat Deegan (2004) argues, we must learn to collectively and strategically respond to people or policies that are oppressive.

An approach to peer supervision (or 'co-reflection') that adopts an anti-oppressive stance can enable this. An anti-oppressive stance 'assumes there are multiple forms of oppression, that oppression is tied to unequal power relations, and that critical reflection on these matters is paramount' (Poole et al., 2012, p. 22). The focus, therefore, is on creating spaces that allow us to collectively identify our shared stumbling blocks (both internal and external), developing alternative ways to understand ourselves and our practices, and resources to resist co-option whilst avoiding exclusion. Such a practice involves creating expertise together, through a process of learning, practising and reflection (Mead, 2014). Within such a practice, the facilitator role is therefore not that of expert, but rather the facilitator creates a space alongside others to allow for reflexivity, complexity, deep curiosity, and solidarity. The peer worker(s) and facilitator must share equally and draw upon each other's knowledge and experience.

Such an approach should make us uncomfortable at times. There are points where, as I learn and unpack the ways in which I internalise and replicate medicalised and deficit frameworks of madness, I wish I could run away from it all. Challenging our frameworks of thinking and critically reflecting on our practices often creates an unpleasant, jarring feeling where we exist between two interpretive worlds. However, these emotional conflicts are the starting point of '[questioning] the things that are self-evident'; questioning our previous acceptance of what others say about us, our madness and our ways of supporting others (Bourdieu, 1998, p. 8). They are vital to breaking through to new understandings of how peer support can be practised within mental health systems in a way that continues to resist oppressive practices.

In any situation of 'unknowingness' it is often tempting to want an 'expert' to determine what the answer is. Yet peer work, and therefore peer supervision, needs to be 'flexible and idiosyncratic'; it is driven 'by the recipient, rather than drawing upon a list of duties' (Rebeiro Gruhl, et al., 2016, p. 82). Part of being a peer supervisor (and peer support worker) is learning to negotiate these meanings together, holding in mind our own frameworks of thinking and our own needs alongside others, and being able to articulate this. This will be different for each person and each context. Thus, I argue that if we are to develop guidelines to support this form of peer supervision, they need to be just that—guidelines—that open up possibilities rather than create limits. Further, while it is mandatory for many health workers to participate in supervision throughout their careers, I propose we collectively need to think through what impact mandatory peer supervision would have on a framework of supervision that embraces an anti-oppressive stance. Peer supervision is potentially no longer a 'third space' once it is mandated, or if peer workers do not get to choose whom they share these spaces with.

Lastly, while there is not the space to explore here, it would be remiss of me not to highlight the vital role that individuals with lived experience have to play in providing interprofessional supervision for services and service managers. It is not enough to expect peer workers themselves to challenge oppressive systems and practices. This responsibility lies with all workers within the sector. There are some worthy examples of this being done in Western Australia, such as the Valuing Lived Experience Project at Curtin University (Dorozenko et al., 2016), and potential for more scope with the emergence of the Western Australian Peer Supporters' Network Community of Practice.

## Moving forward

My own journey of facilitating peer supervision has often involved stumbling around in the dark, potentially replicating power imbalances and oppressive practices within the sector as much as I have simultaneously tried to resist such practices. My experiences have been both enriching and challenging. There are times when I have come away from peer supervision overwhelmed with hope and truly honoured to be learning alongside my peers, and there are times when I have felt hopeless and exhausted. In many ways, these reflect similar challenges I have experienced as a peer worker. My reflective journals speak of the challenges of learning how to negotiate and hold my own space, of feeling unsupported, scared and unsure of myself, of learning to challenge my own practices that sustain my disempowerment, and working to sustain myself through alternative practices. One of the greatest challenges I have found in learning to facilitate peer supervision as a 'third' space has been the lack of literature or education to guide me, and the lack of documented peer narratives to know that I am not alone in my stumbling.

In this chapter I have worked to provide a starting point for considering some of the complexities surrounding peer supervision. I have offered up my reflections on some elements of peer supervision I believe may be important moving forward if peer work is to continue to provide, and advocate for, alternatives to biomedical approaches. My hope is that by offering up my own reflections here, I open up space for heartfelt connections over our shared stumbling blocks, and deep conversations about ways forward for peer supervision.

## References

[AASW] Australian Association of Social Workers (2014). Supervision Standards. https://www.aasw.asn.au/document/item/6027

Bailey, R., Bell, K., Kalle, W., & Pawar, M. (2014). Restoring meaning to supervision through a peer consultation group in rural Australia. *Journal of Social Work Practice, 28*(4), 479–495.

Bateman, J., Henderson, C., & Hill, H. (2012). Implementing practice supervision in mental health community managed organisations in NSW. Sydney: Mental Health Coordinating Council. Retrieved from http://studylib.net/doc/8320658/implementing-practice-supervision-in-mental-health-community

Bates, A., Kemp, V., & Isaac, M. (2008). Peer support shows promise in helping persons living with mental illness address their physical health needs. *Canadian Community Mental Health Journal, 27*(2), 21–36.

Being. (2017). Position statement on the peer workforce. Retrieved from http://being.org.au/2017/07/being-position-statement-on-the-peer-workforce/

Bennetts, W., Pinches A., Paluch, T., Fossey E. (2013). Real lives, real jobs: Sustaining consumer perspective work in the mental health sector. *Advances in Mental Health, 11*(3), 313–325.

Brosnan, L. (2012). Power and participation: An examination of the dynamics of mental health service-user involvement in Ireland. *Studies in Social Justice, 6*(1), 45–66.

Chamberlain, J. (1978). *On our own: Patient controlled alternatives to the mental health system.* London: MIND productions.

Crossley, M. L., & Crossley, N. (2001). 'Patient' voices, social movements and the habitus: How psychiatric survivors 'speak out'. *Social Science & Medicine, 52,* 1477–1489.

Davidow, S. (2017). Downfall of peer support: MHA and national certification (blog post). Mad in America. https://www.madinamerica.com/2017/04/downfall-peer-support-mha-national-certification/

Davys, A., & Beddoe, L. (2010). *Best practice in professional supervision: A guide for the helping professions.* London: Jessica Kingsley.

Deegan, P.E. (1996). Recovery as a journey of the heart. *Psychiatric Rehabilitation Journal, 19*(3), 91–97.

Deegan, P. (2004). Mentalism, micro-aggression and the peer practitioner. Available at: www.patdeegan.com/blog/posts/mentalism-micro-aggression-and-peer-practitioner (accessed 20 June 2017).

Dorozenko, K., Ridley, S., Martin, R., & Mahboub, L. (2016). A journey of embedding mental health lived experience in social work education. *Social Work Education, 35*(8), 905–917.

Elias, P., & Upton-Davis, K. (2015). Embedding peer support using social work values. *Journal of Mental Health Training, Education & Practice, 10*(5), 304–313.

Epstein, M. (2013). The consumer movement in Australia: A memoir of an old campaigner. http://www.ourcommunity.com.au/files/OCP/HistoryOfConsumerMovement.pdf

Gaventa, J. (2006). Finding the spaces for change: A power analysis. *IDS Bulletin, 37*(6), 23–33.

Gillard, S. G., Edwards, C., Gibson, S. L., et al. (2013). Introducing peer worker roles into UK mental health service teams: A qualitative analysis of the organizational benefits and challenges. *BMC Health Services Research, 13*, 188.

Grey, F. (2016) Benevolent othering: Speaking positively about mental health service users. *Philosophy, Psychiatry and Psychology, 23*(3/4), pp. 241–250.

Harper, D. J., & Speed, E. (2012). Uncovering recovery: The resistible rise of recovery and resilience. *Studies in Social Justice, 6*(1), 9–25.

Hawken, D., & Worrall, J. (2002). Reciprocal mentoring supervision. Partners in learning: A personal experience. In M. McMahon & W. Patton (Eds.), *Supervision in the helping professions: A practical approach* (pp. 43–53). Frenchs Forest, NSW: Pearson Education Australia.

Health Workforce Australia (2014). Mental health peer workforce study. http://pandora.nla.gov.au/pan/133228/20150419-0017/www.hwa.gov.au/sites/default/files/HWA_Mental%20health%20Peer%20Workforce%20Study_LR.pdf

Healy, D. (19 February 2018). Being the right kind of peer. Retrieved from https://davidhealy.org/being-the-right-peer/

Kalinowski, C., & Risser, P. (2005). Identifying and overcoming mentalism. InforMed Health Publishing & Training. Available at: www.newmediaexplorer.org/sepp/Mentalism.pdf (accessed 20 June 2017).

Kemp, V., & Henderson, A. R. (2012). Challenges faced by mental health peer support workers: Peer support from the peer supporter's point of view. *Psychiatric Rehabilitation Journal. 35*(4), 337–340.

McWade, B. (2015). Temporalities of mental health recovery. *Subjectivity, 8*, 243–260.

McWade, B. (2016). Recovery as policy as a form of neoliberal state making. *Intersectionalities: A Global Journal of Social Work Analysis, Research, Polity and Practice, 5*(3), 62–81.

Mead, S. (2014) International peer support co-reflection guide. Retrieved from http://www.intentionalpeersupport.org/wp-content/uploads/2015/07/IPS-CoReflection-Guide-2015.pdf

Mead, S., Hilton, D., & Curtis, L. (2001). Peer support: A theoretical perspective. *Psychiatric Rehabilitation Journal, 25*(2), 134–141.

Moran, G. S., Russinova, Z., Gidugu, V., & Gagne, C. (2013). Challenges experienced by paid peer providers in mental health recovery: A qualitative study. *Community Mental Health Journal, 49*, 281–291.

Nickson, A., Gair, S., & Miles D. (2016) Supporting isolated workers in their work with families in rural and remote Australia: Exploring peer group supervision. *Children Australia, 41*(4), 265–274.

Penney, D. (10 February 2018). Who gets to define peer support? Retrieved from: https://www.madinamerica.com/2018/02/who-gets-to-define-peer-support/

Poole, J. M., Jivraj, T., Arslanian, A., Bellows, K., Chiasson, S., Hakimy, H., & Reid, J. (2012). Sanism, 'mental health', and social work/education: A review and call to action. *Intersectionalities: A Global Journal of Social Work Analysis, Research, Polity and Practice, 1*(1), 20–35.

## 6: Specialised developments in peer work

Rebeiro Gruhl, K. L., LaCarte, S., & Calixte, S. (2016) Authentic peer support work: Challenges and opportunities for an evolving occupation. *Journal of Mental Health, 25*(1), 78–86.

Repper, J., & Carter, T. (2011). A review of the literature on peer support in mental health services. *Journal of Mental Health, 20*(4), 392–411.

Rose, D. (2014). The mainstreaming of recovery. *Journal of Mental Health, 23*(5), 217–218.

Sinclair, A. (2018). 'Help yourself to our staff kitchen': A peer worker's reflections on microaggressions. *Journal of Mental Health Training, Education and Practice, 3*(3), 167–172.

Stratford, A. C., Halpin, M., Phillips, K., Skerritt, F., Beales, A., Cheng, V., ... Davidson, L. (2017). The growth of peer support: An international charter. *Journal of Mental Health*. 1-6

Taylor, M., & Harrison, C. A. (2010). Introducing clinical supervision across Western Australian public mental health services. *International Journal of Mental Health Nursing, 19*, 287–293.

Thatchuk, A. L. (2011). Stigma and the politics of biomedical models of mental illness. *International Journal of Feminist Approaches to Bioethics, 4*(1), 140–163.

Vandewalle, J., Debyser, B., Beeckman, D., Vandecastelle, T., Van Hecke, A., & Verhaeghe, S. (2016). Peer workers' perceptions and experiences of barriers to implementation of peer worker roles in mental health services: A literature review. *International Journal of Nursing Studies, 60*, 234–250.

Voronka, J. (2016a). The politics of 'people with lived experience'. Experiential authority and the risks of strategic essentialism. *Philosophy, Psychiatry and Psychology, 23*(3/4), 189–201.

Voronka, J. (2016b). Disciplines, difference, and representational authority: Making moves inclusionary practices. *Philosophy, Psychiatry and Psychology, 23*(3/4), 211–214.

Voronka, J. (2017). Turning mad knowledge into affective labour: The case of the peer support worker. *American Quarterly, 69*(2), 333–338.

Watson, S. (2013). Peer workforce development. Centre of excellence in peer support, May 2015, www.peersupportvic.org/index.php/2014-12-15-22-42-26/2014-12-16-02-20-10/News-and-Events/SandyWatson-Keynote/

# Section 7

# A force for change

# Collated from the proceedings of a workshop held in April 2018

*Leanne Craze and David Plant*

*Leanne Craze AM, based in Sydney Australia, works as consultant in mental health and social policy and is a long-time champion of the peer workforce. Leanne has a PhD and honours degree in social work from the University of New South Wales and a Graduate Certificate in science from Western Sydney University. Some examples of projects conducted and contributions made by Leanne include: being secretary of the Australian Human Rights Commission's National Inquiry into the Human Rights of People with Mental Illness; National Framework for Recovery-oriented Mental Health Services; the NSW Mental Health Commission's Peer Work Hub; the Australian Government's scoping study to establish a new national mental health consumer peak body; and the Australian Government National Mental Health Commission's Engage and Participate project.*

*David Plant, based near Melbourne Australia, also provides consultancy services in mental health and social policy. With qualifications in both social work and economics, David has been on the ground during some pivotal moments in mental health reform in Australia including: the early and heady days of Mental Health Victoria (formerly VICSERV); the establishment of Australia's first non-government community mental health peak body (the Australian Psychiatric Disability Coalition); and the establishment of Australia's first national mental health consumer organisation. David, like Leanne, believes great days are ahead for Australia's mental health lived experience movement and leadership.*

## Introduction

This chapter provides a picture of the depth and breadth of the Australian mental health peer work sector and those who lead and work within it. We present the views of approximately fifty peer workers, peer work pioneers and policy leaders who attended a workshop held in April 2018 in Sydney. Participants contributed experience and learnings from a wide range of positions, roles and settings. There was a spread of age groups including both young and more senior people. Some were new to peer work and others had considerable experience, while others are recognised as leaders or emerging leaders. Participants worked in capital cities, regional, rural and remote areas.

7: A force for change

Others who could not attend the workshop contributed through phone interviews and by email.

A 'world café'-style approach was used to discuss the following questions:

1. Why would a person choose to be a peer worker?
2. Why would a person choose to work with a peer worker?
3. What is the diversity of peer work roles and activities?
4. How does peer work inform or enable people to make genuine choices?
5. How can we promote the benefits of working with a peer worker to people?
6. What strategies are important to develop and maintain the quality, integrity and practice standards of peer work?
7. What should the future of peer work look like?

Throughout the discussion the 'speed thinking' method was used to stimulate discussion in pairs as well as in plenary sessions with all participants.

Participants then identified problems and difficulties in the peer work space, referred to as some 'elephants in the room'. Matters discussed included: human resource practices; industrial relations and conditions; discrimination (including exploitation and abuse); workplace relationships; and incompatible or unacceptable expectations across organisational settings. Participants described the impact of limited understanding of peer work roles and outcomes. They also brainstormed strategies for addressing these issues, and shared their ideas for enabling effective practice and peer workforce development. All shared their vision of the right place for the future of the peer workforce.

This chapter commences by discussing who the mental health peer workforce is and what is known about it. A picture is provided of what the peer workforce is doing, its impact and contribution, and common practices and methods,. An analysis of challenges confronting peer work and future directions then follows. The chapter concludes with the aspirations of peer workers reflected in what keeps them awake at night and gets them up in the morning.

## Who are the mental health peer workforce?

The peer workforce, with a lengthy presence in Australia, is increasingly recognised as a professional grouping in its own right. Peer workers are growing in number and are increasingly being employed across a range of settings. A peer workforce, at this point in time, is just not restricted to members of the mental health workforce. Rather, peer workers are being employed in other workforces and areas including community, disability, justice, corrections, addictions, employment, education, training and housing sectors.

### Who peer workers are

Dr Louise Byrne, a leading consumer academic, explains that peer workers or, as she calls them, 'lived experience workers', are people who are employed to

> work specifically from a lived experience of significant mental health difficulty, Recovery from mental health difficulty and accessing mental health services (2013, p. 15).

Health Workforce Australia provided a similar definition:

> Peer workers are defined as people who are employed in roles that require them to identify as being or having been a mental health consumer ... (2014, p. 5).

Workshop participants emphasised that people undertaking peer work qualifications are also part of the peer workforce and emphasised that the peer workforce has a significant role in transforming services to a recovery orientation.

Participants agreed that peer workers are people who are employed in designated peer work positions where lived experience of mental health issues is a prerequisite.

### Characteristics of the mental health peer workforce

Health Workforce Australia, tasked with supporting the development of new or emerging innovative health workforces, conducted a study in 2011 to describe the peer workforce and to make recommendations for its future development. An online survey of peer workers, the first of its kind, received 305 responses from around Australia. Almost 80% of the survey respondents were women. A majority were aged forty years and over. Over 90% had

## 7: A force for change

previous qualifications including certificate, diploma, degree and postgraduate qualifications.

No further national study of peer work has been conducted. Australia still lacks a national peer work dataset. There was an anecdotal suggestion that there is now a more representative spread of age groups with growing numbers of younger peer workers observed.

*Some key recent moments in the life and journey of this workforce in Australia*

Recognition of peer work as a discrete discipline or profession has occurred frequently throughout the last decade. Examples include the allocation of funding for the employment or training of peer workers within Commonwealth and state/territory funding programs such as the Personal Helpers and Mentors service and the expansion of the lived experience workforce in South Australian public mental health services. Another key moment of recognition occurred with funding for the development and rollout of a nationally accredited Certificate IV in Mental Health Peer Work.

National as well as state and territory policy documents also give official recognition to the mental health peer workforce. For example, the Australian Government stated:

> The Commonwealth ... recognises the value of a mental health peer workforce, and will explore the inclusion of peer workers ... as part of the development and trial of a stepped care approach (2016, p. 12).

Reflecting on different trends across the years, we noted an earlier emphasis on consumer advocate and consumer consultant positions compared to a current emphasis on peer leadership and support positions. An example of this current emphasis is in the announcement by the New South Wales state government in 2017 of funding ($2.7 million) for thirty new peer work positions across the state to provide support during hospital admission and post-discharge support.

*What does this workforce call itself?*

Participants stated that, as yet, a specific name has not been agreed or settled on. Different role or position titles are used around Australia, including mental health lived experience workforce, mental health peer workforce and psychosocial peer workforce.

*What differentiates this workforce from others?*

The personal lived experience of mental health issues and recovery, including a requirement and commitment to openly use this experience and knowledge, is what distinguishes this workforce from others. People also described another important distinguishing characteristic—lived-experience-led change and transformation. The peer workers described their shared vision for transformation across three levels: in people's lives; at the service response and systems level, creating services that people want, need and will use; and then at the community level, creating a society that is accepting and inclusive.

This vision and passion for change is clearly observed in the explanation of why people choose to do peer work. One person explained the choice to become a peer worker is not necessarily an easy one:

> 'Even if someone realises that their experience can be something that they can use ... it is not always easy to become a peer worker. One has to feel empowered to put [oneself] out there. Becoming a peer worker is not an easy decision, you have to acknowledge and take complete ownership of your experience and feel empowered to use this experience/knowledge to inform your work.'

So, if neither choice nor the work are easy, why do people make this decision? A common reason identified was that being a peer worker reinforces the meaning and meaningfulness of a person's experience of mental health issues.

> 'My diagnosis is made the most of, and good comes out of my experience.'

> 'It gives meaning to my experience and is recognition that my experience matters and I can make it count.'

Another emphasised the role of empowerment in deciding to become a peer worker:

> 'One of the reasons (which I think we tend to overlook) is that a person feels empowered to do so. That is a person feels empowered to become a peer worker. Often times people are not aware of their knowledge, they simply perceive it as an experience. Often as a negative experience, often

> due to internal stigma. It requires a shift in thinking (conceptual thinking?) to view the experience as a knowledge.'

Related themes include peer work's contribution to strengthened personal recovery. Similarly, participants noted personal growth and greater self-acceptance. Other common themes included the privilege of being able to give back, to model and support recovery,; to support self-belief and self-agency, and to contribute to change in people's lives and services.

> 'It's a privilege to work with a person to help them not have to go through what I did.'

> 'For me peer work is about striving daily to achieve better services and care—if not their transformation.'

> 'Peer work pays me to be a Trojan horse—to improve services from the inside out.'

The opportunity to be an agent of social change was seen as a key reason why a person chose to become a peer worker:

> 'A priority for me is to work toward the elimination of restrictive practice and to help mental health professionals to learn alternative skills and practices.'

> 'I became a peer worker to use my experience and knowledge to reframe and reform mental health services.'

> 'Peer work is about working for social justice, fighting stigma and discrimination and working toward a more accepting and inclusive society.'

Additionally, identification of their personal preference for peer work's value and practice base including reciprocity and non-judgemental and equal working relationships were significant elements of people's decision to work in this field.

## A picture of mental health peer work today

This part of the chapter provides a picture of the peer workforce through the eyes of those who participated. Identified roles and activities and what's new are discussed.

*Roles and functions*

The Health Workforce Australia peer worker survey revealed that 51% of respondents worked in the non-government sector. Seventeen per cent worked in public mental health services. About half (53%) worked part-time, 29% full-time and 18% were in casual positions. A small number reported they were in voluntary or unpaid positions.

This study concluded that the roles and functions of peer workers could be grouped into seven key functions: individual advocacy; peer support; systemic advocacy and representation; health promotion; education and training; quality and research; and coordination and management.

In contrast, workshop participants identified over seventy-five roles and activity areas including the major categories shown in Figure 1.

| | | |
|---|---|---|
| Peer support | Promotion of wellness and physical health | Representation |
| Service navigation | Policy advice and development | Systems advocacy and service reform |
| Assessment | Change leadership | Veteran support |
| Care and service coordination | Managing and leading teams | Training and teaching |
| Working with specific groups | Individual advocacy | Research and evaluation |
| Peer worker supervision, coaching and mentoring | Staff orientation, induction and professional development | Program administration |
| Accreditation assessment and quality improvement | Facilitating co-production projects | Lived experience academics and casual/sessional lecturers |
| Community development and education | Facilitating engagement and participation | Consultant and advisory roles including policy development |

**Figure 1: Roles and functions of peer workers as identified by workshop participants**

## 7: A force for change

*What's new*

Workshop participants noted the emergence of specialisations and the expansion of peer work into diverse settings. Peer workers now also work within and alongside a wider range of workforces.

Emerging specialisations include: wellbeing and physical health; youth; older people; people experiencing eating disorders; people who are homeless; Aboriginal and Torres Strait Islander people; transcultural, immigrant and refugee communities; lesbian, gay, bisexual, trans and intersex (LGBTI) people; people with physical, intellectual or sensory disabilities; young people, veterans and adults subject to the justice and forensic mental health systems; people with co-occurring conditions e.g. drug and alcohol misuse; family services; people experiencing family violence.

Peer workers are increasingly working alongside workforces other than mental health, including primary health, employment and employee assistance providers, lawyers, police, corrections, disability support, housing, and child, youth and family workforces. Peer workers are also now employed to support people in utilising government social services, courts and tribunals, acute and emergency medical settings.

Although they are still small in numbers in the private mental health service sector, peer workers are establishing their own private practices and consulting businesses. In this capacity, experienced peer workers evaluate programs, conduct accreditation assessments and provide tertiary liaison. Examples of tertiary liaison include lived experience consultants providing advice and training to mental health service staff, for example, introducing and utilising non-restrictive practices. A further example is training staff in trauma-informed and recovery-oriented practice. Lived-experience-owned and -operated services and programs are also taking their place in the service mix. For example, see www.brookred.org.au.

Regarding peer supervision, mentoring and coaching, there are as yet insufficient numbers of skilled peers to meet the demand, but there are experienced peer workers providing peer worker supervision, mentoring and coaching in some sectors. Additionally, some offer training and education to non-peer staff in organisations, in agencies, in recovery colleges and universities.

Further, there are growing numbers of lived experience academics, researchers, trainers and educators;

> 'We are beginning to be able to conduct our own research, build our own evidence base and to communicate its findings.'

> 'We need to write about ourselves and not be written about by others. We need to describe our practice and not have others say what they think it is.'

> 'We need to build our capacity to train our own and not have peer workers being trained by people without peer work experience.'

## How the mental health peer workforce walks, talks and breathes

The roles and activities identified demonstrate the diversity of what peer workers are currently doing. This section describes how the peer workforce works. Put differently, how the peer workforce walks, talks and breathes is described. The practice themes identified by the workshop participants provide a good starting point. The reasons people might choose to work with peer workers provide further insight.

### Some key practice themes

Key practice themes identified included: enabling practice; addressing power imbalance; reciprocity and safety; being rights-based; collegial relationships; and systems advocacy.

Participants described their enabling practice. This practice is trauma-informed, strengths-based and person-centred. Encompassing the values underpinning these approaches, peer workers value lived experience, steadfastly proclaim people's potential and foster self-belief and self-esteem. It's a 'non-deficits' focus—in thought, language and action.

> 'Instead of "What's wrong with you?" ask "What happened to you?"'

> 'Sharing knowledge that recovery is achievable.'

> 'Demonstrating that it is possible to break free from the constraints and low expectations of a diagnosis.'

An important practice skill in peer work's armoury is being able to find and use language that a person understands and is uplifted by. People explained how reflecting on one's own practice, making adjustments, finding meaning and being aware of personal biases help them to support people to explore their different cultural, social or personal constructions of illness, wellbeing and health. Reflective practice of this sort, undertaken singly or in peer groups, requires peer workers to thoughtfully consider their own practice experiences, to identify strengths and weaknesses, and, in particular, to support those they work with to reflect on their own choices and learn from their successes and setbacks.

> Peer workers use their lived experience of relational power dynamics and their impacts to create equal working relationships: 'We pick up on and can anticipate when and why people feel unsafe.'

A practice skill is in understanding how power imbalances can create dependence on 'experts' and a lack of confidence in self. This understanding is used by peer workers to support people to view themselves as experts about their lives and their mental health status. It is also used to shift the thinking of non-peer workers and those who write policy and procedures and design services.

There was reflection on the nature and qualities of the working relationships that peer workers seek to build with people they support. Words used included: trust-based, reciprocal, kind, compassionate and warm. The nature of working relationships is shaped by the underpinning belief in people's capacity and abilities. It is about relationships based on a conviction 'that people are worthy of creating a life they love.'

Peer workers also demonstrate practice skills that support a person in their decision making. They seek to foster curiosity for these people to explore their options and choices. They provide support to help people realise their range of choices and options. To achieve this, peer workers—

> 'emphasise personal choice and encourage people to think about what they want.'

> 'help people work through the strengths and weaknesses, within choices.'

> 'set up a safe space for people to explore options.'

By sharing their own experience, peer workers support people to seek out, obtain, consider and understand information they need to make decisions.

'People find it helpful when I share the small steps that got me started.'

'I help people break down big decisions into smaller ones e.g. to everyday decisions.'

Importantly, peer workers provide reassurance that it is OK to make misjudgements or mistakes and take calculated risks, and, most importantly, to learn from mistakes and failed efforts.

A peer worker walks, talks and breathes rights-based practice. Peer workers understand the personal toll of human rights infringements. Much of their work involves informing people of their rights and providing information about advocacy options and complaints mechanisms. Peer workers in policy, management and leadership roles described this as their key role in preventing rights violations.

There is a tension between the practice of collegial relationships and the practice of systems advocacy. Quite sophisticated practice skills are required to navigate these tensions.

'If we aren't respectful and collegial, it is unlikely that we will change what's happening and win hearts and minds. Yet if we don't talk openly and tell it like it is nothing will change, and we will be co-opted ... into silence and sense of powerlessness.'

Conflict and change management skills are evident as peer workers seek to practise collegially to enable a shift from a risk-adverse framework to one shaped by dignity of risk. The collegial exploration and introduction of non-coercive practices is another area that requires further exploration.

*Why people choose to work with peer workers*

When people discuss their understanding of why people chose to work with a peer worker, their views are drawn from their own experience of working with a peer worker, as well as what people they work with have told them. A key reason identified included the sense of connection and safety that a shared experience brings. Related to this theme was empathy, not feeling alone, being accepted and not rejected nor judged. Other discussions suggested that a peer worker may be less intimidating and be able to relate more readily to a peer. Peer work is a more holistic approach, which is why some people prefer it.

## 7: A force for change

> 'People get that we are welcoming of the "whole person".'
>
> 'People are wanting to explore more than medication and clinical concerns.'
>
> 'Our focus on quality of life and what's important personally is appreciated.'
>
> 'Our approach of supporting self-advocacy and self-esteem helps people to have the confidence to connect with others and to re-engage with the community.'

Another reason suggested for choosing to work with a peer worker is that people understand that a peer worker is trying both to help them and to change services for the better. A peer worker's systemic knowledge and experience with service navigation and negotiation are considered to be very important.

A challenge regarding choice was expressed, as it is unclear whether people actually do have a genuine choice in some environments.

> 'A question is, is there a choice? Ninety-nine per cent of people receiving services do not have a choice. Even if there is a choice, are we able to articulate what a peer worker offers? Many people receiving services are not aware of the difference between a peer worker and another worker. Without this knowledge how can a person make an informed choice. One of our weaknesses, downfalls, as a workforce I think is that we are not very good at articulating what we offer.'

### Change: at peer work's heart

Peer workers seek hope-inspired change. They aim to transform mental health services and practice. They use their personal experience of mental health issues and personal recovery to do this.

This transformation encompasses a normalisation of mental health issues as a human experience. It requires society and service-system-wide early acknowledgement of mental health issues. It seeks positive and supportive responses as the norm. Peer workers envisage a system that validates and nurtures social and emotional wellbeing. One that acknowledges and champions people's capacity for recovery. One which supports people's ability to reach their optimal potential and to live an ordinary life.

Peer workers apply learnings from their own adverse daily life and service experiences to promote change. This is consistent with the Fifth National Mental Health and Suicide Prevention Plan, which identifies the peer workforce as enablers of system reform and performance (Australian Government Department of Health, 2017, p. 48).

This change agenda identifies several practice priorities. These include using lived experience to promote recovery. Promoting self-valuation and empowerment in both self and others. Challenging deficiencies in current mental health practice. It also prioritises recognition for the transforming nature of its contribution.

*Promoting personal recovery, self-valuation and empowerment*

Peer workers use their experiential knowledge base. They build on that in a positive way, for their own recovery efforts and in their peer practice. They apply lifelong learning and learning through sharing. They acknowledge meaning and value in their own experience. They model a meaningful life, participation in and contribution to society. It is a way of translating experience into meaningful knowledge.

> 'Sharing my own experience helps my personal understanding and acceptance of it.'

> 'I got to know me, not my illness.'

Self-valuation, self-empowerment and recovery are key to what peer workers are doing. The personal recovery journey is the starting point for contributing to change—change for individuals, in services and service systems, and societal understandings and response. Davidson, Byrne and Stratford (2018, p. 76), explain this change process:

> Persons in recovery can inspire hope and provide empathy, advocacy, and assistance in navigating the mental health system and the broader community ... This, in turn, promotes the disability rights vision of 'nothing about us without us'.

## 7: A force for change

*Using lived experience to promote recovery, self-valuation and empowerment in others*

Peer workers bring experiential knowledge to the mental health workforce. Their approach encompasses a diversity of life experience and understandings. It is hopeful and positive in its transmission of understanding what is possible. In this way, it counters and fights the impact of negative stereotyping and stigma. It promotes the underlying 'normality' and relational equity of shared experience.

The peer work approach encompasses safety through shared understanding and partnership. It incorporates empathic awareness of relational dynamics. It encourages learning from mistakes and setbacks as well as successes. It is recovery oriented. It values and enables the application of a 'dignity of risk' framework. In this context, dignity of risk refers to people being empowered to make their own choices, to own those choices, to learn from and to live with the consequences.

Peer work challenges systemic limitations, misunderstandings and the power differentials which occur when the coercive attitudes and practices of others contravene individual choice.

The peer work approach is responsive to the destructive impacts of stigma and discrimination. It challenges applied discrimination. It challenges barriers to open acknowledgement of lived experience. These barriers restrict others in the mental health workforce who are unable to use lived experience knowledge in an open and effective manner.

*Progressing the recognition and valuing of peer work while challenging practice and service deficiencies*

Peer workers highlight several 'deficiencies' in current mental health system practice. These deficiencies devalue lived experience and diagnosis dominates practice understandings. Deficiencies include a hierarchical power structure with little collegial practice. The system can be slow to change and often agencies are risk averse. In that framework the system devalues individual choice and personal aspiration and is blind to the socioeconomic context. These deficiencies limit society's capacity to normalise mental health issues. They inhibit the promotion of mental health and wellbeing.

The peer workforce and their allies challenge these deficiencies from a dis-empowered and devalued position. They are agents of change and set out to challenge this risk-averse mentality by using the expertise and knowledge established through processing and valuing personal lived experience. It uses self-belief and builds on a developing evidence base. It challenges risk aversion and coercive practices. It encourages team-based service delivery approaches. Peer workers are cultural agents between clinicians, service providers, service management and those utilising their services.

Peer workers challenge the current distribution of power and role responsibility within services. They seek and utilise opportunities for influencing those in policy and management roles. They build awareness and acceptance of the peer workforce and endorsement of the value of lived experience. They also pursue a 'national change agenda' through systemic advocacy. They promote the uptake of peer work at the service level. They contribute to community understanding and acceptance of people experiencing mental health issues. They emphasise the importance of social and emotional wellbeing.

Peer workers highlight the need to work with groups who experience marginalisation or neglect. These groups include multicultural communities. They include Indigenous communities, the LGBTI community, disability groups, and people subject to the criminal justice system.

Peer workers identify the lack of a unifying national or state/territory peer workforce development strategy as problematic. In this respect governments are missing in action. Services and organisations are slow to act. This lack of action runs contrary to the national change agenda.

Organisational management offers limited acceptance to peer work. The broader mental health workforce applies derogatory language and low expectations to lived experience. Disclosure of personal mental health status for health professionals may come at a career cost. These observations link to the low status and low pay of peer work.

Implementation of the National Disability Insurance Scheme is seen as a 'wrecking ball, a disruptive technology'. Conversely, the Scheme could also offer the biggest opportunity for the growth of peer work in Australia. Limited acknowledgement of the peer work support role risks replacing recovery with a deficits model where workers do 'for' as against 'with'. The introduction of

## 7: A force for change

peer work would provide opportunity for relationship-based recovery approaches that shift the emphasis away from what a person may not be able to do, to one enabling of self-discovery and self-direction, and dignifying risk in a process of moving forward, finding and enjoying a meaningful life.

The current reliance on casual and disconnected peer work positions, or peer workers working alone or in isolation, further impedes effective workforce development.

> 'Peer workers find themselves isolated within work teams; senior people who have identified as having mental health problems also find themselves sidelined.'

> 'In multidisciplinary teams the peer work voice has little influence and peer workers are often involved in client care at the end, not the beginning.'

Peer workers remain a minority within a larger space. They are made 'complicit in mental health practice which is antipathetic to the peer work approach and values system'.

Peer workers seek stronger workforce development processes. They seek recognition as a professional identity, as a discrete workforce. There is conviction. There is momentum. Success will better position peer workers to challenge dominant cultures within service systems.

### What peer work is contributing

Change and leadership define the peer work role. Peer leadership is changing policy and changing practice. It is changing systems, institutions and communities. It is changing minds. It is also leading the establishment of a solid professional identity. The motivation is to change entrenched and negative mindsets. It is to support recovery and inclusion.

The Australian peer workforce envisions and brings change in people's lives. This contribution encompasses all peer workforce roles and positions.

Those in peer positions walk alongside people. They share their recovery experience. They provide living evidence of recovery and potential for growth. In effect, peer workers provide peer-based recovery leadership.

Peer workers change people's lives through their advocacy. Additionally, they may also provide advice, if asked. They research how practitioners and services can better support recovery. They test service provision, its attitudes and practices.

Their leadership improves policy. It redesigns services. It introduces new practice paradigms and programs. Peer work managers reflect the voice of service users and their lived experience and integrate it into reform of organisational practices.

Peer work leadership promotes personal recovery. It promotes service development and reform. It articulates a peer work practice base and professional identity.

There is an inclusive approach to leading peer workforce development. Peer work leadership is leading wider mental health workforce development. It is engaging the hearts and minds of the community.

Such leadership relies on a strong voluntary effort. It entails activity outside designated role descriptions. It involves contributions over and beyond the call of duty. Each of these leadership roles is now discussed.

*Leadership in promoting personal recovery*

Face-to-face peer work values an ability to support and enable people's recovery. It also provide leadership on disclosure. In peer work contexts, self-disclosure of lived experience of mental health issues is a prerequisite for occupants of designated peer work positions. This acknowledgement makes lived experience knowledge accessible, providing a commonality of interest between those they work with and themselves, thereby inviting people to engage. By being approachable, accessible and available, and by being open to appropriately sharing their own experiences to support the recovery journey of others, the engagement in that journey by those they work with is strengthened.

When sharing their own experiences, peer workers might reference the difference that a peer worker has made in their own life: 'working with a peer worker helped me understand that my experience matters and means something'.

## 7: A force for change

Additionally, peer workers role-model wellness. They view people as experts about their lives and mental health. They inspire and instil hope. They support people who may be cast as 'too hard' by others. They are collaborative, working 'with people, not do(ing) things for them or to them':

> 'As peer workers, we do not give up on people. We believe in people's capacity for recovery and to be exceptional.'

Peer workers emphasise quality in relationships. They provide reciprocity. They acknowledge and share their own experiences. They stress the importance of small steps. This is a process which builds trust and emphasises personal preference and choice. Peer work seeks to use language which people understand. It builds self-esteem and confidence. It acknowledges safety concerns and the dignity of risk. It encourages self-advocacy, responsibility and agency. It emphasises an understanding that 'people are worthy of creating a life which they love'.

Peer workers provide leadership in trauma-informed practice. Their values and working methods seek to address the three pillars of providing safety, connection and emotional management (Bath, 2008). They assist co-workers and managers to engage people in their service by acknowledging their experience of trauma. In providing safety to explore it, and finding the tools to manage it, they seek to establish practices that avoid retraumatisation and give power and choice back to the individual:

> 'we understand how traumatising mental illness can be and also understand how the experience of service and treatment can heap trauma upon trauma.'

Peer workers emphasise a collegiate way of working. They apply this to mental health service team work, including at the assessment phase, even where resisted. They identify alternatives to team preconceptions of limited potential in the people they work with. They challenge the use of ignorant or inappropriate language. They question reliance on restrictive practices such as coercive responses and a risk aversion mentality.

Issuing challenges of this sort is difficult for the peer worker; these are some of the very risky elements of this role.

Peer work leaders have a responsibility to develop and share the evidence base. Peer leaders are able to apply the evidence base to their active learning so as to facilitate their recovery practices and to become more effective. Despite this they are used to facing antipathy and misunderstanding within the broader mental health work-force. Peer workers often find themselves 'being the evidence' of what works, and, despite this success, are frequently sidelined or their contribution discounted.

*Leadership in service development and reform*

To build on Byrne, Roennfeldt and O'Shea (2017), it is fair to say that peer workers invest energy in service design and redesign. When feasible, they pursue roles in strategic planning as well as in audit and accreditation, and, especially, in collaborative research and evaluation. They target far greater inclusion and equity in executive and senior management roles. They seek to use their acknowledged existing knowledge and skills in targeting diversity. They aim to promote cultural and organisational change from positions of influence and power.

Peer workers are able to speak from the benefit of their own experience. They provide a communication bridge, enabling their colleagues and managers to hear from people utilising their services. They facilitate the provision of safe spaces and places for people to discuss their experiences and invite their input on how their experience of service might be improved.

Within the peer work ranks, the importance of positions traditionally referred to as 'consumer consultants' and 'consumer advocates' is being emphasised. More often than not, peer workers have felt compelled or have been expected to fulfil this role in addition to their own. There is a growing call for the difference between the positions to be understood and clearly articulated and for organisations to embrace the need for both peer support and consumer consultant positions.

Byrne et al. (2018) reported the value placed on peer work roles by mental health service managers who have employed peer workers. They report benefits to services and people's outcomes. These benefits include improved working relationships, that is, reduced hospitalisation and reduced reliance on mental health community-based services. These managers also report benefits

## 7: A force for change

for the organisation. They report benefits to colleagues. These come from adapting to a recovery-oriented working framework. This adaptation comes from the peer work impact on training and workplace culture.

On the other hand, mental health service managers who have not employed peer workers remain unconvinced or unaware.

It does seem that exposure to peer work can be, of itself, a major change strategy. In this way, peer workers can be effective leaders of change.

There are caveats to the impact identified by Byrne et al. (2018). Organisations must work through the 'learning curve' of effective recruitment. They must learn to apply a flexible and responsive approach to reasonable adjustment in the workplace. For managers with experience of employing peer workers, reasonable adjustment is simply good practice. Reasonable adjustment 'supports the workforce' in general. It is not seen as 'coddling' or patronising peer workers.

Byrne, Schoeppe and Bradshaw (2018) also identify the positive impact of peer researchers. This is shown through valuable contributions to the identification of ethical issues as well as the improved selection of appropriate and viable research methodologies. Peer work's critical thinking, its unique perspective on issues and an increased awareness of those perspectives make it respected by other researchers.

### *Articulating for itself a peer work practice base and professional identity*

Peer work in Australia is in the early stages of articulating its practice base. It is establishing itself as a profession. It has a unique identity. It already holds a value set appropriate to professionalisation. It holds a unique knowledge base established by lived experience. It claims a working method premised upon that knowledge base and values set.

There is clear intent to embed peer work as a core mental health and psychosocial discipline. For peer work in 'every team, every service, and every program'. There is a clear and unequivocal intent for peer work to occur in other settings than mental health.

Peer work entails a holistic conceptualisation of practice. It incorporates a whole of life view of the person. It emphasises personal rights, quality of life, connection to others, and social support. It emphasises safety, life coaching, and emotional attachment. It supports wellness and physical health. It emphasises service coordination and support for transition. It requires individualised and comprehensive service planning. It provides new and innovative directions and solutions. It provides a positive view and vision to all, no matter the degree of difficulty. It supports people to be experts in their own lives.

This professional identity is yet to properly take hold in mental health services. Its take-up is not universal; where it is taken up, it appears to work well. However, it requires policy champions and consequent policy drivers. This professional identity is not yet accepted universally by others with lived experience, nor by some in the community at large. Peer work is not consistently well integrated into mental health service practice. The evidence base requires greater articulation. It is a change agent resisted by its practice context. This resistance results in low status and low profile. This is a clear impediment to establishing peer work as a professional entity.

Even so, peer work is encroaching into broader societal institutional domains. This encroachment includes gaining momentum in education, workplaces and disparate communities. It includes health industry professional and management associations. This encroachment challenges those restrictions by enhancing legitimacy.

The peer workforce is fighting to achieve its professional objectives and to fulfil its capacity. Ways forward include attaining greater role clarity as well as role diversity within services. The peer workforce is also seeking an expanded and upgraded qualifications framework that support the movement of peer workers into management and governance positions. Enhanced professional development opportunities are also being sought.

The peer workforce is aspiring to a system of accreditation and agreed practice standards. Achieving this might involve the development of a professional body to provide oversight and to promote the profession's identity, expertise and capacity. Are all required.

Expanding the range of peer work roles and settings is high on the agenda of the peer workforce at this time.

## 7: A force for change

Peer worker expertise and knowledge is being sought by other professions and disciplines. Peer work also occurs outside primary mental health settings. Examples are 'Mates in Construction' and veterans' support groups.

Peer workers are seeking to develop practice specialisations. These specialisations encompass different needs groups, sectors and roles. These include co-occurring conditions (e.g. alcohol and drug dependency, disability). They include veterans, young people and older people. They include people subject to the criminal justice and forensic mental health systems. Identified specialisations include emergency departments, crisis supports and suicide prevention, perinatal care, borderline personality supports, people experiencing eating disorders. Specialist settings include legal and court systems, homelessness services, child and family services, rural and remote communities, Aboriginal and Torres Strait islander communities, culturally and linguistically diverse and refugee communities, and LGBTI communities. A peer work presence would be viable supporting people to utilise government social services, courts and justice environments.

The professional intent of peer work requires enhancement of the national qualifications framework. Certificate IV in Mental Health Peer Work is a minimalist approach. It does not address the range of roles encompassed by the peer workforce or its potential growth into broader service arenas.

These roles and skill sets include management, industrial relations and human resource management. They include research, policy and planning, service development, and cross-cultural practice. The enhanced qualifications framework required ought to be inclusive of recognition of prior learning. It ought to include peer workers in delivering this education and training agenda.

### *An inclusive approach to leading peer workforce development*

The peer workforce is building for its own future. Each peer worker seeks a community or network of peer workers. The aim is to help others to become peer workers through mentoring and support—'There is excitement about our potential, particularly that which remains untapped'—and for maintaining the integrity of the peer work role—'being as prepared and considered as I can be'.

Building the peer work future incorporates networking and supporting each other. It requires moving peer workers into senior organisational roles. It means contributing to organisational governance. Designing service and support models. Driving strategic planning, policy review and development. It requires systemic advocacy to enable service system change. It prioritises the elimination of discrimination and injustice. It seeks to build a critical mass of peer workers and peer leaders.

The peer workforce has morphed from the early positioning of 'consumer consultants'. There is a growing focus on leadership at all levels. However, formal leadership positions are lacking (Davidson et al., 2018, p. 76, referencing Health Workforce Australia, 2013). Championing change through modelling, collaboration and co-production are the main leadership tools currently available.

## Contributing leadership in wider mental health workforce development

The peer workforce is leading change in mental health workforce practice. They urge staff to move from being risk averse. They embrace dignity of risk and trauma-informed practice. They promote non-coercive practice with other professionals. They encourage, even in involuntary and long-term settings. They input to orientation, induction and professional development within organisations. They input to training courses and programs at universities. This includes universities, technical and further education, schools and other education and training events and venues.

They model strength-based language and the language of empowerment. They share emerging research and evidence. They prove effectiveness through good practice.

They model the value of acknowledging personal lived experience. This often results in staff disclosing their personal mental health status to peer workers, even when they are reluctant to be open with others in the workplace.

Peer work practice challenges inflexible service provision. It challenges stigmatising attitudes and discriminatory practices. Peer workers find themselves providing leadership on cultural change processes. They model cross-disciplinary styles of working. They integrate psychosocial considerations into practice. They show that dignity of risk is a valuable work value and practice construct. They do these things in the absence of broader organisational leadership.

*Leadership with engaging the hearts and minds of the community*

Peer workers raise community understanding and awareness of mental health issues. They engage the community in reducing stigma and discrimination. They develop partnerships to build communities that are inclusive and accepting. They identify psychological distress and mental health issues as part of the normal spectrum of human experiences.

Promotion of recovery and social connection are concepts which enable people within the general community to relate to their own experiences of resilience in the face of trauma and adversity. They understand, respect and find inspiration in their reclaiming of identity and wellbeing following or despite the experience of extreme distress. They draw hope from seeing the walking and talking evidence of (the possibility of) recovery. As reported by Byrne, Schoeppe and Bradshaw (2018), the large majority of one community survey's participants (94%) provided support for recovery as a mental health goal.

The workshop participants provided an insightful glimpse of the workforce's purpose, achievements and contributions to date. They draw a picture of their future aspirations and directions. They also identified several serious impediments to their work.

**Challenges confronting mental health peer workers**

The current mental health system is slow to change. The introduction of peer work programs is often rushed, lacks awareness of core value sets and is frequently rolled out without consultation. The national change agenda is not uniformly evident in service system values and practice. Adequate investment in core peer work ethics and values and in effective consultation practices is lacking.

Training and professional development expectations, and opportunities to participate effectively, are low. Opportunity to build and utilise peer networks is minimal. Roles are not well conceived or developed. In some places confusion exists over the difference between consumer and carer peer work roles as compared to other roles. The specific skill sets associated with peer work receive little acknowledgement. There is little value given to the concept and reality of workforce diversity. The background skills which a diverse peer workforce encompasses are not understood, articulated or used. This includes policy and research skills, education and training skills, recruitment and management experience, and experience within diverse communities.

The peer work voice has little influence in multidisciplinary teams. Menial tasks are often directed to peer workers. There is an implicit assumption that 'they are lucky to have a job'. The broader mental health sector does not understand peer work knowledge and skill. It is not trained or motivated to do so.

For peer workers, professional practice supervision is only rarely provided. Considered workplace adjustment is under-developed and not explicit. Staff appraisal processes do not encourage or enable constructive feedback or organisational learning. Monitoring of wellbeing within the peer workforce is of limited concern to management. This also applies to the mental health workforce as a whole. A peer work values set is not referenced in work contracts. Conflict over workplace values is not addressed. The peer workforce currently has no agreed practice standards to apply. Adherence to national mental health service standards is lacking. Workplace bullying and 'lateral violence' continue unabated. There is little attention to other human resource measures. These include induction, appropriate peer supervision, flexible working arrangements and job sharing.

A small and low-level peer workforce exists within organisations and organisational cultures and practices. These practices gainsay the value of the peer workforce. They limit its development and downplay the specialist expertise. Resistance to change is experienced at all levels and the momentum for change is slow. Jiggins (2018) emphasises this slowness of change by referencing Moore (1991). He identifies that exposure to any change product results in uneven support. Only about 2.5% are innovators—in this case peer workers and supporters; 13.5% will be early adaptors—the first to pick up and adapt to the change. Another 34% may pick up the change once others have. The last 16% are laggards. They will always struggle to accept change.

The peer workforce needs a faster development trajectory. It also seeks acceptance across the Australian community. It has a long way to go.

## 7: A force for change

Byrne, Schoeppe and Bradshaw (2018) found that only 35% of one survey's participants believed in self-directed care. The majority believed medical professionals should direct care needs. Yet a high level of support existed for recovery as a mental health goal: 'regardless of the severity of symptoms experiences and/or the mental illness diagnosis … there is always hope for recovery'.

### Responding to these challenges and shaping the future

Looking at what peer work might do to address key challenges and to shape its own future was interesting. A unifying theme was for peer work to 'be on the front foot', meaning that we be proactive rather than defensive in promoting peer work as a profession.

*Achieving public recognition as change agents and leaders*

Participants discussed their vision of peer work being a household name:

> 'My vision is for peer work achieving household recognition as a discrete profession without compromising values and uniqueness.'

How will peer work become a household name? A key strategy identified is working in partnership with the community to raise awareness of it as a bona fide specialised mental health role, and acceptance and understanding of mental health issues and needs to address stigma and discrimination:

> 'We can do this by modelling and championing recovery and by establishing commonality, as mental ill health is seen and accepted as an everyday human experience.'

Engaging in social media and anti-stigma campaigns were among the activities prioritised.

The strategies of 'being good at we do', 'being approachable, available, readily accessible and inviting people to engage' and demonstrating outcomes were also emphasised.

Further strategies included a continuing yet increased peer work presence in staff orientation, induction and professional development as input into professional training programs e.g. in universities and technical and further education, at both undergraduate and postgraduate levels. Associated with these strategies were those that suggested building a critical mass of peer work leaders, peer workers moving into senior roles and sharing emerging research and evidence.

A further strategy for becoming a household name is the profession striving to reflect community diversity—'peer work viewed as a desirable and attractive vocation'.

*Peer work establishes its own professional identity and association*

Participants spoke of their enthusiasm for a peer work professional identity and association:

> 'A professional body that we create for ourselves will help us to identity as a discipline that brings something unique—articulates that uniqueness.'

Some spoke of a professional association with state and local branches or chapters that works with lived experience peak bodies and representative organisations:

> 'Peer work needs to be recognised as a discipline similar to social work, occupational therapy etc. This will pave the way for the recognition of peer workers under employment [sic] bargaining agreements. Currently peer workers are not recognised and that can sometimes mean consumer workers in managerial positions ... get paid lower rates because they don't meet the qualifications outlined in the employment [sic] bargaining agreements.'

Tasks of such a professional body were said to include establishing national practice standards, accreditation pathways and appropriate employment awards. Also emphasised is the need for an overseeing arrangement for professional supervision and mentoring—adequately funded and resourced; provided by people with experience and expertise as peer workers—'supervision by our own'.

**The peer workforce achieves equitable workplace provisions**

Participants emphasised the need for equitable and sound workplace conditions:

> 'Proper positions not solely fractional—positions that can support a living'

7: A force for change

> 'Career pathways established—peer workers at all levels of an organisation'
>
> 'Flexibility of positions and appropriate workplace adjustments'
>
> 'Peer work industry awards that provide income parity and equity'
>
> 'Not being employed as sole peer worker in isolated and unsafe and ill-described positions.'

Also stressed was the importance of position descriptions and employment policies to written by people with experience of being a peer worker.

*Identity and self-definition*

Workshop participants discussed the risk of peer work in Australia being defined and confined by the terms and condition of funding programs, policy documents and by accredited training programs. A professional body is viewed as key to enabling peer work to define itself.

*Peer work establishes and communicates its evidence base*

Participants spoke of the need for peer work to continue to articulate for itself what peer work is and what its benefits are. Strategies identified included peer workers continuing to move into policy, research and academic positions. The wide yet innovative sharing, dissemination and discussion of research and findings about peer work's evidence base was emphasised. Additional avenues relate to writing for publications and the use of social media as well as engaging info-graphics, multimedia and films.

The negotiation of a national peer work data collection is also thought to be a critical facet of recognition and development of the workforce.

**Peer work provides strong leadership within the mental health and psychosocial disability sectors**

> 'We have expertise and knowledge that is recognised and sought by other professions and disciplines.'

The strengthening of peer work's leadership in a number of important areas was emphasised; areas include: cultural change; the redesign or reconfiguring of mental health services to be inclusive of a psychosocial emphasis, a new remit; the abolition of restrictive practices, ensuring real safety for people in services and services being less risk adverse; and the valuing of disclosure as well as utilising the wisdom of lived experience.

Participants stressed the importance of collaboration and networking instead of the current practice of being isolated from other disciplines.

*Expansion of peer work roles and settings*

A common goal described was to have peer work recognised and embedded as a core mental health and psychosocial discipline and appropriately skilled peers to be employed in all mental health services and programs:

> 'Every team, every service, every program.'

> 'Seeing a peer worker offered to me as a choice is my goal.'

A related strategy was to see peer workers continuing to move into leadership and management positions as career structures and pathways in and out of peer work are becoming established.

*Stronger systemic roles*

Participants were adamant that both peer support and systemic change positions are required. Not one or the other, or one at the expense of the other. There was some discussion of how consumer consultant roles were beginning to be reconceptualised as consumer leadership positions. A vision was painted of systemic positions being routinely included and budgeted for.

*Peer- and lived-experience-run organisations and services*

Participants spoke of the important role lived-experience-run organisations and services as models of service innovation and transformation. For example: peer-run respite or community houses provide alternatives to hospitalisation; peer-run warmlines assist the transition from inpatient care into the community; and peer-run welcoming services provide alternatives to admission via emergency departments. Peer-run self-help and mutual support networks support recovery, increase connectedness and improve quality of life.

7: A force for change

*Recognition of governance and management expertise*

A final strategy identified for addressing challenges is that peer workers need to be appointed to boards and assume executive positions. The movement of peer workers into leadership positions will also assist the profession to shape its own future.

## Conclusion

'Doing the best I can each day for people', 'seeing people fly and achieve more than me' and 'doing my bit to see peer work valued' were among the things that keep peer workers awake at night and get them up in the morning. There is a shared vision of lived experience being recognised and valued and of peer work being viewed universally as desirable and essential. The vision encompasses peer workers in designated positions, as well as those who are undertaking peer work training or internships.

A fierce determination is evident that peer work's time has long since arrived. The workshop participants are resolute that their workforce will take its rightful place and be recognised as key to transforming service and community responses to people experiencing mental health issues.

## References

Australian Government Department of Health. (2016). Summary of actions within the Australian Government response to recommendations to the review of mental health programmes and services. Canberra: Australian Government Department of Health.

Australian Government Department of Health. (2017). The Fifth National Mental Health and Suicide Prevention Plan. Canberra: Australian Government Department of Health.

Bath, H. (2008). Trauma informed care and resilience in fostering futures. Retrieved from www.reclaiming.com

Byrne, L. (2013). A grounded theory study of lived experience mental health practitioners within the wider workforce (PhD thesis). Central Queensland University.

Byrne, L., Roennfeldt, H., & O'Shea, P. (2017). Identifying barriers to change: The lived experience worker as a valued member of the mental health team. Central Queensland University.

Byrne, L., Roennfeldt, H., O'Shea, P., & MacDonald, F. (2018). Taking a gamble for high rewards? Management perspectives on the value of mental health peer work. *International Journal of Environmental Research and Public Health, 15*, 746–758.

Byrne, L., Schoeppe, S., & Bradshaw, J. (2018). Recovery without autonomy: Progress forward or more of the same for mental health service users? *International Journal of Mental Health Nursing*. Online 15 February. doi: 10.1111/inm.12446.

Davidson, L., Byrne, L., Stratford, A. (2018). Speaking out: The global need for lived experience leadership. *Psychiatric Rehabilitation Journal, 41*(1), 76–79.

Happell, B., Gordon, S., Bocking, J., Ellis, P., Roper, C., Liggins, J., ... Scholz, B. (2018). How did I not see that? Perspectives of non-consumer mental health researchers on the benefits of collaborative research with consumers. *International Journal of Mental Health Nursing*. Online 1 March. doi: 10.1111/inm.12453.

Health Workforce Australia. (2014). Mental health peer workforce study. Adelaide: HWA.

Jiggins, D. (2018). What impact could a fully implemented peer workforce have on the mental health system?

# The hearts and minds of the peer workforce

*Leanne Craze and David Plant*

This chapter focuses on the hearts and minds of peer workers. It asks 'what gets you up in the morning?' and 'what keeps you awake at night?'

Information provided is derived from a workshop involving approximately fifty peer workers, peer work pioneers and policy leaders held in Sydney in April 2018. Participants represented a spread of age groups, as well as new and experienced workers. Workshop participants were drawn from metropolitan, regional and remote areas. Additional information was provided by phone interviews and email discussions and submissions involving others who were unable to attend.

Responses to the question of what gets you up in the morning clearly enunciated the primary motivations of the peer workforce. Seven major motivating factors were articulated. These factors were inclusive of self-valuation and skills development, valuation of the people who peer workers work with, valuation of colleagues and workplaces, the ability to lead and to promote improved mental health practice, and the ability to contribute to positive service, system and community change. These factors are discussed below.

A strong motivating factor for peer workers is the self-valuation and pride in translating the knowledge and experience of mental ill health from a negative, stigmatised entity into one which is positively conceived and usefully applied.

> 'In sharing my experience and seeing others helped I can accept myself more.'

> 'It is therapeutic.'

> 'It is empowering.'

> 'It normalises my experience and values that experience.'

Peer workers are also strongly motivated by their understanding of the unique contribution and value of peer work, an offering seen as uniquely different from other mental health professionals.

There is a strong belief in the importance of peer work—'I believe in the work I do'. There is—'excitement about our potential, particularly that which remains untapped'. There is motivation to 'work toward the recognition of peer work' and to play a role in peer work's expansion—'seeing more people become peer workers'. And there is a strongly expressed intent to 'be as prepared and considered as I can be', that is, to 'maintain the integrity of the peer work role'.

Peer workers also express a strong appreciation for 'the people I work with'. They are motivated towards 'standing by them and showing them; I will not give up'. In turn, this translates to being motivated by the achievements associated with making a positive difference in people's lives: 'making a difference by sharing my recovery journey', 'excitement about the difference I can make during the day'. Making a difference—The desire to see my drive and commitment make a difference to people's futures', the privilege of being able to reach out to another person—'Supporting people to fly and achieve optimally and far beyond what I have achieved', using their own experience so that others have better lives—'Making change so that people don't experience what I have'— and helping to give hope—'the opportunity to support a person's recovery'.

Peer workers also get up in the morning to enjoy their interactions with colleagues and workplaces. They enjoy 'being around passionate and caring people'. They value a 'collaborative and caring workplace'. They appreciate their 'interactions with peer colleagues' and are inspired by their 'involvement with peer leaders'.

In response they find themselves helping others to become peer workers—'the peer work students I am teaching' and being part of 'building a community or network of peer workers'.

Finally, peer workers find motivation through their contribution towards systemic change, changing the way services are delivered and changing the way in which the broader community understands and responds to mental ill-health and social and emotional wellbeing. That is, contributing:

7: A force for change

> 'to change and my desire to forge new directions'
>
> 'the knowledge that I am making a difference and that the system is changing'
>
> 'to organisational acceptance and recognition of peer work'
>
> 'by using my experience to help break down stigma'
>
> 'by changing attitudes in multicultural communities'.

It is not surprising that peer worker concerns, or what keeps them awake at night, run parallel to what gets them out of bed in the morning. Some common reasons identified are concern for the people they work with and the desire to support them achieve what's important to them. Other concerns focused on the workplace and on service systems.

> 'Workplace difficulties including negative attitudes toward peer workers and a lack of openness to working collegially worry me.'
>
> 'I worry that I am not doing the best I can to change community attitudes and to bring about systemic policy and practice change.'

Peer workers are also concerned and worried by the self-imposed limitations of the people they work with. They are concerned by the often diminished and disadvantaged lives people live:

> 'people limiting their sights of what's possible in their lives and recovery journeys'
>
> 'people absorbing and taking on board the stigmatising views of others'
>
> 'people who haven't had a cuddle in thirty years'
>
> 'people being unable to say "I have a mental illness" and not be ashamed'.

Peer workers are kept awake by their awareness of community attitudes and understandings which exacerbate these experiences and limited expectations through active discrimination and a lack of shared and effective community response to 'seeing people with mental illness experiencing social disadvantage'.

They are left concerned and worried by workplace failings. These failings include alienating workplace cultures and, in particular, a concern for the impact of this on new peer workers:

> 'experiencing disrespect from co-workers'

> 'alienating and stigmatising attitudes and language used in the workplace'.

They are also kept awake at night by their own desire to 'do better and achieve more' and by their awareness of 'the slow pace of change'. They worry about:

> 'failure to make a big an enough difference'

> 'what can be done better'

> 'how people can be helped more, supported better'

> 'How people might have a greater voice in their treatment and in the services they use'.

They fear lack of effectiveness or giving way to complacency:

> 'a failure to make a big enough difference'

> 'a sense of being a failure or fraudulent'.

They fret about how the peer workforce might be expanded and fear the 'colonisation or bastardisation of peer work' within a larger mental health workforce culture.

They are highly concerned about policy and service development frameworks and the role of peer work within them. In particular, there is a current concern about the impact of National Disability Insurance Scheme implementation through its support for a more casualised, disconnected and activity-focused peer workforce.

Peer workers, as reported by workshop participants, are 'kept awake at night' by workplace cultures which often fail to understand or respect their unique contribution, by the difficulties and slow pace of enacting change, by policy and service frameworks which are inconsistent in concept, and often contradict or limit the contribution which an effective workforce can make. In this context, they are worried about the people they work and concerned that their efforts, no matter how diligently applied, are doing enough.

## 7: A force for change

In conclusion, the peer workforce, as represented by workshop participants, is highly motivated by the acknowledgement and realisation that their own, often negative experiences, of mental illness, community attitudes and service responses provide them with a unique and valuable knowledge base. In their role as peer workers, this experiential knowledge is translated from a negative in their lives to a source of individual and group empowerment—empowerment which enables them to gain motivation and satisfaction through their commitment to and active involvement in facilitating and promoting change. Change which they see as beneficial to individuals whose lives are affected by mental illness, including themselves and other members of the peer workforce. Change which is directed to individual recovery, to radically altered service provision, and to shaping more beneficial community attitudes and responses.

These factors are the primary motivators which enable peer workers to 'get up in the morning', remain focused, and enjoy the contributions they make. And to do so in the face of the many frustrations and fears they face on a daily basis. They are personally aware of the stakes of both failure and success, 'the difference between what is and what might be'.

And so, the night rolls into the next day as the quest of peer workers to achieve more caring and enabling services and communities continues.

# Appendix

**Editorial working group (and chapter authors)**
Janet Meagher AM
Anthony Stratford
Fay Jackson
Erandathie Jayakody
Tim Fong

**Contributing authors**
Aimee Sinclair
Anthony Stratford
Bridget O'Bree
Darren Jiggins
David Plant
Emily Matenson
Emma Cadogan
Erandathie Jayakody
Eschleigh Balzamo
Fay Jackson
Flick Grey
Gerry Naughtin
Hamilton Kennedy
Janet Meagher AM
Jesse Olsen
Leanne Craze AM
Louise Byrne
Michael Burge OAM
Magenta Simmons
Lyn Mahboub
Matt Halpin
Nicholas Fava
Rhianwen Beresford
Rose Randall
Sarah Fitzpatrick
Tim Fong
Tim Heffernan
Vivien Kemp
Vrinda Eagan

Appendix

**Workshop contributors**

Alana Mondy
Annie Sykes
Anthony Stratford
Ben Matthews
Bianca Childs
Cindy Paisio
Daniel Reynolds
Darcy Hale
David Plant
Deslee Matthews
Donna Humphrey
Donna Ingraham
Elida Meadows
Erandathie Jayakody
Evan Fulton
Fay Jackson
Glenn Botfield
Grant Everett
Gwen Scotman-Challenger
Heather Miller
Heather Nowak
Holly Kemp
Immie Wijeratne
Janet Meagher
Jemima Isbester
Justin Caspersz
Kim Jones
Kylie Wake
Leanne Craze AM
Lily Wu
Louise Kelaher
Maurice Corcoran
Mehna Alacozy
Natasha Jones
Peter Farrugia
Peter Schaecken
Sage Green
Scott Williams
Tim Fong
Vanessa D'Souza
Warren Heggarty

www.ingramcontent.com/pod-product-compliance
Lightning Source LLC
Chambersburg PA
CBHW080355030426
42334CB00024B/2880